9.50

The Urban Sublime
in American Literary
Naturalism

The Urban Sublime
in American Literary
Naturalism

CHRISTOPHE DEN TANDT

UNIVERSITY OF ILLINOIS PRESS

URBANA AND CHICAGO

Library of Congress Cataloging-in-Publication Data
Den Tandt, Christophe, 1959–
The urban sublime in American literary naturalism /
Christophe Den Tandt.
p.   cm.
Includes bibliographical references and index.
ISBN 0-252-02402-8 (alk. paper). —
ISBN 0-252-06704-5 (pbk. : alk. paper)
1. American fiction—19th century—History and criticism.
2. American fiction—20th century—History and criticism.
3. City and town life in literature. 4. Cities and towns in litera-
ture. 5. Sublime, The, in literature. 6. Naturalism in literature.
I. Title.
PS374.C5D46   1998
813.009'321732—dc21   97-45409
CIP

To my parents

Contents

Preface

The development of literary realism and naturalism has been so closely associated with the literary exploration of the urban scene that, as Amy Kaplan puts it, we have come to "treat the seamy side of urban life as the touchstone of the 'real' itself" (*Construction* 44). Yet the reappraisal of the realist and naturalist corpus in the last fifteen years has shattered the belief that novels can reveal the truth of the social world merely by offering literary snapshots of urban poverty. Critics like Rachel Bowlby, June Howard, Amy Kaplan, Walter Benn Michaels, and Mark Seltzer have discarded the theory of literary mimesis that takes for granted that social facts can be represented by means of a transparent documentary aesthetic. In the process, the realist and naturalist city, no longer a mere setting for positivistic surveys, has become an intricate field of power relationships structured by interrelated discourses of economic production, population management, and racial and gender definition.

If the naturalist corpus has captured the attention of contemporary readers, it is, I believe, because our own ambivalence toward the world of large-scale urbanization uncannily resembles the emotions of turn-of-the-century novelists who witnessed its inception. At a time when urban space is being refashioned by postindustrial information technologies, we can easily appreciate how naturalist writers, sometimes regarded as crude painters of American life, approached their rapidly evolving environment both with acute sociological intelligence and with a willingness to let themselves be mystified by the promise of new conditions.[1]

I argue here that in the early twentieth century, ambivalence toward the city expressed itself in the authors' tendency to describe the metropolis as a site of terror and wonder, in accordance with Edmund Burke's definition of the sublime. Today, this emotional configuration still influences our perception of urban landscapes in the form of what is now called the postmodern sublime (Jameson, *Postmodernism* 34; Tabbi x). By using the model of the sublime, critics of urban fiction acknowledge that it is simplistic to condemn twentieth-century cities for being alienating: we must take into account the fact that the urban world generates in its inhabitants a dialectic of powerlessness and power fantasies that inspires negative affects, no doubt, but also exhilaration. Through the mirror of naturalist fiction, I wish to analyze the discursive forms that this relation to the city assumes and the historical conditions that shaped its development. At their most utopian, we may venture, the emotions of the urban sublime are rooted in fascinated wonder for what novelist Robert Herrick calls "the realization of multitudinous humanity" (*Together* 185). Yet their mode of expression has been managed and contained by the construction of corporate or political spectacles with the trappings of sublime magnificence.

At bottom, this book investigates how early-twentieth-century literature represents the city's social bonds through various metaphorical idioms, some of which carry affects of fascination and fear. I contend that the aesthetic of sublimity constructs a sociologizing literary discourse particularly suited to articulate the boundary that separates the seen and the unseen, the observable and the mysterious aspects of the city's class, gender, and ethnic structure. As the existence of a postmodern sublime indicates, this field of exploration is not exclusively tied to the literary corpus of realism and naturalism. This book, which covers American literature between the 1890s and the First World War, should be read as an investigation of one moment in the evolution of a broader aesthetic. The sublime as I understand it here—that is, in the tradition of Burke and Kant—is a configuration of the gaze that was elaborated in romanticism and was progressively transposed to industrial and urban settings, determining the evolution of nineteenth-century architecture, literature, and painting. After naturalism, it resurfaced in novelists like Richard Wright, Ralph Ellison, John Dos Passos, and Thomas Pynchon, and also plays a decisive part in popular genres like detective stories and science fiction. The specific contribution of turn-of-the-century fiction to the history of the sublime is the insight that urban locales had, in the early decades of the twentieth century, become mystifying enough to support descriptions in terms of terror and wonder. Also, as literary genres, realism and naturalism initiated what we might call in Bakhtinian terms a pattern of dialogization of the rhetoric of terror: in these texts, the investigation of the visible and hidden aspects of the metropolis is performed by the interplay of several idioms against each other—realism and romance, documentary narration and the sublime, positivism and the gothic, to mention a few subcategories. This plurivocal approach of an unrepresentable social world was handed over to later texts of the urban sublime, which adapted it according to their own generic configuration: it reappears in the discursive discontinuities of Dos Passos's panoramic novels or in the heterogeneous fabric of postmodern science fiction.

Realist and naturalist works also make it possible for me to throw light on the historical logic underlying the persistence of the urban sublime in the literary history of the twentieth century. A large number of texts in the present corpus are novels of initiation to urban life in which protagonists stand on the threshold of the city, beholding it as a mysterious totality. The sublime is, I believe, historically tied to this initiation motif: it proceeds from characters or writers who find themselves in the position of having to investigate a new world, or to reassess a supposedly familiar one. The sublime is therefore the expression of historical changes deep enough to be perceived as a radical mutation in the subject's overall environment—urbanization for Dreiser, African-American migration to the cities in Wright and Ellison, information technologies in Pynchon and cyberpunk.[2] A constant feature of this cultural situation is the need to represent the new objects in totalizing terms—or, more accurately, to test whether they lend themselves to totalizing discourses. In naturalism, I argue, this panoramic imperative leads to the elaboration of a pseudo-totalizing vitalistic rhetoric; in postmodern science fiction, it underlies the elaboration of the concept of cyberspace—the metaphorical site where informational interconnections can be visualized. Through their concern for the unrepresentability of the social totality, the texts of the urban sublime raise questions whose stakes I attempt to clarify here, but which, in my perspective, remain aporetic. They investigate indeed whether the human-made environment of urban life viewed in its totality is understandable in human terms; whether its sociological impenetrability might merely be a tool of ideological control; or, on the contrary, whether the megalopolis is ruled by what Jean-François Lyotard calls a process of "complexification"—a self-propelled development that cannot be monitored by individuals or groups (*Inhuman* 199).

Acknowledgments

This book on American naturalism originated in a graduate seminar paper, developed into a dissertation, and later grew into its present printed form. At all stages of the completion of this project, I have been helped by supportive readers, whose contributions I should like to acknowledge here.

My thanks go to Alan Trachtenberg, who supervised my doctoral dissertation on naturalism, and to Bryan Jay Wolf, who read the initial paper and suggested that the topic deserved to be treated on a broader scale. While a graduate student at Yale, I also benefited from the highly useful comments of Michael Denning, Lynn Wardley, George Shulman, Ann Fabian, Hazel Carby, and Vera Kutzinski. Among the Belgian colleagues who helped me in the completion of the dissertation, I should like to express my gratitude to Gilbert Debusscher, Philippe De Brabanter, Philippe Hunt, and Chantale Zabus. For convincing me that the text deserved publication in book form, I wish to thank Linda Docherty, Ramón Gutiérrez, and James Machor. The contributions of June Howard, Michael Bell, and, at the University of Illinois Press, of Veronica Scrol have been essential in shaping the manuscript into a book-worthy argument.

The collections of the Sterling Memorial Library and of the Beinecke Library proved an essential asset in gathering the sources for my essay. I also wish to extend my thanks to the personnel of the Yale Medical Library, who helped me use their reprographic facilities, and to the staff of the American Studies Center of the Bibliothèque Royale Albert I in Brussels.

Portions of this book have been published separately in an earlier or different form. An early version of the discussion of *Sister Carrie* in chapter 6 appeared in *Belgian Essays on Language and Literature* (*BELL*) 1991, edited by Pierre Michel, Diana Phillips, and Eric Lee (published by L³ Liège Language and Literature). The reading of Sinclair's *The Jungle* was included in *BELL* 1993, edited by Pierre Michel, Andrew Norris, and Eric Lee (also published by L³ Liège Language and Literature). Segments of the discussions of London's *The Valley of the Moon* (chapter 8), of London's *The Sea-Wolf* (chapter 13) and of Dreiser's *The "Genius"* (chapter 14), brought together under the title "Amazons and Androgynes: The Redefinition of Gender Roles at the Turn of the Century," appeared in *American Literary History* 8:4 (Winter 1996), published by Oxford University Press.

Excerpts from Upton Sinclair's *The Jungle*, © 1905, 1906 by Upton Sinclair, are used by permission of Viking Penguin, a division of Penguin Books USA, Inc. Excerpts from Walter Benjamin's *Reflections: Essays, Aphorisms, Autobiographical Writings*, © 1978 by Harcourt Brace & Company, are used by permission of the publisher.

PART I

*Realist and
Naturalist Discourses
of the Urban World*

CHAPTER I

From the Natural
to the Urban Sublime

When characters in turn-of-the-century novels discover the big city, they feel that the urban landscape outreaches their powers of perception. In Theodore Dreiser's *The "Genius,"* for instance, the young painter Eugene Witla is overcome with "the thrill of something big" (96) when, on the final stage of his first trip to New York, he hears the brakemen announce the Jersey City crossing: "He walked out through the gates to where low arches concealed ferry boats, and in another moment it was all before him, sky line, bay, the Hudson, the Statue of Liberty, steamers, liners. . . . It was something he could never have imagined without seeing it, and this swish of real salt water, rolling in heavy waves, spoke to him as music might, exalting his soul. What a wonderful thing this was, this sea—where ships were and whales and great mysteries. What a wonderful thing New York was, set down by it, surrounded by it, this metropolis of the country" (97). The city, which makes "a great noise like the sea," leads Eugene to "[realize] emotionally the mass of people"; he understands that "mere humanity in packed numbers makes a kind of greatness" (97). Likewise, Isabel Price, the heroine of Robert Herrick's *Together,* finds New York as "awe-compelling" as "the Arizona canyon into which she had once descended": the city, which "boil[s] and hum[s]," making her "pulses leap," exerts on her sensibility a similar impact as "the canyon's eternal quiet" (182). In both texts, the spectacle of the metropolis stirs emotions of sublimity anchored in memories of overwhelming nature: Eugene and Isabelle resemble figures in paintings by Thomas Cole, Albert Bierstadt, or Caspar David Friedrich, who encounter sublime vistas at the turn of a mountain path.

Epiphanies such as those described by Dreiser and Herrick constitute the most visible aspect of a vast constellation of discourse that I wish to call the urban sublime. The present interpretation of naturalist fiction is meant to map out the various ramifications of these tropes of sublimity. In this way, we will be able to determine how they inflect our vision of turn-of-the-century writers' attitudes toward the society of their time. What links these late-nineteenth-century city novels to the tradition of the sublime is their tendency to depict "the active life of the great strange city" as a paradoxical experience of terror and wonder (Cahan, *Levinsky* 90). Indeed, in the gamut of affects induced by the metropolis, the spiritual uplift that characterizes Eugene Witla's and Isabelle Price's first experience of the city represents only the sublimated counterpart of a powerful backlog of anxieties. Eugene, for all his sense of wonder, must ward off the impression that Manhattan is "a little shabby" and "physically . . . not distinguished" (98). As subjects for his paintings, Eugene will characteristically favor New York street scenes drenched in a "cold, wet drizzle" (223), with ghostly crowds that show a "buttoned, huddled, hunched, withdrawn look" (219). In a more exuberant vein of sublime imagery, Laura Jadwin, the heroine of Norris's *The Pit*, can enjoy a glimpse of the awesome Chicago Board of Trade only if she dares to brave the "prolonged and muffled roar" of an overwhelming crowd of speculators whose "eddies" and "subsidiary torrents" (380) coalesce into the "tremendous cloaca" (79) of a human whirlpool. Thus, for naturalist protagonists, the otherwise exhilarating contact with the metropolis has been superseded by pessimistic feelings of ambivalence, expressed in the gothic terms of horror and wonder: New York, says the protagonist of James Weldon Johnson's *The Autobiography of an Ex-Coloured Man*, is "the most fatally fascinating thing in America" (89).

⁂

The most often quoted philosophical sources for the aesthetic of sublimity are Edmund Burke's *Philosophical Enquiry into the Origin of Our Ideas of the Sublime and Beautiful,* and Immanuel Kant's *Critique of Judg-*

ment.[1] Burke's definition of sublimity revolves around power and terror: he argues that we should regard as sublime "whatever is fitted in any sort to excite the ideas of pain and danger, that is to say, whatever is in any sort terrible, or is conversant about terrible objects, or operates in a manner analogous to terror" (39). "Visual objects of great dimensions" (39), of great complexity and magnificence are likely to inspire such feelings. For Burke, sublime dread constitutes the initial stage of a scenario of emotional ambivalence that leads the subject from terror to delight. The latter emotion is generated by "the removal and moderation of pain" (42). It represents the reward of enjoying fear by proxy, and of thereby turning a peril into a source of pleasure. The self finds a form of empowerment in delight "when we have an idea of pain and danger, without being actually in such circumstances" (70).[2] Kant's view of sublimity, relying partly on Burke's earlier formulation, is oriented toward the dynamics of cognitive processes and aesthetic perception: for the German philosopher, the emotion of the sublime arises whenever we realize that human reason is liable to produce an idea of infinity that cannot be objectified by our understanding and our imagination: the mind struggles with a representation of an "absolute totality" with which it can never catch up (Kant 119).[3] The philosophical reward of this experience is the assurance that absolutes can manifest themselves to the subject, though in a "supersensible" form that remains undecipherable to the understanding (119).

By describing naturalism as a genre that perpetuates Burke and Kant's aesthetic of dread and fascination, I mean to argue that it stands midway in a cultural filiation that originated in romanticism, spread to the mid-nineteenth-century mysteries of the city, and now informs postmodernism. In its historical development, this tradition of the sublime has focused in turns on nature, the self, the industrial complex, the city, and the postmodern constellation of discourses. Initially, the Burkean and Kantian sublime found a fruitful outlet in the development of romantic literature and painting: it underlies the romantic belief that nature is endowed with infinite, quasi-divine powers, and that it serves as a source of spiritual regeneration.[4] In the course of the nineteenth century, the texts that expressed the sublimity of nature were displaced by a less consistent corpus that portrays the city and the industrial world as overwhelming and fascinating. Elizabeth McKinsey records this change in a study of nineteenth-century responses to Niagara Falls: she argues that Niagara tourists, initially attracted to the wonders of nature, were progressively seduced by the power emanating from the technological environment of the site—the Erie canal, the power plant, the bridges.[5] McKinsey, borrowing a term coined by Leo Marx, contends that the perception of Niagara Falls veered thereby toward the "technological sublime" (Leo Marx qtd. in McKinsey 139).[6]

Among historians of urbanization proper, the belief that cities can inspire dread and wonder has been voiced by Nicholas Taylor. In his study of the "Awful Sublimity of the Victorian City" (431), Taylor chronicles the development of an architectural aesthetic tailored to the goals of industrialism and oriented toward the production of overpowering city structures. The sublime apprehension of urban landscapes described by Taylor has its equivalent in American graphic arts—in what Peter Bacon Hales calls "Grand Style Urban Photography" (69). Hales discerns in portfolios and souvenir books of the post–Civil War period a fondness for grandiose representations of the developing metropolises. Grand Style Photography finds its most significant expression in panoramas, which are meant to "make [the city] comprehensible" and to reduce its fragmentation to "holistic unity" (73). Those panoramas, Hales argues, contributed to the cultural climate that paved the way for the City Beautiful Movement, the post–Civil War drive for the rebuilding of American cities along monumental lines.

Elisabeth McKinsey's claim that urban capitalism initiated a declension in the feelings of sublimity, depriving this aesthetic of its "necessary foundation" in nature (281), finds little resonance in Taylor's and Hales's studies. Unlike McKinsey, historians of the city can, I think, not take for granted the idea that the experience of sublimity leads to authentic empowerment. From the perspective of the human-made urban environment, it is indeed easier to discern that the moment of sublime terror is always to some extent a social construct, that it is a spectacle liable to be harnessed to an ideological agenda.[7] In romanticism, this political appropriation of the sublime leads to the elaboration of rituals of spectatorship that construct nature as an object of desire and conquest. In the city, Taylor and Hales suggest, it works by encouraging subjects to admire overwhelming landscapes of exploitation, or to give their assent to upper-class utopias of urban planning.

Implicit in Taylor and Hales is the idea that the politics of the urban sublime revolves around the issue of legibility—the readability of city space, which conditions both the sociological and the narrative gaze. Theoreticians of urban life have pointed out that the growing intricacy of the modern metropolis may defeat any attempt at description—an approach that makes the city fit the requirements of the Kantian sublime. Michel de Certeau has argued, for instance, that the city cannot be viewed as a field of programmed and controlled processes: it is a human site crisscrossed by a set of illegible power patterns (171). Likewise, in *The Image of the City*, Kevin Lynch analyzes the factors that determine the "legibility" (2) or "imageability" (9) of the urban sphere. Lynch, in an optimistic inspiration shared by few of his contemporaries, contends that town planning should consist in restoring the imageability of urban space (2, 9). The terms of Lynch's description, with their implicit comparison between urban space and texts, have been taken up by Steven Marcus in "Reading the Illegible," an analysis of the anxiety generated by the labyrinthine space of Victorian cities. Among literary critics, the image of the textual city has been vividly evoked by Alan Trachtenberg in his comments on Edgar Allan Poe's "The Man of the Crowd" and Stephen Crane's journalistic sketches. Trachtenberg argues that the city and its obsessive characters "are like a book that does not permit itself to be read" ("Experiments" 139); the reality of fragmented urban space always seems "to flee into the shadows of another street." Quoting Jean-Paul Sartre, Trachtenberg adds that "[a] city is a material and social organization which derives its reality from the ubiquity of its absence" (139). This formula makes urban space an embodiment of Derrida's concept of textuality and *différance:* the city, like the text, is pervaded with the "absence" that, Derrida contends, "belongs to the structure of all writing" ("Signature" 88).

The approach to the legibility of urban space that I follow most consistently in these pages is borrowed from Fredric Jameson's discussion of postmodernity. To Jameson, the interpretation of urban space becomes the index of the readability of a larger entity—the social totality, a term by which the author designates the hypothetical synthesis of all social and economic relations. Less optimistic than Lynch, Jameson contends that postmodernity renders urban space radically illegible: to the members of a postmodern community, he argues, the "contemporary world system" has become an "impossible" totality—a mental image so distended that it cannot be actualized in our imagination (*Postmodernism* 38). Invoking Burke's discourse on terror and Kant's *Critique of Judgment*, Jameson argues that this breakdown in sociological representation fosters emotions of sublime fear. In this logic, the chief object of sublime dread in our urban societies is the labyrinthine information technology of post–World War II capitalism. Yet, as confusing as it is, the techno-structure is the hieroglyph of something even less imageable: it is "mesmerizing and fascinating not so much in its own right," Jameson writes, but because it offers a "representational shorthand" (38) for the social and economic relations of "the whole world system of present-day multinational capitalism" (37).

The urban landscapes that best embody the postmodern structure of feelings characterized by Jameson are those that appear in postmodern science fiction, from Ridley Scott's cult movie *Blade Runner* (1982) to William Gibson's and Bruce Sterling's cyberpunk novels.[8] I believe, however, that Jameson's argument is equally relevant to naturalism because it points out the impossiblity of representing social totalities on the basis of the outward evidence of urban life. Also, Jameson implies that an illegible social scene like our own—or, one might add, like the naturalist metropolis—gives rise to a residual mysticism. In his analysis, the sublimity of the city is liable to express itself not only through the most imposing features of the urban scene, but also through marginal, decentered epiphanies. The uncanny presence of the "impossible totality" (38) informs, for instance, the tendency of postmodern art to endow the squalor of the late-twentieth-century metropolis with an aura of mesmeric seduction. Thus, the fascination exerted by photorealist cityscapes "where even the automobile wrecks gleam with some new hallucinatory splendor" (32–33) has the same emotional basis as the ecstasies of the romantic sublime: it betokens the apprehension of an enigmatic hidden world. Likewise, I wish to show that in naturalism, the literary metropolis is endowed not only with infinite scope but also with unfathomable depths; its sublimity is partly conveyed through a disseminated thematic of gothic uncanniness and secret revelations. Theodore Dreiser's novels, for instance, suggest that the surfaces of the city open out on "the other half of life in which we have no part," or on the "mysteries which may never be revealed" (*Carrie* Pennsylvania 177).[9] This implies that, in naturalism as in postmodernism, we cannot restrict our analysis to the most conspicuous signs of the city's power. Rather, we have to explore how the rhetoric of sublimity marks out the visible from the hidden realms of experience, and how it defines the modalities that allow subjects to gain access to either of them.

∽❨❩∾

In the structure of this book, I have tried to do justice to the problematic of visibility and invisibility that I discern in turn-of-the-century fiction. I have therefore worked from the outward manifestations of the naturalist sublime—the commodity market, the crowd—down to more deeply embedded issues like primitivistic genealogies or artistic empowerment. Thus, after the introductory chapters of part 1, which deal with the theoretical issues of the urban sublime, part 2 analyzes the economics constructed by turn-of-the-century novels. The main object of interpretation there is the representation of urban markets of speculation through a gendered discourse that I wish to call the oceanic sublime. This idiom portrays mechanisms of exchange and production as processes of biological reproduction. Part 3 deals with the sociology of the naturalist sublime and with the idiom in which it expresses itself—naturalist gothic; the main focus of these chapters is the crowd in its grotesque, abject manifestations. I point out that naturalist novelists use uncanny tropes of Darwinian primitivism in order to express their sense that the ethnic or class origins of populations are difficult to trace in an urban context. The texts analyzed in this section also reveal that naturalism elaborates a politics of hypnotic charisma in order to channel the energies of the threatening masses. Part 4 examines how the sublime imagery of the discourse of Darwinism is woven into the naturalist writer's representations of artistic practice. The novels of artistic education interpreted there elaborate scenarios of empowerment for writers who cannot find—or refuse to assume—a stable work or gender identity in the sublime urban scene.

The corpus on which my argument relies ranges from the 1890s to the end of the First World War. This time frame covers the beginnings of naturalism in the United States and stretches to the years when, I believe, the fiction of the sublime metropolis became a spent force and was superseded by modernism. In terms of genre, my readings focus predominantly on texts that fit in the naturalist canon, but they also cover a number of realist works. In the next chapter I contend indeed that, for the sake of the present essay, the boundaries of realism and naturalism need to be redrawn and that the complementarity of the two genres must be redefined. Within these generic categories, another factor that has determined the specific choice of texts is the fact that in the early twentieth century, the writer's prerogative to investigate the public sphere is regulated along gender and ethnic lines. A majority of the corpus is made up of works by William Dean Howells, Frank Norris, Theodore Dreiser, Jack London, and Upton Sinclair—white men who had made the exploration of the new metropolis a test of their writerly masculinity. I contrast their representation of the city with other approaches of urban life, elaborated from the point-of-view of women authors—Edith Wharton, Jane Addams, Charlotte Perkins Gilman, Charlotte Teller—or of black and immigrant writers like Charles Waddell Chesnutt, James

Weldon Johnson, and Abraham Cahan. Also, among the canonical novelists traditionally associated with naturalism, there is one name that I
have not taken into consideration for in-depth analysis—Stephen Crane.
In a later chapter, I explain indeed in what respect Crane does not qualify as a novelist of the urban sublime, and fits rather in a protomodern-
ist tradition different from the corpus of sociological vitalism reviewed
here.

Surprisingly perhaps, not all texts in the present sample qualify as city
novels in the narrow meaning of the term: Jack London's Yukon tales
or Willa Cather's stories of the midwest are on the face of it unrelated
to the story of American urbanization. I have included these works in
the present argument, however, because I believe that in spite of their
rural or natural settings, they handle issues of economic or personal
empowerment from a perspective that would simply be unavailable outside of a cultural context determined by urbanization. In general terms,
naturalist novels establish profound continuities between their representation of city and nature.[10] Environmental historian William Cronon, in
his study of Chicago—*Nature's Metropolis*—suggests that novelists of the
end of the century displayed an intermittent awareness of the "natural
power" embodied in the city. To Hamlin Garland, for instance, "the city
became almost a force of nature itself" (13). Cronon remarks that Garland's "metaphors are all natural" and that, to him, "the city was the great
ocean, to which all fresh streams must flow and become salt" (13). Likewise, June Howard and Mark Seltzer, when discussing Jack London's
works, have pointed out that the paradigms of naturalist sociology apply indiscriminately both to the city and the wilderness: Howard discerns
in the urban field of Dreiser's *Sister Carrie* a set of semantic binarisms
that also informs the universe of London's arctic stories (Howard 50–
51). Seltzer argues that the main political issue of London's Klondike is
"Systematic Management"—the disciplinary norms that are imposed on
industrial workers (169). In these pages, I argue that this blurring of the
boundary between city and nature is due to the deployment of naturalist discourses of the oceanic sublime and the gothic. This phenomenon
is best visible in passages where London, Cather, or others use the elements of the natural world as allegorical signifiers for the metropolis:
when wolf-dog White Fang, in London's eponymous novel, is transplant-
ed from Alaska to San Francisco, he spontaneously views the screeching cable cars as grotesque urban avatars of "the lynxes he had known
in the northern woods" (365). The surprising similarity between land and
city thus brought to light in this gothic passage encourages us to inter-

pret the whole novel as a didactic genealogy of the power relationships at work not only in the natural but also in the urban world. For these reasons, the perimeter of the literary object that we call the naturalist city must be broadened beyond the confines of visible urban space.

The investigation of the sublime generates its own brand of terminological inflation. Because the concept of the sublime is transferrable to different contexts, critics and philosophers have felt the need to subdivide it into ever new ramifications: negative, mathematical, egotistical, natural, feminine, American, hysterical, nuclear, or failed. Some of these subcategories will prove useful for the present argument, and the interpretation of the naturalist sublime will itself contribute a few terms of its own: in addition to the keywords of the urban and the naturalist sublime, I will refer to an "animistic" and a "genealogical" subset of the rhetoric of sublimity, or to the naturalist "politics of charisma." In this, I do not wish to make claims for more methodological neatness than the present argument can accommodate: these neologisms are heuristic tools with a local value. Yet what stands out from the uneven spread of the naturalist discourse of sublimity are the twin terms of the oceanic sublime and of naturalist gothic, as well as the socio-narrative processes to which they contribute—the pseudo-totalization and the dialogization of urban space.

CHAPTER 2

Critical Reassessments
of American Realism
and Naturalism

In the 1980s, critics of realism and naturalism, loosely labeled as new historicists, deeply reshaped our perception of the ideological strategies enacted by turn-of-the-century fiction.[1] Until then, the politics of realism and naturalism had been viewed through the literary-historical narrative elaborated in the 1920s and 1940s by Vernon L. Parrington and Alfred Kazin, or by Warner Berthoff and Donald Pizer in the 1960s. This earlier generation of critics contend that realism and naturalism function as vehicles of democratic emancipation.[2] Parrington, for instance, argues that realism fought against the Puritanical strictures of the Genteel Tradition and denounced the social injustices brought about by "the industrialization of America" (xxvi, 179). Neo-historicists like June Howard, Rachel Bowlby, Mark Seltzer, Walter Benn Michaels, and Amy Kaplan, on the contrary, expose what they take to be the naive assumptions of their predecessors' left-wing-liberal interpretations. For instance, they demystify the claim that Theodore Dreiser and Frank Norris were staunch adversaries of what Parrington calls the "plutocracy" (118).[3] In broader terms, they argue that realism and naturalism remap turn-of-the-century class, gender, and race relationships in ways that consolidate the hegemony of the middle classes, and that ensure the persistence of patriarchal and nativist ideologies.

The 1980s reappraisal of the politics of realism and naturalism proceeds from a rethinking along post-structuralist lines of the logic by which texts are produced within their historical moment. Central to this change in critical perspective has been the concept of textuality—the assumption that historical processes are structured by textual mechanisms similar to those that inform literary texts. At bottom, neo-historicists discard as epistemologically invalid the belief that realism can deliver an accurate, objective record of social conditions. This view, June Howard argues, qualifies as "naive reflectionism" (17); it fails to acknowledge that "representative processes . . . *produce* rather than *transcribe*" their "real object," and that this process of production is itself an ideological act (14). There are, however, divergences among neo-historicists about the specific mode of interaction of history and discourse. June Howard believes that the latter is ultimately fashioned by the "limiting conditions" (127) of a given historical situation; in this, she follows Fredric Jameson, who argues that the impact of history has an extra-linguistic origin, even if it can only be perceived through ideologically oriented discourses (*Political* 35). Seltzer's and Michaels's approaches imply, on the contrary, that by discarding the reflectionist theories of mimesis, we abandon any nostalgic yearning for a qualitative distinction between history and text: the semiotic or pragmatic operations that produce texts construct history as well. In this logic, studying culture means charting the complex interlocking of a plurality of discursive fields, without assuming that one consistently acts as the limiting condition of the other.

Given these theoretical differences, it is possible to distinguish two neo-historicist ways of describing the fictional universes of realism and naturalism. One group of readers—June Howard, Rachel Bowlby, and Amy Kaplan—are close to earlier Marxist criticism in that they regard the sociological categories of class structure, political actor, and historical moment as key elements in the production of texts. For Howard and Kaplan, naturalist and realist novels articulate an ideological discourse that is shaped by social institutions—department stores, middle-class domesticity, labor, the stock exchange—and that reshapes them in return. Mark Seltzer's and Walter Benn Michaels's studies, on the contrary, describe realism and naturalism as a semiotic economy of power—that is, as a textual apparatus that regulates the conditions of existence of subjects and ideologies.[4] Their approaches are both provoking and defamiliarizing because they do not assume that the geography of visible social space—the naturalist metropolis and its institutions—constitutes the primary scene where power relations are established. Instead, the two critics locate the construction of power at the intersection of discourses scattered widely through the novels or through the social science of the day. This method, however, makes realism/naturalism a highly fragmented object, without a locale or an identifiable cast.

Overall, the neo-historicist reappraisal of turn-of-the-century fiction has focused on the construction of ideology and has bypassed the issue of genre definition. Among the 1980s readers discussed above, only June Howard offers a systematic discussion of the distinguishing features and the boundaries of the turn-of-the-century canon. Michael Bell questions the very usefulness of such classificatory ventures: he contends that there is no "coherent formal tradition" underlying the use of "realism" and "naturalism" (4) in American letters: these labels, Bell argues, were used by writers within the framework of cultural or ideological debates unrelated to a theory of genre (5). I believe, however, that the theoretical coyness of Bell's approach is limiting. It has resulted in a situation where the realist and naturalist canons have been taken for granted: critical studies have used corpora selected on an ad hoc basis, and the internal subdivisions of turn-of-the-century fiction have not been reexamined. In these pages, I wish therefore to argue that it is possible to define criteria allowing us to sort out naturalistic from realistic texts; simultaneously, I wish to make this generic model capable of acknowledging both the discursive heterogeneity of the two genres and their complex interdependence.

June Howard's discussion of genre studies brings to light the theoretical hurdles that my own reshuffling of the naturalist canon must clear. Howard, commenting on Northrop Frye's and Tzvetan Todorov's essays, shows that arguments about genre have found themselves locked in an aporia opposing advocates of "theoretical" and "historical genres" (5)— of genres defined as consistent abstract models, transcending actual texts, and genres as they manifest themselves concretely in history, with their heterogeneity and inconsistencies. Howard argues that present-day critics reject the concept of the theoretical genre as impossibly nonhistorical and formalistic. Yet, she believes that studying historical genres outside of a theoretical framework may lead to the crippling nominalism of an antiquarian approach (8). If critics choose to focus exclusively on what she calls the "generic text" (10)—the writers' often conflicting pronouncements on genre categories—they are led to the unconvincing conclusion that texts classified under the same labels were produced without any regulating norm. Howard negotiates this aporia by arguing that literary classifications are neither timeless abstractions nor shapeless groupings of works: they are "distinguishable if not distinct" cultural institutions, produced by "historically specific practices of reading and writing" (9). This amounts to a partial rehabilitation of theoretical genre study: theoretical arguments are, in this perspective, constitutive of the existence of a historical genre, provided one view theoretical activity not as the exploration of a timeless literary system but rather as a form of literary-historical *bricolage* carried out by readers, writers, and critics within their cultural contexts.

Studying American naturalism on the basis of its generic text—along antiquarian lines, as it were—raises impassable problems: the very existence of the movement as a historical entity can, in this case, not be taken for granted—less so in fact than even Bell and Howard suggest. In a surprising statement, Bell describes naturalism as a "less controversial" category than realism (4). Yet, against the idea that a solid naturalist corpus coexisted alongside its less consistent realist counterpart, a strong case could be made that the period was dominated only by the different variants of one single broad realist movement. This classification is vindicated by the fact that the term "naturalism" was hardly a rallying cry for turn-of-the-century novelists. Frank Norris does use the word as a full-fledged generic classification when he points out the romantic features of Zola's fiction (*Criticism* 71–72). Otherwise, the generic text of naturalism is rather patchy. The naturalist label is, for instance, absent from what we might call the turn-of-the-century novels of artistic education—biographical narratives of artistic life like London's *Martin Eden* or Dreiser's *The "Genius."* Indeed, the generic text articulated in these works points toward realism: it is in the name of the latter movement that Martin Eden, Jack London's partly autobiographical persona, wages his struggle against the "bourgeois spirit" (462); likewise, it is by acting on the belief that "only realism" matters for his art that Eugene Witla, the protagonist of *The "Genius,"* is able to make a name in the art world (62).

I do not mean, of course, to refute the critical usefulness of naturalism as a literary category. Instead, I wish to underline to what extent the historical genre of American naturalism was constructed by theoretical arguments coming from outside the writer's practice: even in the beginning of the century, the term was used largely by critical readers often better acquainted than the novelists with the developments of French or

Scandinavian literature. Parrington's notes on "Naturalism in American Fiction," with their remarkable discussion of philosophical determinism, are typical of this effort: they systematize a genre that had so far not been labeled with such consistency in American letters. Neo-historicist readings perform a critical intervention of the same nature: within a horizon of reading informed by post-structuralism and neo-Marxism, the 1980s critics have reshaped naturalism and realism into what Fredric Jameson would call new "semantic" and "syntactic" genres[5] (*Political* 107): they have reinscribed both the object of this corpus and its discursive strategies.

⁓❧❧⁓

In these pages, the change of theoretical paradigm that inspires my attempt to redefine the boundaries of realism and naturalism is the post-structuralist and Bakhtinian effort to acknowledge the discursive diversity of literary texts—the "heteroglossia" of fiction, as Bakhtin himself puts it (*Dialogic* 271). Mikhail Bakhtin argues that the novel is "a phenomenon multiform in style and variform in speech and voice," containing "heterogeneous stylistic unities" (261); as the French translator of Bakhtin puts it, the novel is "pluristylistic, plurilingual, plurivocal" (Bakhtin, *Esthétique* 87; my translation).[6] Likewise, Fredric Jameson, elaborating on Ernst Bloch's concept of the "'uneven development'" of textual structures, describes the novel as a "layered and marbled structure," whose "generic discontinuities" reveal the presence of heterogeneous ideological paradigms within the text (*Political* 141, 144).[7] This conception of fictional discourse applies directly to naturalism, whose disregard of aesthetic homogeneity has repeatedly been highlighted. Charles Child Walcutt characterizes naturalism as a "divided stream" (i), originating both in the realist and the transcendentalist traditions; Donald Pizer lists among the "essential constituents" of naturalism not only the realist analysis of local life but also "sensationalism" and "the melodramatic" (*Realism* 15). Yet Walcutt and Pizer write within a critical tradition that values organic cohesiveness: the recognition of stylistic heterogeneity in their argument resembles a paradoxical apology for what still remain aesthetic flaws. In Bakhtin's and Jameson's perspective, on the contrary, heterogeneous elements are allowed to interact meaningfully within a text.[8] Jameson argues, for instance, that the coexistence of realist and supernatural elements within nineteenth-century romance fiction is not parasitical, but symptomatic: it constitutes the literary manifestation of a tension between industrial and preindustrial outlooks.

The elements that make up the literary dialogization of turn-of-the-century novels could be itemized under a number of different labels—local color realism, sentimentalism, melodrama, and transcendentalism, as in Pizer and Walcutt; documentary discourse, the oceanic sublime, and the gothic, as in the present argument. It is, I think, productive to re-group this plurality of idioms within two broad headings—realist and naturalist discourse, respectively. In the present perspective, these two labels designate not self-contained genres, but epistemological and rhetorical formations that, I believe, coexist with different degrees of dominance in the works traditionally classified as either realist or naturalist. Provisionally, I wish to characterize these terms as follows: the discourse of realism, I suggest, is the literary idiom used by writers like William Dean Howells and Edith Wharton for the investigation of familiar worlds—in many cases, the family itself. The texts where realist discourse is the keynote are wedded to a demystificatory, documentary gaze with a local scope. Because realist discourse focuses on the visible logic of the social world, it must accept the limitations of positivistic vision; it adopts a mode of perception that acknowledges only the tangible evidence accessible to an individual observer or a social group. Rather than encompassing a boundless field of experience, the realist gaze explores what Amy Kaplan, borrowing Raymond Williams's term, calls "knowable communities" (*Social* 47)—the family, the workplace, the neighborhood, for instance.

Naturalist discourse, on the contrary, relies on documentary discourse to a considerable extent, but is also obsessed with the areas beyond the periphery of positivistic discourse. As such, naturalist discourse addresses the totality of its world, whether to attempt to capture it within its fiction or to reveal the impossibility of this task. In this, far from adopting an ironical demystification, it accommodates non-positivistic forms of intuition expressed through romance motifs and imagery, or through the gothic and the sublime. In the present corpus, the realist/naturalist line of division runs not only through literary texts, but also through social science essays: the works of close contemporaries like Fredric C. Howe, Simon Nelson Patten, and Jane Addams are polarized according to what might be called their naturalist and realist epistemologies. We will see below that, in novels as in nonfiction, the intermingling of realist and naturalist discourse is not a random juxtaposition, but obeys preferred patterns of dialogization: while neither realist nor naturalist discourse exists in isolation, texts that are predominantly realist tend to be more homogeneous than their naturalist counterparts. In realist novels, natu-

ralist discourse appears either as discursive slippages—lapses into romance, typically—or as a target for the author's demystifying critique.
No such striving for homogeneity is visible in naturalist texts: all of them
accommodate realist discourse within their plurivocal make-up, yet they
undermine the realist claim to documentary objectivity by implying that
realism stands on the same footing as other non-positivistic idioms.

Logically, the dialogic model developed here makes it harder to cir-
cumscribe realism and naturalism as historical genres with sharply
marked-out boundaries. Accordingly, by "realism" and "naturalism" I
understand genres shaped as blurry clusters of texts where, respectively,
realist or naturalist discourse prevails. There are important advantages
to this fuzzy logic, however. With this dialogical paradigm, it is easier
to conceptualize the uneven historical development of turn-of-the-century fiction—the problems of periodization arising from the close inter-
relationship of realism and naturalism. Traditionally, the boundaries of
the two genres have been drawn on a generational basis: as Donald Pizer puts it, "naturalism comes after realism," and is an "'extension' or a
'continuation' of realism" by writers of a later generation (*Social* 11).[9]
Yet, in the United States even more than in Europe, it is difficult to demarcate the two genres according to a clear historical divide—be it the
crisis of the Haymarket riots or the publication of *McTeague* or *Sister
Carrie*.[10] Indeed, instead of decreeing that naturalism superseded the previous genre as of the 1890s, we must take into account the persistence
of a tradition of literary realism that is embodied notably in the works
of Edith Wharton, H. B. Fuller, Robert Herrick, or David Graham
Phillips, and spills over into the twentieth century with the novels of
F. Scott Fitzgerald, and with immigrant writers like Anzia Yiezerska and
Mike Gold. Also, we must bear in mind that some writers labeled as
naturalists—Jack London, for instance—produced a significant number
of naturalist romances—novels that articulate an explicit sociological
message through romantic narrative strategies. While these works could
be treated as throwbacks to an outdated genre, it makes more sense to
use their existence as evidence that realism and naturalism developed in
parallel—as the two interdependent, overlapping forms of discourse
described above. My description of the turn-of-the-century field assumes,
of course, that realist and naturalist texts are generically discontinuous,
and that they draw, with significant differences in emphasis, on a common stock of literary components: in this view, the line of generic division runs not between historical periods but synchronically across the
turn-of-the-century corpus—in fact within the texts themselves.

An interesting acknowledgment of the continued interdependence of realism and naturalism has come from Amy Kaplan's essay on realism, which, paradoxically, does not acknowledge naturalism in its methodological grid. Her study criticizes Richard Chase's contention that the American novel is essentially oriented toward the romance, and that, as Kaplan puts it, "in the absence of a settled, class-bound society, Americans do not write social fiction" (*Social* 44).[11] Kaplan argues instead that Chase's "romance thesis" is ideologically biased against realism and has helped obscure its existence in American letters. Kaplan's argument must, however, account for the presence of massive amounts of romance elements in naturalist novels traditionally lumped together with realism. For this purpose, Kaplan argues that realism is not homogeneous, but consists in "a debate with competing definitions of reality" (160);[12] this debate is carried out in the clash of several types of discourse—among which are romance and sentimentalism. For instance, she points out that *Sister Carrie*—to her, a realist text—contains an unresolved dialectic between Dreiser's sentimental rhetoric and his documentary discourse. Yet, Kaplan adds, readers of Dreiser would be mistaken in wishing that the author smother his sentimentalism in order to deliver "a more hardboiled, dirty reality" (160): Dreiser's novel needs to express through its romance tropes the utopian yearnings that the documentary discourse cannot articulate. Thus, through this narrative hesitation, the realistic novel "exposes the way in which the terms of the realistic debate have become polarized rather than resolved" (160): it leaves the reader free to interpret the spectacle of its unsolved contradictions.

Of course, Kaplan reads the heteroglot character of turn-of-the-century novels in a direction opposed to what I am attempting here. In her argument, the elements of *Sister Carrie* that seem antithetical to realism—the lyrical outbursts in which characters let themselves be "hypnotized" by the city's "whirlpools of life" (Dreiser, *"Genius"* 103)—are reabsorbed within an enlarged definition of the realist genre. For my purposes, however, these elements contribute to what I call the rhetoric of urban sublimity, and they indicate, as Frank Norris already contended in his literary criticism, that there is a circumscribable segment of so-called realist fiction after Zola—naturalism, in fact—that carries a postromantic or a symbolist outlook.[13] In the readings of Howells's *A Hazard of New Fortunes* and of Dreiser's *Sister Carrie* below, I indicate that the function of the romance idiom of naturalist discourse is not merely to acknowledge the existence of domains that the documentary gaze cannot analyze. What I want to bring out in naturalist discourse is rather a tendency to prolong documentary exploration through the medium of romance or the sublime: when Dreiser hints at philosophical "mysteries which may never be revealed" (*Carrie* Pennsylvania 177) he is doing more than just signaling the limitations of his own power of realist representation.

The Limits of Urban Realism:
William Dean Howells's
A Hazard of New Fortunes

In *A Hazard of New Fortunes* (1890), I propose to highlight how the dialogic heterogeneity of realist/naturalist fiction determines the nature of the sociological gaze that can be constructed in this corpus. The pivotal status of Howells's novel in the literary history of the period makes it a privileged source for this argument. *A Hazard of New Fortunes* was written at the threshold of the naturalist decade by the major proponent of genteel realism in America; Alfred Kazin underlines that the novel, with its depiction of urban crowds and immigrants, made Howells appear as the advocate of naturalism—a form of fiction he actually did not endorse (7, 25). Because of these contradictory characteristics, the novel displays with great clarity how the literary exploration of the American metropolis expresses itself through the interplay of several types of discourse. In *Hazard*, Howells clings to the strategies of realistic fiction for the depiction of a social scene that Dreiser or Norris portray to a large extent through a discourse of romance. Only in a few scenes does the novelist tentatively resort to what I call the naturalist sublime. The choice of this particular dialogic pattern thoroughly shapes the author's attempt to present a comprehensive picture of the urban scene: realism and the naturalist sublime support very contrasted forms of sociological description, with their respective capacities and limitations. By favoring one over the other, Howells reveals which segments of the city are, in his view, imageable and which are not. In this strategy of social representation, I wish to argue, the role of the naturalist sublime is literally peripheral: it marks out the territory where realist narration cannot venture.

A Hazard of New Fortunes is a novel of initiation to urban life. As such, it fits in a turn-of-the-century corpus that includes the writings of people like Hamlin Garland, Theodore Dreiser, Abraham Cahan, Robert Herrick, Upton Sinclair, David Graham Phillips, James Weldon Johnson, or Jane Addams. The leitmotif of the "cityward journey," to borrow William Cronon's term (9), can be read as a literary historical statement: in this light, the decision to move to the metropolis dramatizes the options available to novelists who have chosen to represent social conditions at the turn of the century.[1] For these writers, the inclusion of the urban world into the boundaries of literary discourse fulfills the program of a certain mode of realist integrity. The city is indeed more than their protagonist's destination; it constitutes a literary object whose artistic legitimacy has to be tested against the literary and moral tradition that celebrates the virtues of the frontier and small-town life.[2] The power of anti-urban ideology at the time is mirrored in the fact that Howells and his contemporaries, unmindful of the existence of previous urban fiction, assume that the metropolis has to be described as if discovered for the first time: though American cities had been portrayed in the works of Charles Brockden Brown, George Lippard, Edgar Allan Poe, Nathaniel Hawthorne, and Herman Melville, the urban scene remained a puzzling novelty.

What the writers of Howells's generation found most unfamiliar in the cities of the 1880s and 1890s was, as Vernon Parrington puts it, the rise of the "subjugating power of the mass" (180). This new feature of urban life, Parrington and Alfred Kazin indicate, became highly visible after the Haymarket riots of 1886: the labor explosion laid bare the process of class conflict and class segregation then taking place in the United States (Parrington 245; Kazin 3). Howells's *A Hazard of New Fortunes* provides a middle-class perspective on this social crisis. The novel follows the itinerary of a family, the March household, in their move from genteel Boston to New York. To Mrs. March's Bostonian imagination, the metropolis on the Hudson looms as a threatening landscape, "so *big*, and *so* hideous," swamped under "all [those] millions" of anonymous city dwellers (14, 19). The cluster of characters with whom the main protagonists associate in New York revolves around a biweekly periodical,

Every Other Week, of which Basil March has been named editor. The periodical provides a common meeting-ground for Howells's characters; its socially varied cast allows the novelist to present a cross-class view of the city. Against the background of this island of human connectedness, Howells investigates the feelings of psychological alienation induced by urban living, as well as, in a more tentative manner, the complaints and the rebellion of the immigrant working class.

Amy Kaplan has argued that Howells's very project of mapping the multicultural, class-divided metropolis precipitates in his realist text a situation of constant crisis of representation (see *Social* 44–64). Realist writers, she contends, represent their social scene as a knowable community—that is, as a network "of mutual social recognition that unites diverse members" (47). In the post-Haymarket years, with the advent of socially segregated metropolises, the class-specific aspect of these structures of conviviality became evident; from a literary angle, they could only serve as basis for narratives with a local scope. This implies that the big city must remain irreducible to the narrative epistemology of realism, and that it appears as "'unreal'" (44) in the eyes of those who, like Howells's narrator, aim to survey it.

Kaplan suggests, however, that, in order to overcome the impression that characters in *Hazard* must inhabit this "unreal" (44) urban environment, Howells's novel develops a narrative strategy focused on the reconstitution of the domestic sphere. Like Alfred Habegger, she argues that the structures of kinship radiating from the family are the privileged object of the realist gaze: the home is the most immediate knowable community, and, consequently, the most acutely real segment of the realist universe.[3] Howells's task consists therefore in probing whether, among the multitudes of the metropolis, families can still serve as this yardstick of what is knowable. This is, Kaplan argues, the meaning of the March family's search for a home: their itinerary represents a project of "settling"—or domesticating—the otherness of the city. Through their eyes, we realize how a line can be drawn between the aspects of urban life that can be accommodated within the realist focus, and the perpetual other half—immigrants, strikes, proletarianization—that has to be discarded as useless information.

Because I read *Hazard* within a corpus of naturalist novels containing strong elements of romance, I am led to argue that the urban area that Howells inscribes beyond the boundary of realist vision is not useless and unreal, as Kaplan indicates: it constitutes instead the object of another discourse—the nonrealist idiom that conveys the terror of urban life. The generic discontinuity that this reading choice brings to light is, I believe, the constitutive element of the urban sublime. I wish to highlight the full implications of its presence in the text by showing how it is determined by Howells's project of mapping the urban world as a whole. *Hazard* performs what I wish to call a failed or pseudo-totalization. This term, which I derive indirectly from Georg Lukács's studies on realism, refers to the literary ambition to piece together the unified representation of an object—here, the urban scene—that exceeds a totalizing gaze. I specify in chapter 5 how the concepts of pseudo-totality and retotalization can be used in a reading of realism and naturalism that takes into account the post-structuralist critique of these terms. At this stage, I wish to point out that this terminology accurately describes the unstable narrative dynamic of Howells's novel: *Hazard*, even though it acknowledges the social fragmentation of 1890s New York, keeps trying to present a total picture of its social relations by means of a modified version of the family narrative. It is when this attempt misfires that the text is brought to switch from its realistic narrative mode into romance.

The pseudo-totalizing strategy of *Hazard* focuses on the creation of Basil's magazine *Every Other Week*. Bringing together the staff of *Every Other Week* means indeed opening up the family sphere to a wider circle. In this way, Howells recreates in an urban context the knowable community that makes realist narration possible. Thus, Howells's characters—Basil March, as well as Fulkerson, the public relations agent—manage to gather an incongruous assembly that, as Basil puts it, includes "a fraternity and equality crank like poor old Lindau, and a belated sociological crank like Woodburn, and a truculent speculator like old Dryfoos, and a sentimentalist like me, and a nondescript like Beaton, and a pure advertising essence like Fulkerson, and a society spirit like Kendricks" (291). However, in the socially divided environment of New York, Basil's utopian extended family cannot hope to maintain its cross-class character. Its coming apart is precipitated by a streetcar strike, which exacerbates the opposition that pits Lindau, the socialist, against the millionaire Dryfoos. These two characters had never completely fitted within Basil's group; they are therefore suitably disposed of—one by death, the other by moral chastening. At the end of the novel, the staff of the magazine plans to buy out Dryfoos's unwelcome share in the publication; thus, the community of *Every Other Week* is allowed to survive as an association of self-reliant cultural producers; it can, however, no longer aspire to be a microcosm of American society. This failure corroborates the idea that, from the perspective of Howellsian realism, the city constitutes what Fredric Jameson calls an "impossible totality" (*Postmodernism* 38).

In the light of Georg Lukács's theory of realism, the failure of Howells's totalizing strategy constitutes an American instance of the cultural crisis that turned realism into what Lukács regards as its decadent avatar, naturalism. Lukács, John Frow writes, evaluates the "epistemological" (10) worth of literary genres by reference to their "capacity for aesthetic realization of totality" (10–11). This concern for "the totality of . . . experience" (Lukács, "Narrate" 143) is indeed what allows Lukács to demarcate, both on stylistic and historical grounds, Balzac's realism from the genre initiated by Zola. According to Lukács's Hegelian aesthetic, there should be a close link between the totalizing ambitions of the realist novel and the organic consistency of its narrative techniques. Valuable realist fiction, Lukács writes, must offer a totalizing grasp of "the world in its contradictory dynamics" by means of a "comprehensive, well-organized and multifaceted epic composition" ("Narrate" 143).[4] Lukács means thereby that it is essential for realist texts to make descriptive details and historical narratives merge into a whole that reconciles the abstract and the concrete: only thus are they able to offer a representation of the totality of their object.[5] Naturalism, Lukács believes, deviates from this pattern by substituting theory for vital experience: it portrays social conditions through long descriptions, documentary catalogs, sociological exposés, or lifeless symbolism; these turn the text into a "kaleidoscopic chaos" that never adds up to a fictional totality ("Narrate" 133).

If naturalism initiates a period of literary decline, Lukács argues, it is because the very possibility of writing organically structured fiction is keyed to changes in the history of capitalism. For Lukács, valuable realist texts should be made up of narratives that let us know "the typical agents of a great historical conflict as human beings" ("Narrate" 141). This presupposes that writers are "steeped in vital experience" and therefore directly familiar with all aspects of their subject matter, as if the whole social scene were a knowable community (142). Yet, Lukács contends, such vital realism can only be produced at privileged moments in history: the development of capitalism and the spread of urbanization determine writers' opportunities to produce clear-sighted, totalizing fictions. Lukács argues, for instance, that Balzac, during the rise of the early-nineteenth-century bourgeoisie, was in a position to construct an organic panorama of Paris society still endowed with "dramatic effectiveness" (118).[6] However, such a literary synthesis of the abstract and the concrete was out of reach of late-nineteenth-century naturalists, because in their time, the consolidation of monopoly capitalism had rendered social relations reified and illegible: European society could therefore only be portrayed through the decadent, alienated medium of naturalist fiction, that is through texts hampered by abstract, parasitical theorizing.

Lukács's teleological Marxism requires that the moment of alienation embodied in naturalism should be resolved by a retotalization of experience whose site would be "the consciousness of the proletariat itself" (*Reader* 239). Even in the absence of this utopian framework, I believe that the Hungarian critic's literary-historical narrative remains illuminating, and can be transposed to the late-nineteenth-century American literary scene as it was perceived by Howells. In Lukács's periodization, the failed revolutions of 1848 constitute the cut-off point when the European bourgeoisie, trapped by the social system it itself set up, forfeited its progressive character and started producing literature with a diminished sociological acumen. If we follow Alfred Kazin's account of the genesis of American naturalism, the event that served the same function in the United States was the labor crisis of the 1880s and 1890s, the incorporation of the economy, and, most conspicuously, the "civic murder" of the Haymarket anarchists, which precipitated Howells's crisis of conscience (viii). In the light of this periodization, Howells's choice to investigate New York from the point of view of a composite community is similar to Zola's slice-by-slice depiction of Paris under Louis Napoleon: these are artificial literary contrivances, created as a response to a field of experience that defeats the observer's narrative strategies. Through these devices, the social scene is recomposed artificially, as a pseudo-totality.

৩৫

Lukács's remark that symbolism in the novel constitutes a departure from organic realism is relevant to the passages in *Hazard* where Howells tries to recompose his view of New York no longer by the construction of an extended family, but by strategies that anticipate the naturalist rhetoric of terror. The feature of the urban landscape that makes this pseudo-totalization possible in *Hazard* is the elevated railroad; thanks to its intrusive itinerary through city neighborhoods, the El allows the Marches to discover aspects of urban life that lie outside the middle-class round of life. Thus, the Marches become able to enjoy a distanced, "fleeting intimacy" with people "in second and third floor interiors" (63). To Basil, this opportunity to expand one's knowlegde of "reality"—in fact, of working-class domestic arrangements—is "better than the theater" (63). Less optimistically, Amy Kaplan argues that the El, by performing this spectatorial function, ultimately helps conceal and obliterate the sections of the urban landscape that the realist gaze cannot make sense of (51). The destructive side of the El is indeed aptly summarized in March's statement that the trains "kill the streets and avenues, but at least partially hide them, and that is some comfort"; Basil adds gleefully that the trains "do triumph over [the] prostrate forms [of the streets] with a savage exultation that is intoxicating" (50).

However, I believe that the intense affects generated by the image of the trains are not entirely rooted in their destructive power. In one scene, while waiting at a station, March declares that the El is "the one always and certainly beautiful thing" in New York (145). His wife remains "rapt by the sight" of an oncoming train, and then pulls her husband back in a panic (145). The night trains at the depot look like reservoirs of frightening forces, waiting "like fabled monsters of Arab story ready for the magician's touch, tractable, reckless, will-less—organized lifelessness full of strange semblance of life" (64). In these lines, we recognize what Leo Marx has called the "rhetoric of the technological sublime" (195)—the discourse that transfers the sublimity of natural landscapes to titanic human-made machines. Thus, I wish to suggest that the fascinating elevated trains are more than a symbol ot the realist text's necessity to annihilate what it cannot represent. The "savage exultation," the "intoxicating" manic gaiety that March associates with the El is similar to the sublime affects that seize Dreiser's Eugene Witla in his approach of New York; the grandiloquent rhetoric of these visions of power, instead of contributing to the realist logic of exclusion, expresses the hidden dimensions of the urban scene metaphorically.

Howells's tentative incursion into sublime pseudo-totalization is illustrated in a long description of one of Basil's rides on the East Side line. What we witness there is a change of paradigm—the temporary shift to a different vocabulary of description. So far, the spectatorial pleasure afforded by the train had consisted in the possibility of peeping into alien interiors. The expanded social panorama revealed in this way still had the well-ordered, well-compartmentalized character of the domestic sphere, and, in literary terms, it could be brought into focus according to the conventions of the picturesque. In the East Side passage, on the contrary, we realize how ethnically narrow Howells's family-based model of urban conviviality really is. The narrator, who reflects on the ethnic make-up of the New York crowd, is overwhelmed by his discovery of a surprising gamut of national diversities: "The small eyes, the high cheeks, the broad noses, the puff lips, the bare, cue-filleted skulls, of Russians, Poles, Czechs, Chinese; the furtive glitter of Italians: the blonde dulness of Germans: the cold quiet of Scandinavians—fire under ice" (162). In the dynamic of the enumeration, this cluster of scattered features creates the impression that March's ethnic clichés are vainly striving to keep up with a seemingly uncontrollable proliferation of alienness. The sense of a lack of perceptual control is echoed in the description of the heterogeneous architecture rushing by: the ugly façades of the Bowery dissolve into "an uproar to the eye" made up of "strident forms and colours," floating indifferently over "the life that dwelt, and bought and sold, and rejoiced or sorrowed, and clattered or crawled, around, below, above" (163).

The crisis of representation that manifests itself in these lines resembles a Bakhtinian epiphany—a moment of revelation in which Basil discovers the heteroglossia of American urban space. The city, Basil realizes, is no longer a social field that one single social class can control and submit to its cultural norms: it is a plurivocal environment filled by the discourse of social and ethnic Others. However, Bakhtin's model leaves open the possibility that subjects might negotiate the heterogeneity of social space by appropriating the Other's voice or language. This form of intersubjectivity, Alan Trachtenberg has argued, is not envisaged in Howells's novels, whose narrators can only speak in the voice of Anglo gentility ("Experiments" 144). I would add that Howells, for lack of a fully egalitarian cross-class and cross-ethnic dialogue, stages his character's confrontation with immigrants as an encounter with radical, sublime otherness: Howells anticipates naturalism in that he is tempted to represent the socio-ethnic fragmentation of the city in radically irreconcilable—and therefore more intensely fascinating and terrifying—terms.

Basil's elevated train epiphany brings about a dialogization of familiar experience and uncanny discovery—hence also of realism and romance. This process can be described on the basis of Thomas Weiskel's analysis of the dialectic of the romantic sublime. Basil is indeed threatened by the realization that the object of his contemplation radically exceeds his gaze—that the new city of immigrants generates a welter of information that cannot be assimilated within any existing cultural categories. In Weiskel's semiotic reformulation of the sublime experience, this perceptual confusion is interpreted as the sudden occurrence of an overflow of signifiers—the visual features of a sublime landscape, for instance—which dazzle the observer's capacity to reduce the sensory overload to a recognizable set of signifieds (26). Thus, in such a case, the surplus of stimuli outpaces the observer's ability to transform perception into meaning. The resolution of the disruption caused by the excess of the signifier over the signified, Weiskel argues, is effected through the recourse to metaphor: the crisis itself—the experience of excess—becomes the sign of a hitherto hidden, encompassing presence; indeed, if perceptual chaos cannot be understood in its own terms, it can still be interpreted as the manifestation of a higher order of being or thought, beyond the evidence of the senses.

In Howells's text, the shift into metaphor described by Weiskel takes the form of a change in models of representation—from the picturesque cast of Basil's initial vision to evolutionary reflections on the chaos of social life: "Accident and then exigency seemed the forces at work to this extraordinary effect; the play of energies as free and planless as those that force the forest from the soil to the sky; and then the fierce struggle for survival with the stronger life persisting over the deformity, the mutilation, the destruction, the decay of the weaker. The whole at moments seemed to him lawless, godless" (163). In these lines, the novelist manifests his protagonist's loss of sensory and intellectual control in the face of what Ronald E. Martin has called the naturalist "universe of force"— the social and biological energies that underlie the naturalist polity.[7] Weiskel's model suggests, though, that in a second moment, the feelings of powerlessness must be transmuted into a new sense of recovered mastery, based on the consciousness of having gained a privileged insight into these chaotic forces. In Howells, this sense of empowerment is expressed in two ways: on the one hand, the text adopts a vocabulary of description—the rhetoric of social Darwinism—endowed with a totalizing sweep, and, on the other hand, it asserts the narrator's epistemological privilege over his character. Indeed, Howells's narrator boasts that a "self-enwrapt" (163) personality like March can only imperfectly awaken to the realization of "the chaos to which the individual selfishness must always lead" (163). Only the writer and the reader can enjoy the full depth of the sublime epiphany.

Of course, the enclaves of sublime rhetoric have a marginal status with regard to the novel as a whole. As a realist text, *A Hazard of New Fortunes* tends to conceal the fact that it contains heterogeneous discourses. Characteristically, Howells shows how Basil, after the "vague discomfort" (164) induced by his inchoate social awakening, is again in a position to view the city as a picturesque spectacle, full of "neglected opportunities" for local painters (164). We might deduce from this that the sublime discourse, because it provides a glimpse of a larger field of experience, points out the limitations of the character's vision. Yet, the text as a whole is also determined by these boundaries: the representational strategies of Howells's novel are by and large grounded in the aesthetic of the picturesque endorsed by March, and they reproduce the character's ethnic prejudices. Ultimately, the main vehicle of narrative closure in Howells's novel turns out to be not the sublime, but religious quietism. Dryfoos's son, the religiously inclined Conrad, is killed in a labor fight and Margaret Vance, a member of the New York upper class, decides to join an Episcopalian sisterhood. Thus, to the unrepresentable chaos of the New York world, Howells opposes a utopian withdrawal from economic strife that is easier to reconcile with realist narration than the fascinated acceptance of struggle offered by the rhetoric of sublimity.

Overall, Howells's *Hazard* is representative of turn-of-the-century realist novels in that its pattern of dialogization marks out an area of realist discourse surrounded by a horizon of romance—both in dark and in utopian accents. This configuration of discourse recurs, for instance, in Edith Wharton's *The House of Mirth* (1905) and Kate Chopin's *The Awakening* (1899). These texts develop a family-centred realist narration, which they make interact with sentimental and sublime discourses, expressing a sense of threat or wonder. *The House of Mirth* chronicles the progressive estrangement of young Lily Bart from her social class, the New York aristocracy. Old New York constitutes the anchoring ground of Wharton's realist vision; thus, when her heroine is relegated to less fashionable circles, she finds herself surrounded by characters who have "no more real existence than the poet's shades in limbo" (274). Unreality reaches its climax in the depiction of Lily Bart's drug-induced death: in sublime tropes of dissolution, the text shows how Lily reaches "the dizzy brink of the unreal" (322). Yet, as in Howells, the author introduces a less pessimistic romance discourse to counterbalance this moment of despair: shortly before her death, Lily enjoys a vitalist epiphany—a sentimental revelation of the solidarity of life. In Chopin's *The Awakening*, the depiction of the family world of Creole society is constantly matched against the seduction of the ocean, which attracts the heroine, Edna Pontellier. The romance universe of the sea offers, in Chopin's perspective, the prospect of a freedom that eventually requires Edna's self-inflicted death. In these texts, the logic of urban realism consists in securing—or, in Chopin's case, escaping from—the family-rooted perimeter of realist discourse, which is fragilized by sublime uncertainties.

While I believe that most turn-of-the century novels revolve around the dialogization of familiar and uncanny social space, I must also point out that this structure of feeling does not inform the fiction of Stephen Crane—one of the canonical proponents of naturalism. On the face of it, Crane's stories rework the thematics of his realist and naturalist contemporaries: *Maggie: A Girl of the Streets* or Crane's journalistic sketches—his contributions to the New York *Press* and the New York *Tribune*—are crammed with chaotic crowds, dysfunctional families, or grotesque city dwellers. Yet, in Crane, these features of the city are viewed neither according to the literary logic of the middle-class knowable community nor through the romance sensibility of the urban sublime. Crane's departure from Howells's class-based apprehension of the city, Alan Trachtenberg contends, is visible in the fact that the author of *Maggie* "writes from a curiously asocial perspective" (147): his writing is immune to the ideological prejudices that lead Howellsian narrators to mark out the safe confines of middle-class existence from the threatening urban wasteland in the margins of gentility. For this very reason, Trachtenberg suggests, Crane manages to create the conditions for "a true exchange of point of view with the 'other half'" (144). Thus, Crane, unlike Howells, makes perceptible the subjectivities of "'low life'" characters (145), with their little dramas, their "imaginative world," and their escapist assent to the alienating forces of their urban environment (145).

More pessimistically than Trachtenberg, I believe that Crane's gaze is classless insofar as it embodies a stance of radical alienation—an existential commitment that places the writer in the tradition of Melville's and Hawthorne's city fiction and of Sherwood Anderson's and Ernest Hemingway's (proto)modernist works. Trachtenberg is quite right in describing Crane as a realist "in the phenomenological sense" (147): phenomenology, which provided the epistemological basis for existentialism in the mid-twentieth century, supports an absurdist gaze that strips human situations of the emotional investment they elicit in everyday observers. For Crane, adopting this phenomenological gaze means that there is a thin line between his ability to let subjectivities express themselves regardless of class and, on the other hand, his frequent temptation to dismiss all of his characters' feelings as uninformed, self-deceiving, or futile within a larger cosmic perspective. Crane's success in adopting the perspective of childhood—in city sketches like "An Ominous Baby" or in *Maggie*, for instance—betokens a predilection for representing beings who, though at the lowest level of power relations, are still pathetically intent on forming their own self-serving interpretation of their predicament.

It is, I believe, Crane's willingness to speak with the ironical authority of despair that most radically marks him off from the corpus of naturalist fiction discussed in the present essay. In the readings that follow, I repeatedly show that naturalism does not foster detachment or existential alienation but rather a fascinated grasp of the urban world, informed by the sensibility of the gothic or of sentimentalism. Crane's texts, on the contrary, are at pains to signal that there is nothing in the human-made environment of the city that warrants this form of fascinated rapture. Sublimity in Crane's sketches of New York is occasionally stirred by the spectacle of nature. In "Mr. Binks's Day Off," the Binks family, escaping from New York for a weekend, experience a cosmic epiphany when they behold a sunset over the mountains: the trees, stirred by the wind, produce an awe-inspiring "song" whose "infinite sorrow" speaks to the characters of "the inevitable end" (565). Crane's metropolis itself, however, cannot inspire such a dignified *Weltschmerz*. Typically, while other writers depict urban crowds in sublime terms, Crane grants them the status of bizarre aggregates that can be surveyed from an ironical, defamiliarized perspective: in "The Broken-Down Van" the traffic jam of furniture vans and horse cars that constitutes the object of the story does not appear, as it would in Dreiser or Norris, as an expression of overwhelming energies; it is rather an odd geometric tangle described by means of playful rhetorical symmetries and repetitions (51). Thus, Crane's city is situated outside of the naturalist universe of force that worries Howells, and that other naturalist writers wish to explore.

Sublime Horizons, Vitalist Mysteries: Theodore Dreiser's Naturalist Metropolis

By stating that a realist novel like Howells's *A Hazard of New Fortunes* covers up the heterogeneity of its narrative discourse, I imply that naturalism turns the same lack of discursive homogeneity to profit. Indeed, in the following discussion of *Sister Carrie* I indicate that Dreiser uses a mixture of documentary and romantic discourse in order produce a pseudo-totalizing spectacle of the urban scene. The literary mapping thus obtained is broader in scope and more overtly dialogized than Howells's: Dreiser's sublime depictions of the city round off the fragmented, local vision of his novel's own realist idiom. The novelist suggests thereby that, if the totality of the city cannot be made visible in the sharp light of realism, his text can at least make it apprehensible to a romantic imagination. This naturalist tendency to paint the metropolis as an immensely large or unfathomably mysterious field is, I believe, a compensatory gesture: against the prospect that the apprehension of the city is to remain fragmented, Dreiser endows the cityscape with what we might call, after Walter Benjamin's example, an artificial aura. *Sister Carrie* reveals that the enigmatic aura of naturalist cities is constructed by means of the oceanic and gothic varieties of the sublime. These idioms offer a metaphorical representation of what the writer takes to be the hidden foundations of urban life—a mysterious netherworld of instincts and life forces that cannot be objectified in realist discourse.

Sublime pseudo-totalization in Dreiser is determined historically by the migration from small towns to the new metropolis. In depicting Chicago or New York as dangerously fascinating, Dreiser acknowledges that his characters have moved to an environment no longer held together by the conviviality of shared, familiar space. Portraying the urban universe as a scene of glamor and sublime mysteries alleviates the fears raised by this change of locale. The strained optimism that underlies this literary strategy may be traced in the novelist's willingness to discard the negative view of urban life that was common sense in his own day: unlike in Howells, Dreiser's Chicago and New York are endowed with the allure of magic. This fascination is partly due to the fact that Dreiser portrays the city as a radically novel form of enchantment: his novel obliterates the small-town past of its characters and makes the urban scene appear as self-generated. In Howells's *Hazard*, Boston still stands as a haven of conviviality from which the characters depart with reluctance. In *Sister Carrie*, however, when we are introduced to Carrie Meeber boarding the Chicago train, we see her leaving behind a world about which we will learn very little. Also, contrary to Howells's characters, the hopes of Dreiser's heroine are entirely set on the opportunities of the metropolis. To her, the "familiar green environs of the village" are hardly worth anything more than the desultory show of feelings of a family separation (1).

The eclipse of the small town and the departure for the city are obsessive motifs for Dreiser; the scene recurs in various guises in his other fictional works as well as in his autobiographical narratives. In each case, the novelist records the experience of people whose lives have been influenced by the urban world from a distance. In the account of Carrie's journey, the city asserts itself over the horizon long before the train has reached the Chicago suburbs. "Since infancy," Dreiser writes in the manuscript version of novel, Carrie's "ears had been full of its fame" (Pennsylvania 3). For years, it seems, the pull of this "giant magnet" (*Carrie* 11) has been radiating into the heroine's life, defining her fantasies and her prospects of personal development. Likewise, in Dreiser's autobiographical accounts, we learn that the "gleam of a thousand lights" and the "roar" of urban life had torn the author from his own native surroundings long before he contemplated writing his first novel (*Newspaper* 1).[1] Carrie's trajectory is thus clearly Dreiser's as well: the young woman's aspirations closely parallel the author's dreams of journalistic and literary fame in the city, and her soaring career as an actress functions as a wish-fulfilment equivalent of the author's more troubled course. Thus, the migration from country to city is placed under the sway of a strongly dominant urban pole, which serves as a standard of value for an unromanticized rural world.

Against this vision of an irrepressibly attractive city, we detect in the first pages of *Sister Carrie* Dreiser's self-conscious efforts to provide a demystifying sociological variant of the urban initiation motif: as our reader's gaze is led away from the familiar outline of the small-town environment, we are submitted to a course of education that allows us to empathize with people and situations that a genteel reader would have discarded as scandalous or alien. This expository strategy requires catalogs of documentary evidence traditionally associated with naturalist narration. Accordingly, Dreiser indulges in games of psycho-sociological classification: Carrie's person is detailed to the very way she has of setting her feet flatly. The heroine's moral choice is defined along deterministic lines: in her situation, the narrator states, Carrie can only do "one of two things" (1)—stay on the path of virtue or stray from it, a difficult choice for one possessed with "a mind rudimentary in its power of observation and analysis" (2). Likewise, Drouet, the traveling salesman Carrie meets on the Chicago train, is viewed as the representative of a "type," an "order of individual" or a "class," acting according to his usual "method" (6).

Yet, contrary to what we might expect of a genre that has been accused of legitimating a mode of documentary surveillance, the reader's urban initiation in *Sister Carrie* is not carried out chiefly through catalogs of visual details.[2] Dreiser's Chicago is, on the contrary, all the more impressive when it is described in distant, abstract terms; its blurry seduction is generated not by concrete particulars and classificatory portraits, but by the sublime rhetoric of the author's essayistic prose poems, which attempt to capture the city as a spiritual totality:

> To the child, the genius with imagination, or the wholly untravelled, the approach to a great city for the first time is a wonderful thing. Particularly if it be evening—that mystic period between the glare and the gloom of the world when life is changing from one sphere of condition to another. Ah, the promise of the night. What does it not hold for the weary. What old illusion of hope is not here forever repeated! Says the soul of the toiler to itself, "I shall soon be free. I shall be in the ways and the hosts of the merry . . ." Though all humanity be still enclosed in the shops, the thrill runs abroad. It is in the air. The dullest feel something which they may not always express or describe. It is the lifting of the burden of toil. (6–7)

In this crepuscular panorama, we detect a hesitation between, on the one hand, the demystificatory attitude of a realist narrator, here acting as the voice of adulthood, and, on the other hand, the awakening to the seduction of urban romance. The city offers to the newcomer both a sense of elation—the prospect of freedom, the hosts of the merry—and the darker suggestion of a quasi-narcotic release from toil. These dissonant overtones have an effect of distancing and postponement: the text points toward the revelation of an essence, but this epiphany is thrust backward into the perspective of childhood, or forward into the realm of the visionary.

The epistemological wavering of Dreiser's vision is produced by having the text depict the urban world now as an inexhaustible, open-ended field, now as a unified selfhood. On the one hand, the novelist presents the city as literally incomplete, half-built. Chicago, he writes, is "a city of over 500,000, with the ambition, the daring, the activity of a metropolis of a million" (11); open to future development, the metropolis includes uninhabited "regions open to the sweeping winds and rains, which [are] yet lighted throughout the night with long, blinking lines of gas-lamps" (12). On the economic plane, the department stores' "remarkable displays of trinkets, dress goods, stationery, and jewelry" (17) stir in the heroine a chain of endless desire, perpetually pointing ahead of their material object. Yet, against the suggestion that the city disseminates itself, Dreiser indicates that it can be represented allegorically as a personified entity: it is a "tempter" (*Carrie* 1) or, as Dreiser implies in his eponymous novel, a "Titan" (*Titan* 13). Overall, the oscillation between the fragmented chart of the city, and its embodiment as a larger-than-human being endows the city with an aura: it remains unapproachable either way.

⁂

The dialectic that Dreiser's text establishes between documentary observation and supra-sensible intuition can be analyzed in the light of Walter Benjamin's writings on the aura of the work of art (see *Baudelaire; Illuminations* 217–51). Benjamin's concept of the aura is useful here because it is both cognate and diametrically opposed to the naturalist aesthetic: on the one hand, it carries religious overtones comparable to the blurry mysticism of the naturalist sublime; on the other hand, it describes a mode of artistic reception that characterizes pre-industrial, organic communities. Therefore, it constitutes a foil to the urban-industrial outlook of naturalism, which partakes in the cultural fragmentation that Benjamin associates with modernity.

In "The Work of Art in the Age of Mechanical Reproduction," Benjamin argues that the foundation of the aura lies in the inescapable distance that separates an observer from an object endowed with ceremonial value, and whose magical authenticity suffers from being exhibited indiscriminately (*Illuminations* 225). Benjamin believes that the aura in its ceremonial form cannot survive in the culture of industrial societies—a disappearance he welcomes in his essay on mechanical reproduction but deplores elsewhere. The German critic contends that the movement toward mechanical reproduction in art originates in "the desire of the contemporary masses" to bring things "closer spatially and humanly" (*Illuminations* 233)—an impulse that must necessarily destroy the aesthetic of unapproachability associated with the aura. The contribution of modern urban culture to the decline of the aura is further characterized in Benjamin's essays on Baudelaire, where the critic reads the French poet in conjunction with Poe's "The Man of the Crowd": there, the random agitation of street scenes—the "experience of shock"—is singled out as a spectacular manifestation of the logic that brings about the decay of the aura and the abolition of distance (*Baudelaire* 154). Benjamin argues that Baudelaire attempts to create a form of poetry that renders the *flâneur*'s sensation of being jostled by the metropolitan masses. The poet thereby had to pay the price of precipitating the disintegration of the aura.

The relevance of the concept of the aura to realism and naturalism can be deduced from Benjamin's critique of journalism and the novel—the two cultural channels of the urban masses in which most naturalist writers were active professionally. In "The Storyteller," Benjamin contrasts the rhetoric of the press with storytelling, which he pictures as the cultural form of organic communities of craftsmen. Storytelling is there described as a ritual in which a charismatic narrator helps a community relate to their own cultural values. Through the ceremonial process of storytelling, stories retain an element of distance and mystery. This fascinating aura is the narrative trace of the fact that they exist only in the form of a social exchange—no individual in the group can appropriate the tale as his or her own. Only stories exchanged in this way are able to make experience communicable, thus to provide what Benjamin calls "counsel" (*Iluminations* 87). Under industrialism, on the contrary, stories are transformed into the individualistic form of the novel, which announces the advent of the era of information. Journalistic information embodies the culture of fragmentation: it pursues truth, not "experience," creates a proximity without genuine bond, and offers no "counsel" (*Illuminations* 86–87; see also *Baudelaire* 112).

Benjamin's argument implies that a literary unveiling of urban life on the basis of journalistic shock tactics, as occurs in naturalism, cannnot compensate for the loss of a shared arena of discourse induced by modernity. My point here is that naturalist writers do respond to the same concerns as the German critic. Yet their exploration of urban life follows opposite directions. The naturalist practice of endowing cityscapes with a romantic glow reverses the terms of Benjamin's aesthetic of the aura: when the naturalist text evokes the city's sublime splendor, it acknowledges indeed the fragmentation of its object, but also utters the ineradicable fantasy that the urban field could be perceived in unifying terms; this form of gaze seeks to prevent the city from being further shattered by the fragmentation of experience associated with journalism or scientific discourse. Benjamin himself, in his famous characterization of Baudelaire's *flâneur* aesthetic, does highlight the possibility of the pseudo-totalizing gesture I detect in naturalism, but condemns it as vacuous:

> Baudelaire's genius, which is fed on melancholy, is an allegorical genius. In Baudelaire Paris becomes for the first time a subject of lyric poetry. This poetry is not regional art; rather, the gaze of the allegorist that falls on the city is estranged. It is the gaze of the *flâneur*, whose mode of life still surrounds the approaching desolation of city life with a propitiatory luster. The *flâneur* is still on the threshold, of the city as well of the bourgeois class. Neither has engulfed him; in neither is he at home. He seeks refuge in the crowd. Early contributions to a physiognomics of the crowd are to be found in Engels and Poe. The crowd is the veil through which the familiar city landscape lures the *flâneur* like a phantasmagoria. In it the city is now a landscape, now a room. Both, then, constitute the department store that puts even *flânerie* to use for commodity circulation. (*Reflections* 156)

Baudelaire's poetry, Benjamin implies, is a de-realizing form of discourse that signals the absence of any organic wholeness in the urban landscape. There is, however, a compensation for this alienating experience—namely, the *flâneur*'s immersion into the crowd. By characterizing the mass as a "phantasmagoria" or as an hypnotic presence that "lures" the artist from a distance, Benjamin acknowledges that the city can generate an aura of an artificial kind: for the sake of the *flâneur*, the urban crowd can display itself as landscape or as room—thus, respectively, as an object of ceremonial contemplation and as a site of rootedness. In these guises, the crowd appears as a pseudo-totality that answers the emotional and aesthetic needs of the uprooted *flâneur* artist.

The idea that the city and its masses are endowed with an essence—an artificial aura—that remains concealed behind an inaccessible horizon is, of course, redolent of self-delusive mysticism. Yet, dismissing Dreiser's romanticizing of the urban world—as would be the case if we followed to the letter the logic of Benjamin's and, particularly, Lukács's interpretations—might lead us to disregard the complex ideological work performed through this discourse. In the remainder of this chapter, I wish therefore to provide a schematic survey both of the heuristic and the mystifying aspects of the pseudo-totalizing gesture of the naturalist sublime. In what follows, I argue that the function of the rhetoric of sublimity is, first, to give utterance to the writer's doubts about the very possibility of portraying the city as a totality comprehensible in human terms; simultaneously, in an act of rhetorical substitution, the sublime fills the epistemological and existential void of the city's fragmentation by producing its pseudo-synthesis of the urban field; as Thomas Weiskel's semiotic analysis of the sublime indicates, the totalizing representation thus created is a metaphorical token for the unrepresentable object—in this case, the whole of city life. In naturalism, I wish to argue, the metaphorical medium through which the pseudo-totalization is performed is a social Darwinian discourse of instinctual energies that constructs the city as an uncanny totality moved by mysterious "forces wholly super-human" (*Carrie* 1–2).

The literary gesture of pseudo-totalization that informs Dreiser's vitalism is quite literally of a rhetorical nature: sublime metaphors are in this light sublimity speech acts, used in a rhetorical power game. Peter De Bolla indicates that in the earliest critical discussion of the aesthetic of sublimity—Longinus's first- or third-century *Peri Hypsous*—rhetoric is described both as the object and the vehicle of admiration and terror (De Bolla 32, 36): the emotions of sublime "transport" are ranked among the tools available to powerful orators.[3] This rhetorical dimension of sublimity subsists, I believe, in the (post)romantic variety of the idiom of terror: on the one hand charismatic oratory is an important issue in the corpus of naturalist works that depict political struggles; on the other, in naturalism at large, the novels' narrators themselves deploy their pseudo-totalizing rhetoric with the force of what Kenneth Burke in his theory of symbolic action calls "magical decree[s]" (6): they rely on a power immanent to words, not on a presumably transparent process of realistic reference.

The speech acts of Dreiser's vitalistic idiom are, in the first place, meant to manifest the very existence of a metaphysical netherworld. In highly melodramatic terms, the novelist acts as a master of ceremonies disclosing the unknowable forces hidden in the wings of his characters' limited round of life (*Carrie* 1–2).[4] In so doing, Dreiser's rhetoric of sublimity provides what Thomas Weiskel calls an "intuition of depth"—a glimpse of essences beyond phenomena (Weiskel 24). This theatrical strategy informs the scene of the manuscript of *Sister Carrie* in which the heroine senses that, beyond the worldly charms of Drouet, her seducer, lie the uncanny powers of the metropolis:

> Under the influences of . . . the fine invisible passion which was emanating from Drouet, the food, the still unusual luxury, [Carrie] relaxed and heard with open ears. She was again the victim of the city's hypnotic influence, the subject of the mesmeric operations of super-intelligible forces. We have heard of the strange power of Niagara, the contemplation of whose rushing flood leads to thoughts of dissolution. We have heard of the influence of the hypnotic ball, a scientific fact. Man is too intimate with the drag of unexplainable, invisible forces to doubt longer that the human mind is colored, moved, swept on by things which neither resound nor speak. The waters of the sea are not the only things which the moon sways. (Pennsylvania 78)

Here, the rhetorical thrust of Dreiser's gothic and oceanic tropes immediately distracts our attention from whatever doubts we may entertain about the existence or representability of the urban totality: instead, we are dazzled by the display of its imputed contradictory qualities—seduction and terror. As such, these lines perform what Kenneth Burke calls a "chart" (6)—the symbolic action that leads readers to acknowledge that the author's "sizing up" of a given situation is adequately realistic, even though it is inflected by a certain "quality of namings," that is, by a set of tropes (6).[5]

As Dreiser's "chart" of unknown fields of experience unfolds, it constructs a sublime pseudo-totality through metaphorical means: the utterly unrepresentable mysteries that underlie the city's "strange, insensible inflowings" are named as manifestations of the "forces of life" (Pennsylvania 78, 73). This metaphorical moment is, I believe, the ideological fulcrum of the sublime: it provides the subject with a pseudo-totalizing view of his or her universe that is epistemologically more manageable than the supposedly unrepresentable object of terror and fascination first evoked by the sublime discourse. When he analyzes this mechanism of metaphorical substitution, Thomas Weiskel does not imply that the sublime is in itself rhetorically, much less ideologically, biased: in Weiskel's formulation, the very intensity of the subject's emotions of dread gives a stamp of existential authenticity to the sublime experience (26). Unlike Weiskel, however, I do not believe that the dynamic of the terrifying intuition of depth stops short at the awe-struck contemplation of blurry absolutes, thus remaining innocent of any power agenda. In the sublime moment, Nature, the city, the space program—to mention a few historically attested sources of fascination, come to be viewed no longer as signifiers of something that exceeds them, but as glamorous fronts for more prosaic ambitions—the search for exploitable lands, the development of urban-based capitalism, or of military space research, say. This ideological co-optation of the experience of sublimity is inevitable because the metaphorical language through which pseudo-totalities are expressed is bound to be shaped by the ideology of those who piece the pseudo-synthesis together.

The ideological task performed by the naturalist rhetoric of sublimity consists in advertising a vitalistic sociology of urban space articulated in gender terms: naturalist novels pass off as common sense the idea that the forces at work in the city are not only vital, but also sexualized. Dreiser performs this gendering of the sublime when, in his portrayal of Chicago, he presents the urban world as a seducer of sublime proportions: the city, he writes, has its "its cunning wiles no less than the infinitely smaller and more human tempter" (1–2); its "thousand lights" are "as effective . . . as the persuasive light in a wooing and fascinating eye" (1–2). Likewise, Jack London develops a gendered sociology of vital force in his documentary essay on the London East End: there, the author compares the urban population to a "flood of vigorous strong life" that pours from the country into the city, where it becomes "so cheap that perforce it perishes of itself" (*People* 28). In this rhetoric, class, economic, and racial issues are phrased through an idiom of biology and desire.

At the turn of the century, the emotional configuration of the sublime constituted an appropriate vehicle for a gendered sociology because the discourse of terror and wonder, in its previous romantic form, also carried sexual undertones. The sexual components of the romantic sublime, Thomas Weiskel has argued, manifest themselves in the guise of oedipal and preoedipal narratives: the emotions of sublimity originate from, respectively, the fear of the castrating father or the ambivalent desire to fuse with the mother.[6] The gendered sociology of naturalism, I argue below, privileges the maternal, preoedipal scenario of the sublime: the texts are concerned with the creation or the multiplication of money and bodies in the urban scene, and they represent these social phenomena through tropes of sexual reproduction.

The preoedipal idiom of naturalist sociology is channeled through the two interrelated subsets of the rhetoric of terror—the oceanic sublime and naturalist gothic—which I identified in the introductory chapter. The oceanic sublime is the keynote of Dreiser's ponderings over hypnosis quoted above: Dreiser pictures the city by means of oceanic metaphors that evoke a preoedipal, maternal totality—a virtual chain of life whose energies are comparable to a "rushing flood" submitted to lunar cycles (Pennsylvania 78). The ubiquitousness of these oceanic tropes in naturalist novels has been underlined by June Howard (49):[7] visually, the sea constitutes a fair metaphorical equivalent of city crowds; the turbulence of the ocean, which Kant designates as an important icon of the natural sublime, can easily be made to evoke the threat emanating from the unstable economy of the metropolis (122).

Naturalist gothic applies the discourse of vitalism to a different object than oceanic discourse: instead of panoramas of crowds and speculation, urban gothic offers a grim vitalist portrayal of the abject physiologies and living conditions of city dwellers. This gothic view of urban life underlies, for instance, Jack London's claim that slum dwellers are "twisted monstrosities" with "an elemental economy of nature such as the cave-men must have exhibited" (*People* 164). Historically, naturalist novelists derive these tropes from romantic or postromantic sources: they are imported from late-Victorian urban gothic—from Robert Louis Stevenson, for instance—or from the mid-century mysteries of the city, a genre named after Eugene Sue's *Mysteries of Paris* and practiced in the United States by Charles Brockden Brown, Edgar Allan Poe, George Lippard, and Herman Melville.[8]

The status of the gothic within the vitalistic economy of naturalism can be determined by examining how both varieties of the urban sublime express the writers' awareness of the fragility of their own pseudo-totalizing sociology. Anxieties—both over the nature of urban life and over the possibility to represent it—can be traced in the fact that the oceanic vistas of naturalism can easily veer into the uncanny. We will see in the following chapters that, compared to romanticism, naturalist works handle the sexual scenarios of the sublime in a pessimistic light, without achieving what Weiskel calls the transcendence of the sublime—the enlargement of consciousness triggered by the confrontation with terror. In a mid-century text like Walt Whitman's "Crossing Brooklyn

Ferry," the sublime expanses of the American continent still make up a well-integrated maternal cosmos—a "well-joined scheme" into which subjects may immerse themselves in the confidence that they will be "disintegrated . . . yet part of the scheme" (*Leaves* 128). The nineteenth-century city, portrayed negatively by advocates of anti-urban pastoralism, can, however, not support this optimistic epiphany. It is therefore portrayed in uncanny terms that preclude Whitman's utopian synthesis. Dreiser's Carrie, when she is seduced by Drouet, responds to a mesmeric call that, if we take the oceanic metaphors at face value, crosses threatening abysses of engulfing waters. Likewise, in Norris's fiction, the oceanic currents that keep the urban market in motion take the form of a mind-numbing vortex that reduces men to "a pinch of human spawn" (*Pit* 79).

In naturalist gothic, the pessimism that underlies oceanic panoramas manifests itself in highly dramatic terms through an obsession with pathological degeneration—unnatural twists both within literary language and in the city's masses. The linguistic paroxysms of the gothic help the novelists convey their belief that vital currents are submitted to abject transformations when they circulate through the urban scene, that the gendered economy gives birth to, as London puts it, "a new species, a breed of city savages" (*People* 164). Simultaneously, the shrillness of the gothic imagery reveals, by default, the falterings of the vitalist idiom when it serves as a means of economic representation: whatever rhetorical energy is channeled into the gothic tableaux proves insufficient to objectify the horrors of the city. Inadequate to its overwhelming object, the gendered economics of naturalism is exposed as a pseudo-totality.[9] The writers' project of sociological exploration remains therefore an instance of what Patricia Yaeger has called the "failed sublime" (201)—a flash of "dazzling, unexpected empowerment followed by a moment in which this power is snatched away" (Yaeger 201).

CHAPTER 5

Domus versus Megalopolis:
Local and Global Epistemologies
of the City

In psychoanalytical readings like Patricia Yaeger's and Thomas Weiskel's, the "failure" of the sublime is measured by reference to a standard that can be apprehended intuitively—personal empowerment: the subject's confrontation with terror and fascination is expected to lead to the broadening of the self that Edmund Burke calls "delight" (42) and Weiskel calls "transcendence" (23). It is, however, far more paradoxical to allude to a failed sublime in the present interpretation of early-twentieth-century city novels, where the naturalist discourse of terror functions as a sociological and epistemological tool: doing so implies indeed that this rhetoric, which expresses the writers' inability to represent their own environment, could be measured against a hypothetically successful version of itself—or against another, purportedly truer totalizing map of the urban scene. Such form of evaluation is impossible here: while totalizing discourses are the object of my argument, I share the post-structuralist skepticism about their epistemological claims. Statements that aspire to a totalizing status are, I think, not falsifiable.

In order to specify the methodological guidelines that are productive within the epistemological framework thus defined, I first wish to address an objection Fredric Jameson has leveled against what he takes to be the post-structuralist bias of neo-historicism. Jameson argues that neo-historicism, in the absence of a totalizing theory of history transcending its object of study, is led to a "valorization of immanence and nominalism" (*Postmodernism* 190). Such a critical discourse, Jameson contends, relies disproportionately on homologies—arguments based merely on similarities and not on dialectic relations. Neo-historicism is therefore reduced to "a collage or montage of multiple materials" (189) and, insofar as it handles history, to what filmmaker Sergei Eisenstein calls "'a montage of historical attractions'" (qtd. in *Postmodernism* 190).

Jameson's argument, though impassable in its own terms, would overshoot its mark if it led us to regard montage as a euphemism for randomness. The present readings of naturalism, because they are not geared to a historical foundation transcendent to language, do fall within the critical aesthetic Jameson deplores. Yet it is, I think, possible to point out regularities, affinities, and contrasts that inform the linkages they establish among literary texts, genres, and theoretical idioms. The guiding principle—one might even say the rhythmic pattern—that emerges from the present book is the very logic of dialogization that I detect in naturalist novels: what I take to be the core issue of the naturalist urban sublime—the dialogization of local space and absent urban totality, of realism and romance—directly determines the mutual relations of the theoretical paradigms used here—namely, Marxism and postmodernist theory.[1] Indeed, in the readings below, I assume, on the one hand, that naturalism, like Marxism, structures its discourse around the issues of reification and totality; on the other, like postmodernist theory, it expresses these concerns through the discourse of the sublime, thus seemingly refuting the possibility of reducing the urban world to a totalizing model. On this basis, I attempt to play off these two theoretical frameworks against each other without assuming that one can ultimately gain dominance over the other. In this chapter, I argue indeed that little is gained by decreeing, as Lukács does, that the naturalist representation of urban life can in all respects be demystified in the name of a non-alienated, self-transparent vision of social space. Conversely, I contend that one cannnot take for granted the insight, expressed in the critical discussions of the postmodern sublime, that social experience is fragmented, and that the work of naturalist fiction consists therefore exclusively in making this fragmentation visible.

So far, I have used Marxist models—Lukács and Benjamin—as foils to naturalist sociology. More accurately, these two critics have provided on a theoretical level a realist anchoring ground from which the demystification of naturalism could be carried out. From a Marxist perspective, it is indeed politically crucial to deconstruct the aspects of naturalist discourse that endow with magical seduction what is literally a modern landscape of alienation; urban capitalism, which naturalism inventories, is a realm where labor and its products are reified, reduced to the status of things; it is a social configuration where, as Marx puts it, "all is under the sway of an inhuman power" (156) and where "the complete return of man to himself" is radically thwarted (135). The importance Lukács grants to the concept of totality in his reading of naturalism is in this light indissociable from the Marxist premise that "human self-estrangement" must be overcome (Marx 135), and that this revolutionary upheaval will establish a utopian society where each individual's concrete existence develops into what Marx calls "a totality of human manifestation of life" (138). Thus, Lukács criticizes naturalism because he believes that it exacerbates the logic of reification and impedes the advent of "society as a concrete totality" (*Reader* 226). Both Lukács and Benjamin argue that works of art that assent to alienation end up depicting their universe in the shape of false totalities—be it the documentary catalogs of naturalist novels or the spurious seduction of the crowd in Baudelaire.

The Marxist critique of alienation, as illuminating as it is for the understanding of the urban environment, relies on categories—human nature, the teleology of the historical dialectic, totality itself—whose metaphysical groundings have been deconstructed by post-structuralist theory. According to Jean-François Lyotard, the impulse toward philosophical totalization that underlies Marxism is untenable in the postmodern context: the evidence of social and political fragmentation in our situation is so overwhelming that it leaves no room for theoretical discourses oriented toward epistemological or political syntheses. Against the Marxist project of creating a "teleology in the first person plural" (Lyotard, *Reader* 361) for the sake of an "emancipated working humanity" (Lyotard, *Differend* 171; also *Condition* 54), Lyotard advocates a philosophical exploration of discontinuities in discourse. Only in this way, he implies, can we do justice to the constraints of a historical predicament that provides no validation for the unified *we* of Hegelian Marxism (Lyotard, *Reader* 373).[2]

The break-up of totalizing discourse is for postmodern theorists the very moment of fascination and terror of the postmodern sublime. Subjects in the postindustrial period, Lyotard contends, are confronted with "*the infinity of the heterogeneous*" (Lyotard, *Reader* 409). For Jameson, late-twentieth-century individuals are assailed by "a perceptual barrage of immediacy" (*Postmodernism* 413) that leaves them split between a "multidimensional set of radically discontinuous realities" (413). Likewise, Slavoj Žižek, in *The Sublime Object of Ideology*, argues that, contrary to the totalizing impulse of Marxist theory, we must acknowledge "a fundamental antagonism" (6) in the world of politics and philosophical discourse. Jameson, for whom postmodernity equals alienation, contends, however, that the postmodern sublime wages a "'war on totality,'" inspired by an anti-Marxist "fear of utopia" (*Postmodernism* 401)—a nominalist skepticism that hampers a commitment to left politics.

Jameson's distrust of theories of fragmentation is to some extent useful in the present context. I believe indeed that the dynamic of the sublime in naturalism is best described from a critical approach that does not gloat over the deconstruction of totality. Instead, it is more productive to align my readings on those aspects of the theory of the postmodern sublime that express a desire to preserve the possibility of a panoramic grasp of the postindustrial constellation, be it in less ambitious forms than full-fledged totalization. Such contrasted authors as Jameson and Lyotard are indeed tempted to examine the conditions of validity of what might be called pseudo-totalizing discourses—theories mapping the contours of postmodernity without pretensions to absolute truth. This postmodern nostalgia for totality follows a dynamic of the sublime similar to what I have brought out in Dreiser's fiction—namely, a movement that runs from the dislocation of totalizing representations to some form of recomposition.[3] In Jameson, this effort has led to the elaboration of a so-called aesthetic of "cognitive mapping" (*Postmodernism* 54), which offers a substitute for the now absent totalizing framework. Cognitive mapping refers to the elaboration of charts of postmodern space that take into account their own status as ideologically inflected semiotic constructs: they are expected to make visible "the nature of [the] representational codes" that inform both their own procedures and their object of inquiry (52). Cognitive maps make up a provisional metadiscourse— a pseudo-totalizing chart whose "representational failure" (409) has a heuristic value. This procedure assumes that the validity of a cognitive map—a turn-of-the-century novel, say—is tested against "an impossible concept of totality" (409).

Jameson's call for cognitive mapping provides, however, more a heuristic imperative (indeed an admirable and highly evocative one) than a working method. It also tends to take for granted that the postmodern plurality will dissolve of itself into a totality articulated along Marxist-Hegelian lines. Lyotard's discussion of pseudo-totalizing discourses, on the contrary, is more cognate to the narrative strategies of naturalism because it takes discursive heterogeneity more seriously. Specifically, it indicates that the same field of inquiry can be mapped only by means of an epistemological negotiation involving several incompatible paradigms. These detotalized idioms are separated by a pattern of epistemological and quasi-judicial conflict that the philosopher calls the "differend" of postmodernity (*Differend* xi). In his discussion of Kant's essays on the sublime, Lyotard represents this fragmentation of postmodern subjects and discourses in the shape of a textual "archipelago" (*Differend* 130). In this view, the insular character of each idiom in the archipelago should never be ignored, lest one give in to the elaboration of totalitarian syntheses (see *Differend* 252). Yet Lyotard points out that the insularity of discourses can be, if not mended, at least negotiated (133); the discourses of the archipelago are linked by the very ocean that keeps them separate. Interconnections—"passages" (131)—can be built between them, for instance by confronting the deficient mapping of totality obtained in one idiom with what is elaborated in other discourses. Thus characterized, these epistemological connections can clearly never become solid bridges: they are at best "arrangement[s]" or "compromise[s]" (133) through which totality can never be represented literally but is glimpsed only metaphorically, as if through "symbols" (131).

In order to make Lyotard's archipelago paradigm transposable to naturalist fiction, it is useful to rewrite its problematic of pseudo-totalization into the terms of Bakhtinian dialogism, a model with which it shares basic presuppositions. Bakhtin and Lyotard both contend that the field of language is the effect of the interaction of a plurality of idioms, each with its specific prerogatives and its area of validity. In the light of Bakhtin's concept of "heteroglossia" (*Dialogic* 271), which the French translators of Bakhtin evocatively transpose as "plurilinguism" (*Esthétique* 96), Lyotard's archipelago of discourse appears as a set of dialects without a global, normative language. Yet even Lyotard's fragmented postmodern constellation is submitted to what Bakhtin calls the "centripetal forces of language" (*Dialogic* 270)—the unifying tendencies that compete against centrifugal heteroglossia. Indeed, the "passages" that the French philosopher wants to build between fragmentary idioms play the part of what we might call (pseudo-)totalizing dialects. By this oxymoronic label, I refer to detotalized idioms that vie to express a lost unifying text; their task is of necessity unfulfilled: totalizing dialects or idioms, we infer from Lyotard, must remain metaphorical.

In the present discussion of urban fiction, I will in turn write from the perspective of three totalizing dialects: the gendered rhetoric of vitalism; the dialect of the knowable community, of which, I argue below, Marxism is a subset; and the dystopian vision of a fragmented megalopolis, which is the hallmark of postmodern descriptions of urban space. I should like to differentiate these idioms by exploiting—figuratively, that is—the socio-geographical rationale that ties dialects to a specific area of experience. Though totalizing idioms purport to represent the whole social field, they proceed from a given epistemological vantage point— from an anchoring ground—from which they drew the tropes that allow them to encode all other domains of knowledge.[4] I have shown how the discourse of the knowable community emanates from the familiar spaces of families, neighborhoods, communities of labor. The megalopolis, on the other hand, is the embodiment in concrete architectural and communicational space of Lyotard's postmodern "differend"; as a methodological vantage point, it is therefore a metaphor for the epistemological perspective from which we can survey the saturation and dissemination of postmodern discourse. In this threefold division, vitalism occupies a middle territory wedged between local space and global fragmentation: it links reproduction in the domestic sphere to an uncanny "web of life" (Herrick, *Web* 365) that is either a vision of an enlarged community or of a dislocated one.

The idioms demarcated in this figurative topography are simultaneously objects of analysis and methodological tools. In other words, I do not mean to grant any one of them the epistemological privilege of subsuming the other two. Instead of looking for a master narrative, I want to follow Jameson's practice of theoretical "transcoding" according to which totalizing idioms must be criticized in the light of "the conceptual possibilities of [their] competitors" (*Postmodernism* 393). This reading method defuses, for instance, the unrealistic expectation that a Marxist/positivistic reading could totally demystify the gendered vitalism of naturalist fiction. Vitalism, for all the bad science that it generates, legitimates a discussion of urban space in terms of gender. Moreover, from the point of view of the postmodern idiom of the megalopolis, the sublimity of naturalist vitalism expresses through its gender metaphors a sense of social dislocation that cannot be reduced to a representation in terms of familiar space or through the intermediary paradigm of a Bakhtinian, harmoniously plurivocal city.

Marxist criticism, especially in its Lukácsian form, enjoys in the present perspective the status of a totalizing dialect whose utopian aspirations convey the image of a reconciled local space. It may seem paradoxical to characterize Marxism, a theory of industrial capitalism wedded to a universalist politics, as a local-oriented idiom. In fact, in making this claim, I wish to read Marxism as a discourse that emanates from what Lyotard calls the *"domus"* (*Inhuman* 191)—the social and epistemological configuration of domesticity. Lyotard uses the *"domus"* and its opposite term, the "megalopolis" (191) as metaphors designating, respectively, societies before and after (post)modernity. According to this dichotomy, the pre-postmodern *domus* is "a community of work" whose social practice is based on "labour"—the "service" of nature—and "being-together-as a whole" (*Inhuman* 192, 193, 195). Under these terms, Lyotard characterizes a structure of feeling that fits the Marxist aspiration to make coincide by means of collective work "the *human* essence of nature" and "the *natural* essence of man" (Marx 143). Conversely, the Marxist utopia is antithetical to the "megalopolis," which, Lyotard indicates, is ruled by "a process of complexification . . . which is desired by no-one, no self, not even that of humanity" (199).

Phrased in Lyotard's terms, the community of human labor is the metaphorical vehicle through which the totalizing dialect of Marxist criticism expresses its utopian aspirations. In the same way as Howellsian realism makes the family the paradigm of the whole of society, Marxist critics make visible the figure of an equitable community in contexts where, according to other discourses, human nature is doomed to alienation, self-absence, and reification without end. This gesture is, epistemologically, an act of demystification, anchored in a form of common sense that, Lyotard underlines, is a prerogative of the *domus* (*Inhuman* 191). It is illustrated in Lukács's desire to see the underlying forces of society express themselves with organic explicitness through the surfaces of social life and through literature.[5] The limits of this totalizing script are defined by the fact that, as Lyotard puts it, the *domus* is "too simple" (199): we cannot unify the totality of discourse under the single metaphor of a familiar world reshaped through praxis and explored by positivistic perception; this operation remains an incomplete "compromise" (*Differend* 133). On the other hand, we might add that it is impossible to prejudge the extent to which this demystificatory enterprise can be attempted.

Equally surprising may appear the decision to ascribe to the post-structuralist discourse of difference and heterogeneity a methodological status similar to Marxism and vitalism, whose totalizing ambitions are explicitly advertised. I do so out of the belief that an approach that is systematically on the look-out for discontinuities in texts and in the social environment acts according to an axiomatic judgment on the totality of experience. However intuitively compelling any pessimistic assessment of present-day fragmentation may be, there is indeed no verifiable grounding for the decree according to which postmodernity resists a synthesis of knowledge; therefore, a description of the world in terms of fragmentation functions as a totalizing dialect.[6] The idea that the discourse of difference generates its own objectifiable structure of feelings, subsuming its whole field of enquiry, is corroborated by Lyotard's decision to define an intuitively accessible historical correlative of postmodern fragmentation—the megalopolis, namely. Yet the megalopolis differs from the totalizing metaphors of vitalism and Marxism—respectively, the biological chain and the community of labor—in the fact that it does not claim to have a utopian side: the "megalopolis" of postmodernity is, Lyotard writes, "uninhabitable" (*Inhuman* 200); it is the site of a deployment of discourse that constrains people "into becoming inhuman" (2) by confining them within an environment characterized by an ever-deepening lack of self-presence. As expressed through this metaphor of urban space, Lyotard's post-structuralist skepticism acts as a dystopian reminder: it makes visible the process of sublime complexification in social or textual objects that could still be naively perceived as organically consistent or totalizable.

PART 2

Mysteries of
Production and Exchange

The Discovery of the Urban Market: Theodore Dreiser's *Sister Carrie*

While naturalist fiction constructs its visual background—the oceanic cityscapes—on the basis of tropes derived from romantic nature poetry, it develops narrative strategies for the exploration of urban life reminiscent of the mysteries of the city. This genre, by its very name, conjures up the image of an urban world in which mystification and social opacity are structural principles, not local aberrations. By mentioning this literary filiation at the outset of a discussion of naturalist economics, I mean to indicate that the literary investigation of the urban scene in the 1890s, even if practiced in the name of social science, grants a lot of importance to the gothic and the uncanny. However, unlike in mid-nineteenth-century fiction, the enigmas investigated in naturalist novels are not the issues of crime, confusion of social identities, and political intrigue: they are the secrets of economic production and biological reproduction. The present section investigates indeed the cultural and historical logic that prompted naturalist writers to articulate their vision of economic production in terms of elusive vital forces and secret agencies. In readings of Theodore Dreiser's *Sister Carrie* (1900); Frank Norris's *The Octopus* (1901) and *The Pit* (1903); and Jack London's *The Valley of the Moon* (1913), I attempt to show that the conflation of economic and gender categories that resulted from this literary choice constitutes the primary rhetorical gesture of the naturalist sublime. The influence of this gendered view of market relations radiates throughout naturalist texts beyond the areas specifically associated with economics.

After decades of taking the mechanics of urban life for granted, it is difficult to grasp the sense of newness conveyed by naturalist narratives of initiation to city life. The disenchantment of late-twentieth-century observers with urban conditions cannot approximate the sense of awe and of outrage that William Cronon detects in nineteenth-century travelers on their way to Chicago (1–19). The cultural history of the last decades of the nineteenth century suggests indeed quite literally that the urban market represented a mystery for which no readily available system of description yet existed. Robert Wiebe, in *The Search for Order*, argues that in the late nineteenth century, no social group—except corporate leaders—was in a position to understand the social changes of urbanization. In barely a few decades, Wiebe argues, this process had transformed the United States from a loosely connected confederation of "island communities" into a continent-wide urban-based sphere of exchange (xiii). Wiebe's explanation pits the chaos of social and geographical fragmentation against the rationalizing efforts of government or corporate bureaucracies. As such, his argument is sympathetic to the ideologies of the business and professional elites of the early-twentieth-century Progressive Era, which contributed to the establishment and the regulation of the continental market. This historical scenario assumes that the new bureaucracies correctly understood that even in the absence of a totalizing understanding of social processes, industrialism could at least be competently managed by a rule of middle-class experts.

In *The Incorporation of America*, Alan Trachtenberg provides a more disenchanted account of the rise of urbanization in the Gilded Age. The literary genre of the mysteries of the city, Trachtenberg argues, registered the bafflement of the new urban population. City dwellers were unable to grasp the pattern of market relations that regulated the organization of urban space and the new hierarchies of labor: the market logic "proved difficult to grasp for all city consumers, owners and tenants alike, precisely because of its changing forms in everyday life, of the mysteries it generated (how goods were made, for example, or how they appeared neatly packaged on store shelves), of the spectacles of consumption it produced" (22). Trachtenberg implies that the new set of mystifying relations, as undecipherable as they appeared to contemporary reformers, were nevertheless constructed for the benefit of the corporate elites. The cultural and commercial channels of the new metropolis—mass journalism, advertising, and the department store—functioned as educational agencies that trained the city dweller into the logic of a market where commodities acquire a magical life of their own, totally separated from their origins in production (*Incorporation* 132). In Trachtenberg's interpretation, the chief mystery of the cities is therefore the fetishization of the commodity. Because middle-class reformers of the Progressive Era failed to question the culture of commercialism and the private ownership of the means of production, their attempts at rationalization and clarification only worked to turn the confusion of the market into the mystification of consumerism (139).

The concept of fetishization of the commodity offers a crucial theoretical framework for the analysis of naturalist texts because, like Dreiser's *Sister Carrie*, most of them attempt to construe the logic of urban economics on the basis of the spectacle of commercialism. I wish to indicate in this chapter that Dreiser's path-breaking novel seems to take the logic of fetishization so literally that it articulates a system of vitalist economics reminiscent of animism. My reading is based on the belief that the romance or sublime components of Dreiser's novel develop a utopian view of urban life that stands in a paradoxical relation toward the pessimistic, realist strains of the text: the magical portrayal of urban life coexists with the descriptions of economic violence but it is never explicitly contradicted by them.[1] We are offered both the tale of Carrie's quasi-supernatural ability to negotiate the urban environment, and the realist story of her lover Hurstwood's downfall and eventual suicide.

The oscillation of Dreiser's novel between documentary discourse and romance is marked by the presence of conflicting impulses toward elucidation and mythologizing. This dialectic between positivistic enquiry and magical fascination is illustrated in the passage of *Sister Carrie* where the heroine, only recently arrived in the metropolis, confronts for the first time the vistas of urban industry:

> She walked bravely forward, led by an honest desire to find employment and delayed at every step by the interest of the unfolding scene, and a sense of helplessness amid so much evidence of power and force which she did not understand. These vast buildings, what were they? These strange energies and huge interests—for what purposes were they there? She could have understood the meaning of a little stone-cutter's yard at Columbia City, whittling little pieces of marble for individual use, but when the yards of some huge stone corporation came into view, filled with spurs and tracks and flat cars, transpierced by docks from the river and traversed by immense trun-

dling cranes of wood and steel overhead, it lost all significance and applicability to her little world. It was concerned with something of which she knew nothing, and was doing things which she could not understand. . . . The great streets were wall-lined mysteries to her. The vast offices, strange mazes which concerned far-off individuals of importance. She could only think of people connected with them as counting money, dressing magnificently and riding in carriages. What they dealt in, how they labored, to what end it all came, she had only the vaguest conception. That it could vitally concern her, other than as regards some little nook in which she might daily labor, never crossed her mind. (Pennsylvania 17)

These lines perceptively analyze the mystifying complexity of the relations of interdependence generated by the urban market. The small-town economy—here the "little stone-cutter's yard"—stands as a pole of complete economic transparence, composed of recognizable interpersonal relations. On the contrary, the urban marketplace, magnified by Dreiser's oceanic rhetoric, is mystifying: fascinated by its spectacle, the protagonist loses all sense of her insertion in the city's social structure.

This economic epiphany represents one of the few moments in *Sister Carrie* where urban complexity is explicitly associated with the obfuscating presence of big corporations. The passage recalls the antitrust debates of Populism, which, Bruce Palmer argues, were waged in the name of the "simple market society" (111), here embodied in Dreiser's image of the "little stone-cutter's yard" (12). The Populist program aimed at maintaining, even under the conditions of industrialism, a system in which the economic cycle between producer and consumer would be both transparent and fair (Palmer 109). By the turn of the century, though, the development of incorporation spelled the decline of this agrarian utopia. Martin Sklar has pointed out that the growth of the trusts to hegemonic status brought about a shift in social relations that affected the very image of what the American polity should stand for (34). The evolution from the "proprietary-competitive" system (23)—the early-nineteenth-century market of competitive producers—to the corporate model, with its concentration of capital and its monopolistic price-fixing, meant in the first place a redefinition of the class of people who owned America (44). Simultaneously, the legal amendments that made the creation of corporations possible sanctioned a new definition of property and personality: "intangible" values like shares became legitimate objects of property and the corporation, a legal construct, was granted the status of "natural entity" (50). This resulted in a dissemination of economic and social identity as well as in a dissociation of the economic chains of cause and effect. The mystifying urban landscape that dazzles Dreiser's heroine is the architectural expression of this new, elusive polity.

In the following chapter on Norris, I point out in more detail how Populism, in its eagerness to reestablish a simple, Jeffersonian commonwealth, produced a perceptive critique of the capitalistic market system. In *Sister Carrie*, however, I want to show that Dreiser's impulse toward economic demystification does not play itself out. Rather than single-mindedly exposing the mechanisms of the market, *Sister Carrie* traces the heroine's growing ability to manage these mysteries, and to turn them to her own advantage. In this logic, the transparence of the simple market society turns out to be more a lack than an asset: the labyrinthine surfaces of the urban scene are experienced as a source of magnificence and power; the "strange mazes" of the "vast offices" and the "trundling cranes of wood and steel" contribute to the sublime display of "strange energies and huge interests" (12–13). The magical epistemology that supports these sublime visions requires that the naiveté of Dreiser's protagonist be at first heavily foregrounded, but, against all narrative expectations, never completely dispelled: Carrie enters the city as a "half-equipped little knight" (2) and ends up as a romantic dreamer, fantasizing to the motion of her rocking chair. As Walter Benn Michaels demonstrates, no other voice in the novel ultimately disproves Carrie's sublime perception of economic relations (32). On the contrary, the voices of restraint and traditional common sense carry a relative, if not a negative, authority in the novel. Robert Ames, a midwestern electrical engineer whom the heroine meets through her New York friends, is sometimes presented as a mentor who could lead Carrie toward higher ideals;[2] yet there is little evidence that his valued advice will inflect Carrie's own market-oriented ambitions. More damagingly, Hanson, Carrie's brother-in-law, who preaches the doctrine of thrift and character, is branded as a petty libidinal miser—a character who takes pleasure in smothering other people's legitimate desires. Hanson offers Carrie lodgings only as long as she is willing to pay board; his denunciation of commercial leisure—the very area where Carrie will thrive—comes out as a sign of his intellectual limitations.

As he endorses his character's mystified perception of city life, Dreiser turns his back on the epistemology of realist novels, which make it a priority to puncture economic fantasies. In contrast to Dreiser's Carrie, Lily Bart, the heroine of Edith Wharton's *The House of Mirth*, pays dearly for her limited insight into both economics and sexual politics. Lily initially looks like an upper-class equivalent of Carrie: she is a poor relative of an Old New York family, who, by the standards of her set, can only hope to trade her exceptional beauty for a wealthy husband. Dissatisfied with this prospect but ignorant of the economic technicalities through which money is made, she becomes entangled in a scandal involving Gus Trenor, a married Old New Yorker who deals in stocks: Trenor had volunteered to pay the young woman's gambling debts out of a sum that Lily thought was obtained by speculating on her own assets; the money was actually a gift meant to seduce her. If there is any mystery to Lily's transactions with Trenor—to the young woman, the whole business is enveloped in a welcome "haziness," a "general blur" (85)—it is only due to the heroine's faulty understanding of the financial underside of conspicuous consumption.[3] Trenor, who knows the nuts and bolts of money making, claims that "it takes a devilish lot of hard work to keep the machinery running" (81). His remark self-pityingly refers to his own efforts as a speculator. Implicitly, however, the novel alludes thereby to the existence of a hidden but nevertheless quite real scene of production: in less privileged social circles, workers spend their lives making the commodities used by the idle rich.

What Dreiser opposes to the literary sociologies of demystification is an ambitious form of naturalist science that integrates unconscious or even quasi-supernatural factors within its methodological paradigms. As such, *Sister Carrie* offers a non-positivistic resolution to the issues that plagued early practitioners of sociology. In a study of the early decades of these disciplines, Thomas Haskell argues that the development of nationwide market relations brought about a radical blurring of social intelligibility. This situation, Haskell contends, induced American social scientists to move away from models of behavior hinging on personal will and autonomy, and led them to elaborate paradigms of social causality that take unconscious agencies into account (41). *Sister Carrie*, I believe, rewrites this discourse of the social unconscious along the lines of the romance. Unconscious impulses are made a predominant focus of concern in *Sister Carrie*, be it in the sentimental guise of the "blind strivings of the human heart" (369) or in the form of "subtle, strange and wonderful" forces that "require refinement of thought in the observer" to be understood (Pennsylvania 119). By marshalling a whole set of sublime tropes for the representation of the characters' hidden strivings, Dreiser's text constructs a form of the unconscious that has little in common with an individualized libido. In this system, all forces are interchangeable: the silent suggestions channeled through Carrie's and Hurstwood's dialogue are consubstantial with "the voices of the so-called inanimate" (75) issuing from commodities, with the mesmeric operations of the "super-intelligible forces" (Pennsylvania 78) that lure the young woman to urban luxuries, and with the voice that prompts Hurstwood to escape with his employer's money. According to the pseudo-totalizing momentum of Dreiser's sublime discourse, these voices seem to originate from the areas beyond the characters' horizon of perception; they appear as audible signals issuing from the aura that Dreiser's text constructs around the outline of the urban scene. The sublime idiom, by linking the protagonists' unconscious to this ill-defined totality, ensures that all these punctual stirrings eventually merge and become identified with the power of the economic arena as a whole. June Howard remarks that, in the discourse of naturalism, the inscrutable universe of deterministic forces seems to emanate from the urban sphere, and can actually be identified with it (47). I wish to add to this that the retotalizing representation of social causality in *Sister Carrie* results in the elaboration of a psychology of forces that merges psychological and social determinants. The urban market is thereby represented as an animated field, endowed with an unconscious soul.

By arguing that Dreiser constructs a cosmic soul for his urban scene, I depart from interpretations that stress the dehumanizing aspect of the novelist's deterministic views. True, the author's own contention that "science knows nothing of a soul or spirit" since man is only "an atom in a greater machine" seems to fly in the face of an animistic vision of the urban arena (Dreiser qtd. in Elias 240). However, Rachel Bowlby argues that the rhetoric of determinism in *Sister Carrie* follows a more complex logic than strictly positivistic interpretations acknowledge. She remarks that the author manages to render his anti-humanist cosmo-sociology alluring by turning the workings of cosmic laws into a spectacle that seduces the artistic imagination of those submitted to blind evolutionary forces (53). Bowlby's argument reveals an epistemological duality at the heart of naturalist science. This ambiguity, Charles Walcutt argues in his account of the cultural genealogy of naturalism, is due to the fact that the fiction of Dreiser and Norris straddles the divided streams of positivism and transcendentalism (vii). While it appropriates the deterministic outlook of positivism, naturalism inherits from transcendentalism a reluctance to deny the existence of free will, and, one might also add, the nostalgia for a world view that accommodates the presence of an encompassing spirit.

The epistemological ambiguity of Dreiser's science is visible in the novelist's appropriation of the Spencerian concept of the Unknowable—

the term with which the positivist philosopher designates the domains beyond positivistic perception (Bannister 43). Dreiser inclines toward a mystical interpretation of the Unknowable energies he discerns in the cosmos. In the terminology of the aesthetic of terror, we might argue that, against the nihilistic view that would equate the Unknowable with pure nothingness, he is receptive to the sublimity of the full, embodied void. Therefore, he paradoxically suffuses his professions of scientific determinism with nostalgic yearnings for a retotalized social body: in his invocations to mysterious forces, Dreiser suggests that the presumably empty shell of the Unknowable does accommodate cosmic forces whose influence can be sensed, if not described. Once these pseudo-totalizing agencies are named—either as "Nature" (*Carrie* 356) or as "the forces of life" (56)—they can easily become personalized. Thus, the "greater machine" of determinism becomes animated with influxes of desire that make up a huge, disseminated spiritual field. Carrie's example illustrates how the voices of that hypothetical soul resonate within a few intuitive beings, who can identify with, or even appropriate the deterministic flows. By tuning in to a realm beyond mechanical laws, some privileged human atoms can regain some degree of control over their existence.

Dreiser's temptation to name the unknowable totality of the urban world transforms what are originally distinct economic and psychological energies into a city-wide vital substance. This leads the novelist to deploy a relatively consistent vocabulary of vitalism. Vitalistic rhetoric is most clearly noticeable in later texts such as *The Titan* or *Newspaper Days*, where the desire to give voice to the feeble stirrings of the urban market leads to a proliferation of enthusiastic outbursts celebrating the embodiment of Life in the figure of the city. To Dreiser's autobiographical persona in *Newspaper Days*, for instance, the pit of the Chicago Board of Trade constitutes a fascinating "roaring, yelling, screaming whirlpool of life" (2). Likewise, when Frank Cowperwood surveys the panorama of Chicago for the first time, he reflects that, in this "seething city in the making . . . Life was doing something new" (*Titan* 11–12). Here as in *Sister Carrie*, vitalism functions as the conceptual operator that allows Dreiser to give if not a visible shape, at least a generic name to the scattered voices and drives that let themselves be heard throughout Chicago and New York.

The narrative apparatus that Dreiser's discourse of life forces constructs in *Sister Carrie* might be described as a vitalist theater. Not only does the novelist's animistic economy express itself most explicitly in the actual institution of the theater, but it models the whole urban space as a stage for the voices of the life forces. The significance of this economic paradigm can be brought to light by pointing out by way of contrast that a theatrical configuration is an essential component of the realist representation of the urban class system. Edith Wharton's Old New York, for instance, is, like Dreiser's Chicago, organized as a staged spectacle. In Wharton's text we are, of course, dealing with a theater of demystification, whose logic of exploitation can be exposed: Lily Bart is raised in a class so engrossed in parading their social rituals for the benefit of the "gaping mob" (70) that its members forget that "real life is on the other side of the footlights" (70). Eventually, however, Lily sees through her earlier delusions—an awareness that aggravates her estrangement from Old New York. Lily's narrative is, in this respect, informed by a sociological vision similar to Veblen's satire of the leisure classes (see *Theory* 119–28, 58): Wharton indicates that the rituals of consumption performed by Old New Yorkers are financed by the activities of a hidden world of working-class drudges who can in turn act as dazzled spectators of the magnificence generated by their own alienated work.

Dreiser's urban theater is, by contrast, not a world where it is possible to peep behind the surfaces of the class system and to discover its hidden mechanics of exploitation. First, what is heard on this urban stage is not primarily a set of human actors. In a gesture that thoroughly upsets Veblen's realist critique of vitalist sociologizing (see *Theory* 26; *Instinct* 53), Dreiser fills his novel with the mysterious and floating voices "of the so-called inanimate" (75; Pennsylvania 98) or with the movement of "the things of which we are the evidence" (Pennsylvania 119).[4] These voices emanate from the elements of the city's market whose meaning Carrie can grasp intuitively—money, sartorial display, and all the signs of conspicuous consumption.[5]

> Fine clothes to her were a vast persuasion; they spoke tenderly and Jesuitically for themselves. When she came within earshot of their pleading, desire in her bent a willing ear. Ah, ah! the voices of the so-called inanimate. Who shall yet translate for us the language of the stones.
>
> "My dear," said the lace collar she secured from Pardridge's, "I fit you beautifully; don't give me up." (75)

This passage reads like a bitterly ironical representation of the fetishism of the commodity—a satire of an economy in which the relations between marketable objects usurp the attributes of relations between people to the fantastic extent that commodities acquire audible voices. Yet Dreiser's text is not ironical here: Carrie's ambition to decipher the language of the "inanimate" (75) constitutes the inchoate form of the visionary and artistic sensibility that ensures her later success as an actress.

Within this vitalist landscape, the role of the theater, as a cultural and commercial institution, consists in mediating between the visible "superficialities" (75) of the urban market and the elusive forces of Life or "the world" (356). Commodities do speak to Carrie, but only "Jesuitically" (75); likewise, the brilliant mansions of the upper class only inspire the young woman with "awe and distant wonder" (129). The voice of the theater, on the contrary, beckons to her in friendly and trustworthy accents: the stage takes "her by the hand kindly, as one who says, 'My dear, come in'" (129). When Carrie accompanies her friend Mrs. Vance to the "showy parade" (226) of the Broadway crowds, the organized display of affluence strikes her as an awe-inspiring but harsh and slightly humiliating experience, where she finds herself "stared at and ogled" (226) by people who can detect her economic inferiority. The matinee performance, however, immediately heals those wounds. Here, the "gilded surroundings" (228) are a given, a convention, and the tormenting questions about the origins of other people's wealth—"Whence came the rich, elegant dresses, the astonishingly colored buttons, the knicknacks of silver and gold?" (228)—can be laid to rest.

What Carrie discovers in the world of the theater is a "mingled atmosphere of life and mummery" (128) that fulfills her "innate taste for imitation" (Pennsylvania 157). Her habit of intuitively modeling herself on those that she regards as her social betters becomes in this context refined into "the first subtle outcroppings of an artistic nature" (Pennsylvania 157). The array of cosmetics and clothes that play a crucial role in the construction of the everyday personality of Dreiser's city women is transmuted into "the nameless paraphernalia of disguise"—"rouge, pearl powder, whiting, burnt cork, India ink, pencils for the eyelids, wigs for the head" (128). Like the corresponding commercial artifacts, these stage props exert a form of enigmatic fascination: they "breathe of the other half of life in which we have no part, of doors that are closed, and mysteries which may never be revealed" (Pennsylvania 176). In this case, however, we are dealing with a fascination of a higher order: "Here was no illusion. Here was an open door to see all of that. She had come upon it as one who stumbles upon a secret passage, and, behold, she was in the chamber of diamonds and delights!" (129). The image of the hidden treasure implies that the theater spontaneously divulges the secrets that the things of the market could only express in mystifying terms. As

Carrie's intellectual mentor, Robert Ames, puts it, the stage constitutes the site where "the world is always trying to express itself" (356)—hopefully in a language shorn of the vulgarity of material interests. Accordingly, Carrie's growing affinities with these mysteries, combined with her acting talent, will render her able to perform what the positivistic discourse of the novel deems impossible—circumventing the monolithic determinism of the sublime field of forces—or the iron logic of the urban class system.

Yet even Dreiser's text itself sends signals that the world of the theater cannot so easily transcend the economic arena on which it feeds. Rachel Bowlby and Philip Fisher have argued compellingly that the stage in Dreiser can be regarded neither as a haven of anti-capitalist authenticity nor as a higher aesthetic realm. On the contrary, theatrical conventions are paradigmatic of the city's economy in so far as they mimic—and in fact naturalize—the commodification of objects and personalities on which the market relies (Bowlby 62–65; Fisher 266–70). Bowlby concludes therefore that, in spite of the author's claims, "no qualitative distinction exists" between Dreiser's view of the realms of drama and of the economy (63). To a certain extent, Dreiser himself concedes that the drawing-room melodramas Carrie attends are mere compensatory fantasies that misrepresent economic conditions. He comments ironically on his character's eagerness to be gratified by a make-believe world of wealth: "Who would not suffer amid perfumed tapestries, cushioned furniture and liveried servants? Grief under such circumstances becomes an enticing thing" (228). Still, in those very words, he outlines the scenario that allows Carrie to achieve the material and artistic success she is longing for. The heroine wants indeed "to take her sufferings, whatever they [are], in such a world, or failing that, at least to simulate them under such charming conditions upon the stage" (228). Fisher infers from this that, by providing a positive portrayal of simulation in the theater and the market, Dreiser depicts an economy perpetually in transit toward its own future: the stage helps actors rehearse "anticipatory states of the self" (270) in exactly the same way as clothes help Carrie in the constant remodeling of her personality. This view precludes any functional distinction between art and economics.

In view of this, Dreiser's insistence that an invisible line be drawn between the theater and the parade of consumption stems, I think, from the necessity to preserve the aura of vitalist splendor of the urban scene. The narrator's allusions to the mysteries of the stage may indeed be read as a rhetorical decoy: they might, by compensation, cover up a void—a lack of substance—at the heart of the urban world. The novel must indeed fend off the suspicion that it fails to establish the substantiality of its sublime field of forces in the description of the economic scene alone. In this logic, the stage, because it provides an extra channel of expression for the voices of life and of the world, offers the ultimate guarantee of the presence of hidden forces in the urban domain itself. Drama is a doubly powerful—and thus superlatively real—wellspring of mysteriousness. It exorcizes the anxiety that the urban economic scene could be unmasked as a mere showcase of the commodity. Indeed, without the aura of magic supplied both by the market and by the theater, the characters would be trapped in a groundless labyrinth of deceitful surfaces; Carrie's gift of social imitation would remain pure mimicry, and not the dim artistic intuition of a larger order of being that it is purported to be.

In the questions raised by the status of the theater, we may discern the ambivalent configuration of the failed sublime—the form of sublimity where power is simultaneously asserted and subverted. In this light, Carrie's trajectory as an actress is a precarious bid for empowerment. On the one hand, it projects an aspiration toward a release from the constraints of the market; on the other hand, its frailty is brought to light by the fact that it is hemmed in by the author's recurring emphasis on the hardships of life in the city—violent strikes, unemployment, homelessness, soup kitchens. It is, I think, impossible to resolve or interpret this contradiction through an intrinsic reading of the text: this would leave us perpetually wondering whether or not the sentimental tropes that articulate the empowering discourse of animistic economics are meant ironically. An approach that seems more promising for the interpretation of this sublime ambivalence is Kenneth Burke's theory of "symbolic action" (8). Burke argues that literary texts work like magical "'spells'" (8) meant to effect a change in the situation of the author, or of his or her community. Burke suggests that writers cannot face dangerous or painful experiences head-on, but can shape their texts as "a strategy for confronting or encompassing" a difficult or terrifying situation (64).

Burke's approach can easily be transposed to *Sister Carrie* if we choose to read the text as a displaced autobiography. I have mentioned that the narrative pattern of Carrie's initiatory voyage to Chicago and New York recurs, with a few inevitable modifications, in overtly autobiographical texts like *The "Genius"* and *Newspaper Days*. If we assume that Carrie is a probe that Dreiser sends out into the metropolis, it is crucial to determine what symbolic act is achieved by substituting an inexperienced provincial young woman for the novelist himself. One major aspect of this question will be further developed in the discussion of novels of artistic education in part 4. I argue there that naturalists postulate an uncanny affinity between women, the urban scene, and the field of art. In Dreiser, this gendered vision of the access to urban culture is elaborated in a thematics of androgyny; in *The "Genius,"* particularly, the artist best attuned to city life is the one who can develop the feminine features of his personality.[6] This issue is illustrated in *Sister Carrie* in the pair formed by Ames and Carrie at the end of the novel: Carrie and Ames *together* make up the two sides of the naturalist artistic personality, and Carrie qualifies therefore at least to some degree as an autobiographical figure.

For the rest, the main component of the symbolic strategy centering on Carrie lies in the author's strategic manipulation of his heroine's alleged naiveté and caricatural passivity. In this scenario of autobiographical self-dramatization, I want to argue that Dreiser uses Carrie's naiveté as a shield for the dazzlement he may have felt as a visitor to the city and, by compensation, as a tool for his own empowerment.[7] Because she is pictured as a stereotypical "half-equipped little knight" (2), Carrie is allowed to give in to ecstasies of wonder that are highly beneficial for the literary exploration of animistic economics, but that might be awkward in an autobiographical hero, and, more particularly, in a man. This results in a difficult balancing act in which Dreiser must present Carrie as both more insightful and more limited than his narrator: with her intuitive grasp of the city's magic, she is allowed to explore the sublime wonders of Chicago and New York further than a fictional author might; yet the narrator must simultaneously establish his superiority over the young woman by pointing out the limitations of her understanding.

The language game through which Dreiser constructs Carrie's implied passivity is, I think, the centerpiece of the displaced autobiographical scenario enacted in the novel. Passivity is a keyword in Dreiser's deterministic cosmo-sociology: it is induced both by the forces of nature and by the mechanisms of the urban market. Hurstwood is the most striking representative of the passive city dweller, resolved to let himself be carried away by the "Lethean waters" (252) of the city's entropic influence. In this, Hurstwood is the sacrificial victim of Dreiser's narrative strategy. His powerlessness needs to be exorcized.

Carrie is at first characterized as a victim of the same kind of powerlessness; the subtitle of the first chapter describes her as "a waif amid forces" (1); for a long time, she remains a puppet at the mercy of the city's intrusive voices—"She was as yet more drawn than she drew" (57), Dreiser comments. By virtue of an unaccountable metamorphosis, however, her passivity discreetly evolves into a tool of social ascension. Her intuitive grasp of the mechanisms of the market—her understanding of "fortune's superficialities" (75)—is at bottom a passive gift of sartorial and social mimicry; yet it constitutes the basis of her sexual attractiveness, which guarantees her livelihood as a kept woman, then as an actress. The most spectacular instance of magically felicitous passivity occurs in the narrative of Carrie's artistic breakthrough on Broadway. Still only a chorus girl, Carrie is given the role of "a silent little Quakeress" (325) in a new play; feeling that the author wants to shelve this minor part, the young woman goes through the whole dress rehearsal harboring a perfectly unpremeditated "disconsolate" frown (325); the expression catches the eye of the author, however, who encourages Carrie to "frown a little more" (325). The "quiet, unassuming drollery" of the young woman's expression turns out to be the "chief feature of the play" (326). An enthusiastic critic, commenting on the meteoric rise of Miss Madenda—Carrie's stage name—reflects with unwitting perceptiveness that the "vagaries of fortune are indeed curious" (327).

By conjuring up the vision of an actress whose chance gestures are in harmony with the flow of deterministic forces, Dreiser performs a symbolic act meant to exorcize the helplessness that affects his characters—and arguably himself—in the commercial metropolis. The fact that Carrie's passivity works as a form of empowerment in disguise is brought to light very suggestively in a conversation between Ames and the young woman that appears in the Pennsylvania manuscript; Ames—here clearly speaking for the author—defines the actress's role in the cosmic scheme of things:

> "I know why, if you tried, you would be a success, because I know the quality of that thing which your face represents. The world is always struggling to express itself—to make clear its hopes and sorrows and give them voice. It is always seeking the means, and it will delight in the individual who can express these things for it. That is why we have great musicians, great painters, great writers and actors. They have the ability to express the world's sorrows and longings, and the world gets up and shouts their names. All effort is just that. It is the thing which the world wants portrayed, written about, graven, sung or discovered, not the portrayer or writer or singer, which makes the latter great. You and I are but mediums, through which something is expressing itself. Now, our duty is to make ourselves ready mediums." (Pennsylvania 485)

Ames's belief that a vague cosmic spirit is struggling to express itself through Carrie represents the ultimate statement of animistic economics. It is indeed impossible to take for granted the engineer's contention that the world is dominated by passivity, that "all effort" consists in making oneself the "medium" of cosmic currents. Through these words, Dreiser defines the form of activism open to those who live in a universe of paralyzing inequality: in a paradoxical strategy, the text implies that an artist in late-nineteenth-century New York should completely identify herself or himself with cosmic and market forces, as Carrie does through her gift of intuitive apprehension; on the other hand, the whole discourse of fortune and good luck that runs through the novel sends the much more important signal that the whole cosmic framework can be made to conform magically to the character's and the writer's aspirations. Dreiser, as a writer, has the latitude to manipulate luck: at the cost of a breach of realistic verisimilitude, he can ensure that his heroine's frown of frustration yields a magical reward. Therefore, the overall image that the novel constructs of Carrie Meeber's development, beyond the ironies and the cautionary warnings, is one of effortless, though arguably limited, empowerment.

To sum up, the symbolic calculus of *Sister Carrie* functions in several stages: as an acknowledgment of the destructive power of the city, Hurstwood has to be sacrificed so that the heroine may succeed; on another level, Carrie's naiveté is ritualistically denounced so that her intuitive sensibility may thrive; the passivity of the heroine, on the other hand, is magically metamorphosed into a positive faculty. Ultimately, the vision of a successful pseudo-passive female artist secures the empowerment of Dreiser, the male novelist, whose sense of economic stability and identity is all but assured. It is through this give-and-take logic of sacrifices and gains that the basic ambivalence of Dreiser's sublime vision is spread out through the text—and, to some extent, alleviated.

CHAPTER 7

Sublime (Re)production:
Frank Norris's *The Octopus* and *The Pit*

Dreiser's efforts to make visible the economic underpinnings of the spectacle of urban life do not probe further than the perimeter of the city. Even in *The "Genius,"* which devotes some attention to life on the land, the novelist does not suggest that small-town people—picturesque icons of agrarian virtue, most of them—vitally contribute to the welfare of the urban realm: the city remains a world sui generis. By comparison, Frank Norris's *The Epic of the Wheat*—a trilogy of which only two volumes, *The Octopus* (1901) and *The Pit* (1903) were completed—works on a broader base, tracing the display of urban wealth to its origins in agriculture—namely, in the activities of California field hands. Yet, despite the dissimilarities in scope, Dreiser's and Norris's fictional projects are linked by important continuities, both in literary discourse and economic concerns. Like *Sister Carrie*, Norris's *The Epic of the Wheat* is a work whose politics have been radically reinterpreted in the last decades: described in its own days as a critique of the newly developed trusts, it is now read as a prime example of what Walter Benn Michaels calls "corporate fiction" (189). As in Dreiser's case, Norris's ideology has been reappraised by critics who felt the need to take into account the political dissonances and discontinuities present in his texts: in these novels, the realist critique of capitalism coexists awkwardly with the urge to provide a quasi-mystical celebration of the new corporate forces in America.

A central aspect of the pro-corporate bias of Norris's fiction is what June Howard and Mark Seltzer call, respectively, "the erasure of the laborer" (Howard 122) and the "radical emptying of the category of production" (Seltzer 26). Howard and Seltzer imply thereby that the representation of economics in naturalist fiction obscures the role of human agency in the process of production. Their argument can, I think, be extended to Dreiser's novels as well, where factory work or other working-class jobs are synonymous with degrading proletarianization. In the present chapter, I contend that it is through the medium of what I have called the rhetoric of sublime life forces that the marginalization of production is effected in naturalism. Thorstein Veblen, a staunch critic of vitalism, argues that proper work—the task of the engineer—consists in a confrontation with "brute matter" (*Instinct* 196). There is little room in Dreiser's sublime economics for such a dialectic of inert matter and instrumental reason. The essential business in Dreiser's city is indeed ultimately the action of "super-intelligible" cosmic forces (*Carrie*, Pennsylvania 78). Likewise, Norris's cosmo-sociological discourse anchors the urban economy directly in the generative power of the land. The main economic actors in this scheme of things are "Titanic" (*Octopus* 46) vital powers like "the Wheat" (*Octopus* 651), "Life" (635), or "Force" (634). This metaphysics marginalizes the scene of industry and even turns farmers into secondary actors in the development of their own crops.

After analyzing Norris's economic vitalism, I will be led to argue that his novels do indeed indulge in pro-corporate proselytizing, yet do not display a sufficient degree of ideological closure to be read exclusively as pro-business tracts. The dissonances of Norris's texts—which justified their being ideologically reevaluated in the first place—are too resilient to be perceived merely as necessary moments of hesitation, destined to be sublimated into a final political epiphany. It is precisely through these unresolved tensions that the texts reveal their inability fully to map the urban economy and to utter consistent sociological pronouncements about it. Conversely, by paying attention to the novels' lack of closure, we can retrospectively better understand how turn-of-the-century readers were incited to read those works along left-wing liberal lines.

The persistent instability of Norris's politics can be briefly brought out in the way he handles his political and literary sources. By adopting an agrarian view of turn-of-the-century economics, Norris picks two sets of political and literary interlocutors for himself: on the one hand, the Populist movement of the Farmers Alliance and, on the other hand, the literary tradition of American pastoralism. As far as politics go, the belief that Norris endorses the Populist agenda has compellingly been criticized as a misreading of the historical context in which *The Epic of the Wheat* was written (see Howard 120; Seltzer 26; Michaels 175–77). Norris's gendered economics, I point out below, stand indeed at odds with the producer-oriented ethos of agrarian politics. It would, however, be simplistic to consider that the novelist, in his pro-corporate treatment of agrarian insurrections, could conjure up a *consistent* chart of 1890s economics merely by replacing the radical discourse of Populism with a mystifying gendered discourse. For one thing, nature romanticism, from which Norris's gender tropes are derived, is no neutral tool: in the reading of Norris's *The Pit*, particularly, I suggest that this discourse generates ideological instabilities of its own. Indeed, by drawing on the pastoral tradition, Norris transposes to the uncharted domain of urban-industrialism an epistemological grid that was certainly familiar to his reader, but was also inadequate to the city context: in pastoral discourse, the urban world is likely to be portrayed in gothic terms, as an anti-natural environment. Accordingly, Norris's novels end up modeling the economy of the city as a wellspring of fertility whose (re)productive power is matched only by the uncanny fascination it inspires. As I mentioned in part 1, I believe in this case that gothic characterization does not limit itself to making the city landscape glamorous in its fearfulness. It also performs the function Vijay Mishra ascribes to the Gothic sublime: to be *"the embodiment of pure negativity"* (Mishra quoting Žižek 17, emphasis in original). The proliferation of gothic prose manifests therefore the residual doubt that prevents the texts from articulating their ideology consistently.

The Octopus

Based on an historical event—the 1880 Mussel Slough incident—*The Octopus* presents the narrative of a violent rebellion that opposes a group of California wheat ranchers to the railroad trust. The farmers accuse the railroad of burdening them with unfair rates and of using legal maneuvering to expropriate them from the land they have been working for years. Ultimately, the farmers' insurgency misfires: they are utterly defeated by the trusts. This central narrative is surrounded by a number of important subplots. Most of the novel is viewed from the eyes of an initially neutral witness—Presley, a poet who strives to find the literary form that will do justice to the social upheaval that unfolds in front of his eyes. Presley's outrage at the plight of the ranchers leads him to write a poem of agrarian rebellion—"The Toilers"—and to take part in the activities of the Farmers' League. In a more fantastic vein, Norris develops the tale of Vanamee, a mystical shepherd whose psychic powers all but allow him to resurrect his deceased sweetheart. The novel's conclusion offers a number of paradoxical possibilities: a farmer's wife and daughter are led respectively to starvation and prostitution in the city; one of the most repulsive agents of the trust dies buried in a flood of wheat. Chastened by the defeat of the farmers, Presley disowns his freshly developed agrarian radicalism: he is converted to the cause of the corporation, seemingly against the logic of the narrative.

Presley's eventual political about-face is the most visible manifestation of the uncertainties that affect Norris's economic vision. While the novel is for the most part focused on the farmers' economic complaints, the poet's unexpected pro-corporate conversion is facilitated by the fact that, from early on, the text also positions itself in ambiguous fashion toward the agrarian/pastoral tradition.[1] *The Octopus* draws on two strands in the agrarian constellation—the political tradition of Jeffersonian republicanism and, on the other hand, the literary discourse that defines American nature as "a goddess of fertility and a dispensatrix of inexhaustible bounty" (Smith 193). Thus, the Jeffersonian legacy is no ideological anchor for Norris: it weaves in and out of *The Octopus* as the author presents the ranchers from opposite perspectives.

If we follow the literal logic of the text, the Jeffersonian world of the yeoman farmer belongs in a nostalgic past. Kevin Starr pointedly remarks that Norris's California ranchers, by their very labor practices, are only distantly related to the Jeffersonian ideals of the Populist insurgency.[2] Norris, Starr contends, provides an accurate appraisal of a social situation that differed in many respects from agricultural conditions in the Populist South or the Midwest: from the 1870s on, wheat ranches in the San Joaquin Valley resorted to thoroughly mechanized agricultural forms of organization. Holdings were huge and machines were numerous and powerful (xiv–xv). In the "new order of things," Norris writes, the California wheat farm works like "a principality ruled with iron and steam" (*Octopus* 60). Its farmers are characterized by a toughness and recklessness that fits their industrial methods. In the description of Magnus

Derrick—the chief rancher of the region, who started off as a gold miner—Norris even raises the suspicion that the novel does not deal with farmers at all:

> Magnus remained the gambler, willing to play for colossal stakes, to hazard a fortune on the chance of winning a million. . . . the miner's instinct of wealth acquired in a single night prevailed in spite of all. It was in this frame of mind that Magnus and the multitude of other ranchers of whom he was the type, farmed their land. They had no love for their land. They were not attached to the soil. They worked their ranches as a quarter of a century ago they had worked their mines. To husband the resources of their marvellous San Joaquin, they considered niggardly, petty, Hebraic. To get all there was of the land, to squeeze it dry, to exhaust it, seemed their policy. (298)

Thus, the San Joaquin Ranchers, as they gamble and squeeze their resources dry, seem to straddle the line of demarcation that separates them from the hated railroad men.

However, this apparent indictment of the industrial farmer weighs relatively little against the narrative momentum of the novel, which, except for the very last pages, directs the reader's sympathies toward the farmers and their families. To Vanamee and to Presley, the ranchers represent "the People" (377). By focalizing its narrative from the point of view of the embattled ranchers, the story automatically remobilizes the positive ideological valuation that attaches to farming. Norris's ranchers are therefore two-faced: in their losing battle against the railroad, they still appear as late embodiments of the independent husbandmen of the agrarian republic; at the level of their actual economic practice, however, they have already joined the new order of industries and trusts.

If we follow the drift of Norris's cosmic philosophizing, it is the task of the gendered economic discourse to heal the contradictions illustrated in the double-edged characterization of the ranchers. A major ambition of the text consists indeed in making us accept that the generative power of the Wheat—of the mighty Earth, then of Force itself—can function as a sublime operator that miraculously dissolves all contradictions. At the most spectacular level, this logic of sublime conversion can vanquish death: in a process depicted as a form of resurrection, Vanamee reclaims his lover Angèle, who supposedly died when she was raped twenty years before. She now returns in the shape of her own grown-up daughter. On a more mundane plane, the humiliation of the proud ranchers and the sufferings of their families is somehow made good by the fact that cosmic energies that were once invested in farming have been rerouted toward expanding corporations. At that moment in history, these constitute indeed the site where the cosmic force, the pressure of the Wheat, has elected to embody itself. Norris intimates thereby that the political fractures or urbanization will be healed by having the trusts serve as visible symbols for the new totality of the American nation.

The conversion process by which *The Octopus* tries to doctor its narrative inconsistencies has been perceptively described by Mark Seltzer. What Seltzer detects in Norris and in naturalism at large is an attempt to defuse all possibilities for oppositional politics whatsoever (see Seltzer 25–44). In this perspective, the totalizing momentum of *The Octopus* is an ideological ploy: Norris's textual mechanism of conversion and expropriation of energies is meant to create a unified field of political discourse that serves the ideological interests of men. Texts like *The Octopus*, Dreiser's *Sister Carrie*, or Henry Adams's "The Virgin and the Dynamo," Seltzer argues, emulate the thermodynamic principle according to which "matter and energy may be converted and exchanged but can neither be created nor destroyed" (29). Cycles of conversions that function on this basis, he points out, are able to co-opt the power of both industrial production and female reproduction, and to sublimate them into an "autonomous male technology of generation" (31). The latter does not need any external principle to perpetuate itself and cannot be subverted by outside influences.

Though extremely insightful, Seltzer's description of Norris's economics makes, I think, impossible claims for the degree of ideological consistency that can be achieved in *The Octopus*. To take up his thermodynamics metaphor, I believe that Seltzer does not do justice to the considerable ideological entropy involved in Norris's manipulation of gender and economic energies: the crisis of social imageability with which Norris is struggling is powerful enough to oblige his text to stage not only its retotalizing gesture but also the spectacle of its faltering: the process by which the trusts supplant the agrarian cosmos as totalizing embodiment of America remains precarious.

In what follows, I wish to show that Norris's pseudo-totalizing strategy consists in a grandiose, though unstable rhetorical manipulation of gender thematics, first deployed in the novelist's gendered representation of agriculture. In this logic, Norris reshuffles the pastoral imagery of the fertile American continent along naturalist lines. The novelist first sets up a vision of Nature as an inexhaustible feminine power of reproduction; yet, at a later stage of the novel, this feminine potency is converted into more abstract and de-gendered cosmic agencies. This gesture of transcoding necessitates the definition of several modes of intercourse with nature. One of these is presented through the memories of Mrs. Derrick, and is characterized as peripheral to the world of the ranchers: it is the "cosey, comfortable, home-like" (59) universe of the Jeffersonian husbandmen of the past "where the farmers loved their land, caressing it, coaxing it, nourishing it as though it were a thing almost conscious; where the seed was sown by hand, and a single two-horse plough was sufficient for the entire farm" (59–60). Here, as in no other point in the text, the relation to the land evokes the ideal of a heterosexual marriage, with its traditional implications of stability and self-sufficiency.

Compared to this pastoral parenthesis, the gender configuration of California wheat farming already belongs to the industrial order: it mobilizes forces beyond any human control. The ploughing scene reveals that magnitude, specialization, and hierarchical discipline constitute the basic principles of the ranchers' mechanized agriculture. The closest simile Norris offers for this type of organization of labor is a military one: the line of ploughs, "thirty-five in number, each drawn by its team of ten," resembles "a great column of artillery" (127–28). In instinctual terms, ploughing becomes a heterosexual copulation of sublime proportions:

> It was the long stroking caress, vigorous, male, powerful, for which the Earth seemed panting. The heroic embrace of a multitude of iron hands, gripping deep into the warm flesh of the land that quivered responsive and passionate under this rude advance, so robust as to be made almost an assault, so violent as to be veritably brutal. There, under the sun and under the speckless sheen of the sky, the wooing of the Titan began, the vast primal passion, the two world-forces, the elemental Male and Female, locked in colossal embrace, at grapples in the throes of an infinite desire, at once terrible and divine, knowing no law, untamed, savage, sublime. (131)

Male aggression and rape fantasies are the keynotes of this vision of agricultural work. In the literal sense of the terms, the wheat farmers in their alliance with their crude machines are no longer husbandmen, but disciplined carriers of an awesome male principle that confronts a no less formidable female force.

Our expectation that this bipolar gender system might be the ultimate achievement of gendered agriculture is defeated, however: Norris introduces a third mode of relating to the land that defuses his vision of cosmic heterosexuality. This new element is the sheer dread of the wheat itself—the "undefinable terror" (60) Mrs. Derrick experiences when confronting the vast expanses of the ranch: "The direct brutality of ten thousand acres of wheat, nothing but wheat as far as the eye could see, stunned her a little. The one-time writing teacher of a young ladies' seminary, with her pretty deer-like eyes and delicate fingers, shrank from it. She did not want to look at so much wheat. There was something vaguely indecent in the sight, this food of the people, this elemental force, this basic energy, weltering here under the sun in all the unconscious nakedness of a sprawling, primordial Titan" (60). Passages like these corroborate Seltzer's insight that Norris singles out the offspring of agricultural copulation—the wheat itself—and not the "pains of labor" of "the great earth, the mother" (47), as the major source of power. The bipolar logic of the plowing scene is thus replaced by a pattern where one primordial principle suffices, and where a mode of feminine reproduction is expropriated for the benefit of a non-female, neutral force.

Viewed as a rhetorical gesture, the process of transcoding that leads to the enthroning of the wheat as a cosmic force fulfills the logic of what I have called the sublimity speech act. This rhetorical procedure stirs the dread of absolute magnitude only to soothe it by an ideologically oriented gesture of crisis resolution. In other words, it conjures up through its hyperboles the vision of an open-ended field—a semantic abyss, as it were—and then replaces this unsettling vista by a more easily imageable metaphor of infinite power—the Wheat, later, the corporation: in this fashion, the sublime boundlessness is superseded by a pseudo-totality. Norris's sublime idiom reveals that this rhetorical gesture is the more impressive if the construction of the pseudo-totality is presented as the outcome of a painstaking moment of hesitation: the text displays its movement of oscillation between the various possible metaphors that will help contain sublime dread.

Norris's manipulation of semantic indeterminacy is noticeable in his systematic reliance on the polysemy of hyperbole. Characteristically, Norris's sublime idiom thrives on repetitiousness, and it revolves around a limited set of keywords—"colossal" (104, 577, 634), "gigantic" (46, 180) "leviathan" (51, 179, 180, 577), "monster" (51, 179, 616), "Titan" (369, 128)—applied to sometimes incompatible objects. It is the ambiguity of the term Titan, for instance, that makes possible the transfer of power from the earth to its offspring, the wheat: the cosmic copulation of the ploughing scene is presented as the "wooing of the Titan" (128)—the fertile earth—at the hands of masculine farming machines. Yet the "sprawling, primordial Titan" (60) dreaded by Mrs. Derrick is the wheat

itself. This discreet semantic shift is facilitated by the fact that the term
Titan traditionally carries a masculine connotation; thus, the gender
value of Norris's earth figure had been blurred from the very beginning,
in a way that smoothly paves the way for the conversion of energy.

It is the same mechanism of hyperbolic interchangeability that allows
Norris to cancel the opposition between the basic antagonists of the narrative—the world of farming and the railroad monopoly. This conversion is established through Mrs. Derrick's fear of the threatening trains,
which, in a tell-tale association, is made indistinguishable from her own
dread of the Titanic earth. To Annie Derrick, the railroad is a "gallop-
ing terror of steam and steel" (179), a "symbol of a vast power, huge and
terrible" (179) that roars through the California night. Her imagination
blows up the railroad to the dimension of a *"leviathan with tentacles of
steel"* (179, emphasis added) that condemns its opponents to be "ground
to instant destruction beneath the clashing wheels" (180). In the same
breath, the text reverts to "the terror of sheer bigness" (180) which Mrs.
Derrick experiences when she faces the "limitless reaches of spaces" (180)
of the California ranch. The indifference of Nature turns out to be as
awesome as the train: if the human insect rebels against her, Nature turns
into a "relentless, a gigantic engine, a vast power, huge, terrible; a *leviathan with a heart of steel* . . ." (180, emphasis added). Thus, long before
Presley's conversion to the discourse of the monopoly, the equalizing
logic of Norris's sublime rhetoric has already neutralized the distinction
that seemed to preclude the reconciliation of pastoral values with the
order of corporate technology.

Overall, the ideological impact of Norris's sublime rhetoric consists in
acknowledging the defeat of individual agency and of individual economic producers. The revolving-door logic of the novelist's sublimity speech
acts elevates in turns the power of the earth, the Titanic trains, the wheat,
and the trust to the dignity of pseudo-totalizing agents of the American
economy. As June Howard and Mark Seltzer point out, these are principles over which individuals—small producers, typically—have no hold.
Therefore, Norris's decision to depict an economy moved by a constant
uprooting and displacement of power ultimately enfranchises economic
middlemen. Because there is no origin, only transit, in Norris's economic
system, producers are sidetracked: the ceaseless traffic of energies obscures
the role of human agency in production since it delegates ultimate power
to the "unassailable, undefiled" wheat (*Octopus* 651)—"that mighty world-
force wrapped in Nirvanic calm, indifferent to the human swarm" (651).
By turning power itself into a sublime, disembodied entity, the novel works

to the benefit of those who control the flow of exchange—tradesmen and speculators. This point is made plain to Presley by Cedarquist, a San Francisco capitalist: "The great word of [the] nineteenth century has been Production. The great word of the twentieth century will be . . . Markets" (305).

However, when reading this resounding rhetoric, it is useful to bear in mind the fact that Norris did not quite manage to put across the pro-corporate accents of his text in his own time. Indeed, the contention that Norris wrote for the benefit of the trusts, and that he therefore depicted Populism as "a dangerous force" (Howard 127), flies in the face of previous traditions of reading—left and right—which associated *The Octopus* with the anti-trust Farmers Alliance. Richard Chase contends indeed that Norris was heavily influenced, if not by the concrete demands of the farmers' movement, at least by the "folklore of populism" (200–201). In Norris's own time, the novelist was either celebrated or reviled for making the term "Octopus" a rallying cry for anti-trust campaigners inspired by Populism. A socialist activist portrayed in Upton Sinclair's *The Jungle* (1906) is warmly praised for setting out "on the trail of the Octopus" for most of his life (380). From the opposite political corner, the antisocialist David M. Parry thought he could turn the tables on Norris's alleged anti-trust views when, in his own reactionary dystopia *The Scarlet Empire*, he pictured a socialist Atlantis where individualistic opponents are fed to a giant Octopus—the living embodiment of the smothering State.[3]

By emphasizing these odd dissonances in critical reception, it is not my intention to argue that Norris's novel is purely and simply ambiguous—that it speaks as compellingly on both sides of the agrarian issue. Rather, I wish to bring out a more complex pattern of ideological faltering, inherent to Norris's ambition of providing a "larger view" (651) of 1890s economics by means of a text that mingles the epistemologies of realism and romance. We have seen that the narrative mechanics of *The Octopus* frame local communities and individuals in such a way that they seem destined to be integrated—in fact dissolved—within a larger entity, namely, a corporate-managed America depicted in the accents of sublime romance. In this sense, the novelist's merger of realistic analysis, esotericism, and corporate ideology rewrites Robert Wiebe's theory of modernization in mystical terms: the novel stages a dialogue between the claims of the pseudo-populist "island communities" (Wiebe xiii) of California farmers and, on the other hand, the sublime discourse of the trusts.

Populism, in this perspective, may be viewed as the proper realist foil to *The Octopus*, whose romance discourse promotes an esoteric form of sociological description. The Farmers Alliance appears as the realist pole of 1890s agrarianism notably because it proves markedly less beholden than Norris to the literary mystique of the fertile American land. The tie to the land in Populism is essentially a matter of economic survival and political identity. The political literature of the movement is often much too matter-of-fact to wax nostalgic about the passing of pastoralism. Henry Nash Smith, in the interpretation of Hamlin Garland's *Jason Edwards* (1892), suggests, for instance, that farmers of the western settlements had by the 1870s come to regard pastoralism as an alienating myth: some of the agrarian revolts after 1870 were fueled in part by the realization that the utopia of the garden of the American West concealed a reality of droughts, sandstorms, and grasshopper infestations (see Smith 193).

As a response to this crisis of rural life, the populist Farmers Alliance developed strategies meant to safeguard the "simple market society" (Palmer 109)—the commonwealth of producers based on intelligible, democratic relations between work, consumption, and government (125). The blueprint for the simple market economy was Charles W. Macune's subtreasury plan, which sought to eliminate the stranglehold that, according to Populist doctrine, bankers and all other middlemen had secured on the American economy (see Goodwyn 92, 23). The centerpiece of this project was the struggle for the control of the currency—the "financial question" broached by many Populist tracts (Goodwyn 8). The main cause of poverty for farmers was indeed the unavailability of cheap credit, exacerbated by the government's decision to peg the dollar to the gold standard. Therefore, Populists endorsed the greenback movement's dream of establishing a flexible currency, whose expansion could be controlled democratically, according to the needs of the nation's economy.

Lawrence Goodwyn shows that the originality of Macune's plan was to fuse the greenback critique of American capitalism with the cooperative tradition of the Farmers Alliance. Macune collaborated in the creation of the Texas exchange (Goodwyn 88), a statewide farmers' cooperative that sought to substitute itself for the network of local merchants and bankers. Cooperatives, in Macune's subtreasury plan would retail the farmers' cotton without intermediaries, at full market price, and would cover the farmers' credit needs by means of greenbacks issued by the federal government (Goodwyn 92). The economic circuit defined thus ran from the producer to a producer-controlled medium of exchange—the cooperative—and to a democratically elected federal government, which would modulate the flow of the currency according to the needs of the producers; by the standards of an industrial society, it was economic simplicity itself.

Simplicity and democratic control are, however, not the political goals pursued in Norris's romance assessment of the American economy. *The Octopus* reveals instead that elitism and mystery are prerequisites of the sublime view of social processes: the rhetoric of gigantic forces is crudely presented as the carrier of esoteric truths, and it presupposes the existence of a mode of visionary consciousness accessible only to a few privileged minds. There are three of these in the novel: Shelgrim, the railroad magnate, Presley, the poet, and Vanamee, the mystic. The mystery that these three characters are allowed to perceive consists, not surprisingly, in a full grasp of the ultimate equivalence of all forces in Nature. With this comes the insight that individuals are impotent to dominate or influence sublime forces, which work for "the greatest good to the greatest numbers" (651). When Shelgrim states to Presley that *"Railroads build themselves"* (576) just as "the Wheat grows itself" (576), or when he contends that not even the president of the P.&S.W. "can stop (the railroad) or control it" (576), he expresses the wisdom of the "larger view" (651)—the enlightened perspective of corporate life. Presley converts to this stance when he becomes able to understand Vanamee's mystical insight that the Wheat is a Nirvanic power above the human fray.

Still, in Norris's celebration of continental corporations, the rhetorical gesture that enacts the dissolution of the local into the cosmic is not fully effective: the reception history of the novel indicates that Norris's text never managed completely to silence the voices of local life, of agrarian communes, of producers to which it partially gives voice. By decreeing that *The Octopus* succeeds in giving absolute primacy to its romancing of the trust, we would indeed take for granted that the pro-corporate sublime idiom is persuasive as such. There is, however, a basic instability in a rhetoric that invests all objects with an aura of terror: since Norris's hyperboles render their various sublime objects interchangeable, the author cannot expect his readers automatically to agree that, for instance, the trust rather than sublime farming is the proper pseudo-totalizing entity for the new economy. The fragility of Norris's rhetoric of sublimity has been emphasized from a different angle by Michael Davitt Bell, who argues that Norris's language is so addicted to "abstract, melodramatic cliché" that it makes "the impulse to raucous laughter . . . often irresistible" (123, 125). I cannot, of course, concur with an evaluation implying that Norris's sublimity speech acts are simply not functional—or not even significantly dissonant—within the text. Still, critics who, like Bell, are diffident of the romantic strains of naturalism suggest how easily Norris's paeans to the trust may have been overlooked in the past. Texts as heterogeneous as *The Octopus* lend themselves more than other works to the reader's prerogative of partial appropriation. Thus, in a historical context where anti-trust feeling was predominant, it must have been common sense to focus on the story of the farmers' sufferings, and to screen off the rest.

The Pit

Paradoxically, the second part of the unfinished triptych of *The Epic of the Wheat* is less triumphalist than *The Octopus* in its political support of urban-industrialism, though more explicitly antithetical to the Populist program. In this work, Norris tackles an issue that might be regarded as a blind spot in Populist economics—the creation of wealth on the urban market. Bruce Palmer suggests that the concern for economic rationality that is so essential to the Populists' critique of the financial system may have partly hampered their understanding of the workings of industrial processes and urban markets. He points out that Populist economics measures efficiency by the production of tangible wealth (18); therefore, Populists picture banking as a thoroughly parasitical institution that drains the economic resources created through the legitimate channels of production. In this perspective, bankers are "leeches on the business body," who "prosper when the people mourn" (18). Characteristically, Charles Macune's subtreasury plan aimed at short-circuiting the flow of exchange. Yet, Palmer argues, this radical gesture is grounded on theoretical principles that refuse to take into account some important mechanisms of the economic arena they seek to supplant. Palmer indicates, for instance, that the greenback analysis of the money system fails to grasp the importance of velocity in money transactions—a factor that directly influences the volume of the money supply and the availability of credit (82).

Given the stark opposition between Populist politics and Norris-style sublime economics, it is hardly surprising that *The Pit* should make the velocity of the currency flow one of the cornerstones of its representation of speculative markets. Indeed, this text attempts to provide a literary investigation of the mechanisms of creation of *in*tangible wealth— an economic process that naturalism presents as the prerogative of the urban domain. Far from disempowering the middlemen, Norris's eco-

nomics depicts in sensationalist terms the financial practices by which
the metropolis turns its channels of exchange into sites of (re)production
in their own rights. In so doing, Norris's city novel reverses the premises
of the agrarian tradition and endorses the discourse of sociologists like
Fredric C. Howe and Simon Nelson Patten, whose theories greeted the
advent of the urban-industrial order with enthusiasm and hope.

The Pit transfers the apparatus of forces pieced together in *The Octopus* to the confines of the urban arena. Its narrative centers around
titanic speculation deals; it traces the rise and fall of Curtis Jadwin, the
master speculator who seeks to corner the wheat market and fails, precipitating the defeat of all chief protagonists. Laura Dearborn, Jadwin's
wife, and Corthell, an ineffective artist, witness the speculator's downfall from the sidelines. The pessimistic drift of the narrative highlights
the fragility of the urban social order: neither the superhuman strivings of the speculators nor the claustrophobic decorum of the upperclass universe can shield the characters against the destabilizing welter of the Board of Trade, where the flow of the wheat is ceaselessly
exchanged and transformed into money. In the end, the novel restates
the claim, already voiced in *The Octopus*, that market forces remain out
of human reach.

The main structural device of *The Pit* is an elaborate set of parallels
and contrasts established between the domestic sphere—the world of
upper-class marriage—and the male-dominated arena of exchange. On
the surface, these two realms are sharply segregated: when Laura Dearborn first meets Jadwin at the Chicago opera, she has barely ever lent
any thought to what lies outside her genteel, feminized world of music
and entertainment. Yet, the intrusive whispers of men talking about a
financial failure, as well as the impressive physical presence of Jadwin,
precipitate in the young woman an artistic and economic epiphany: she
realizes the importance of the struggle in the world of business—"that
other drama that . . . was working itself out close at hand, equally picturesque, equally romantic, equally passionate, but more than that, real,
actual, modern" (34). The city that Laura discovers outside the theater
pulsates with "a life where women [have] no part" (64): a world of men
in shirt-sleeves, of messengers scurrying to and fro—a jungle of males
"freed from the influence of wife, mother, or daughter or sister" (64).
Above all, she experiences the power of Jadwin, a businessman with
"broad strong hands," who knows "how to grip and how to hang on" (34).
While passages like these seem to trace impassable boundaries between
the men's and the women's world, their sublime rhetoric also makes plain

that the hysteria of the market and the coming apart of family life are subtly linked: Norris's insistent efforts to foreground the dissimilarities of the private and the public spheres fail to conceal that, in the gendered economics of this Chicago novel, discontents in the domestic world and the perils of economic life can be referred to a single logic of economic exchange and kinship.

The nature of the link between public and private in Norris can, I think, be clarified by using Gayle Rubin's anthropological concept of "the traffic in women" (157). In her definition of the sex/gender system, Rubin provides a feminist rereading of Claude Lévi-Strauss's theories of the social function of kinship ties. Lévi-Strauss, Rubin explains, regards marriage—the basic element of kinship structures—as a particular case of gift exchange. The social meaning both of marriage and of the prohibition of incest resides indeed in the fact that women, like gifts, have to be exchanged among the different clans of a given community. By establishing this traffic in women, the structures of kinship cement a system of social relations that, Lévi-Strauss argues, are characterized by solidarity and reciprocity. However, against this utopian vision, Rubin points out that the social grammar described by Lévi-Strauss institutes an asymmetrical gender system in which women serve as inert and unwilling currency in the establishment of social ties between men: "If it is women who are being transacted, then it is the men who give and take them who are linked, the woman being the conduit of a relationship rather than a partner to it" (174).

Rubin's theory is relevant to the interpretation of naturalist economics because it points to similarities between gender relations and economic circulation. Indeed, she describes a grammar of gender modeled on an economic concept—the notion of traffic itself. In so doing, her description of the sex/gender system integrates the rationality of economics: there must, in this logic, be something like an economy of sexual relations. Naturalist city novels, on the other hand, use the language of kinship and sexuality as a metaphor for economic processes.

Viewed from Rubin's perspective, there are in *The Pit* two different but interrelated traffics—one in the private sphere, the other in the public world. The former is the traditional object of theories of kinship: it consists of the rules that regulate Laura Dearborn's and Curtis Jadwin's marriage, and prevent Laura from taking part in the world of men. In Norris's social allegory, the young bride serves as currency in a symbolic alliance between two camps of the capitalist classes—the older New England middle class and the new breed of midwestern speculators. Thus, the Jadwin household symbolizes the alliance of the eastern world of feminized culture with the western universe of male competition. That this traffic of kinship is at the mercy of the vicissitudes of the urban market is illustrated in the fact that Jadwin's speculative schemes bring about the death of his friend Cressler: there can be no solidarity among capitalists, even on the basis of kinship ties. Likewise, the bargains enacted in the family circle are unstable: the novel describes Laura's progressive estrangement from her husband, her attraction to the artist Corthell, and her final resolve to support Jadwin after his bankruptcy. In this, her marriage proves as frail as the bond established among the men in the public scene.

The textual element that makes possible the destructive interference of the public on the private sphere is Norris's sublime idiom. In their tentative love affair, Corthell stirs in Laura "troublous, unknown deeps" (136)—metaphors that recall the abyssal depths of the speculation vortex. More explicitly, Jadwin is depicted as the character who imports the sublime idiom of speculation into the bounds of the home. When he returns exhausted after a whole night of trading, the flood of commodities keeps running on in his very blood; still awake at dawn, he hears "the faint tides of blood behind [his] eardrums" murmuring "ceaselessly to [his] overdriven brain, 'Wheat—wheat—wheat, wheat—wheat—wheat. Forty million bushels, forty million, forty million'" (283).

Conversely, what the private sphere offers to Norris's economic idiom is its gender logic and its discourse of reproduction. In its panoramas of speculation, *The Pit* describes what, in Eve Kosofsky Sedgwick's terms, one might call an arena of self-destructive male homosocial bonds. Sedgwick, on the basis of Rubin's theory of the traffic in women, contends that social relations between men, like all other kinship ties, need the mediation of a feminine term—that is, that they are based on a literal or figurative exchange of women (see *Between* 29–33). In the sublime economy of *The Pit*, the mediating term that links men together is their relationship to the city's apparatus of production—that is, their common interests in the financial circulation of the sphere of exchange. Thus, the triangular configuration of male bonding takes the form of a traffic between speculators, in which the third term is the apparatus of the urban economy itself, in its gendered, feminine representation.

By describing Norris's view of speculation as a displaced form of gift exchange—a concept that, ironically, projects an image of solidarity—I mean to indicate that the novel's rhetoric of sublimity performs its ambiguous function of evoking the fantasy of a pseudo-totalized economy, while pointing to its constant dislocation. What keeps the men's arena of economic strife in motion is the movement of speculation originating in the Board of Trade Building—that is, the whirlpool of the wheat pit. The chaotic movements of the mechanisms of exchange, symbolizing both an economic bond and its dislocation, are subsumed under the sublime trope of the maelstrom—the vortex of a stormy sea, which rumbles through Chicago and shakes the whole world beyond. This metaphorical representation of market forces is first introduced into the text through Jadwin's own reflections on the power that drives the stock exchange crowds:

> Often Jadwin had noted the scene, and, unimaginative though he was, had long conceived the notion of some great, some resistless force within the Board of Trade Building that held the tide of the streets within its grip, alternately drawing it in and throwing it forth. Within there, a great whirlpool, a pit of roaring waters spun and thundered, sucking in the life tides of the city, sucking them in as into the mouth of some tremendous cloaca, the maw of some colossal sewer; then vomiting them forth again, spewing them up and out, only to catch them in the return eddy and suck them in afresh. (79)

The whirlpool represents a form of traffic, albeit in caricatural form: its wild gyratory circulation, which reverberates "all through the Northwest," in "the elevators of Western Iowa" (79), and "as far as the streets of New York" (80), appears as a grotesque simulacrum for the larger, incomprehensible economic traffic of the American nation. According to Norris's explicit economic doctrine, it embodies the reproductive capacities of the titanic earth itself, displaced to the bounds of the city.

In *The Octopus*, Norris reshuffled the discourse of fertility of pastoralism; here, the presence of a thundering vortex at the heart of Jadwin's Chicago suggests that *The Pit* mixes tropes of pastoral fertility with the gothic accents of Edgar Allan Poe's stories. Norris's depiction of the urban market recalls indeed Poe's "A Descent into the Maelstrom," as if Norris had transposed Poe's "Moskoe-ström" ("Descent" 129) from its setting in the Norwegian seas to the building of the Chicago Board of Trade. Poe's story is reported to a dazzled listener by a Norwegian fisherman who survived a trip to the vortex; it describes how the Norwegian narrator and his two brothers miscalculated their trip, so that they found themselves on the maelstrom site when the whirlpool was forming. At that moment, the storyteller was granted a sight that is truly sublime: "The edge of the whirl was represented by a broad belt of gleaming spray; but no particle of this slipped into the mouth of the terrific funnel, whose interior, as far as the eye could fathom it, was a smooth, shining, and jet-black wall of water . . . speeding dizzily round and round with a swaying and sweltering motion, and sending forth to the winds an appalling voice, half shriek, half roar, such as not even the mighty cataract of Niagara ever lifts up in its agony to Heaven" (129). The awesome spectacle swallows two of the brothers, though the storyteller survives the descent by virtue of his ingenuity, and also, probably, because he is sensitive to the dark beauty of the maelstrom. Norris's and Poe's texts share the narrative motif of the descent into the vortex, the exacerbated sublime intensities, as well as numerous descriptive features—the gyratory motion, the appalling noise "half-shriek, half roar" (Poe 129), and the comparison with the floods of Niagara. More intriguingly, Poe, like Norris, associates the figure of the vortex with reproduction and economic gain. The trip to the dangerous destination of the maelstrom is indeed motivated by the high fertility of dangerous waters: "In all violent eddies at sea there is good fishing, at proper opportunities, if one has only the courage to attempt it; . . . There fish can be got at all hours, without much risk" (131). Norris's vortex, on the other hand, carries reproductive connotations in that it constructs a vision of economic exchange that conflates gothic terror and pastoral bounty. The terrifying aspect of the commodity market signals the fact that it is endowed with uncanny powers of productivity; it is a pathological substitute for natural reproduction.

In their allusions to unnatural reproduction processes, both Poe and Norris mobilize a consistent constellation of maternal metaphorics. In this, Norris and Poe activate the sexual component of the sublime. In his discussion of the psychology of terror, Thomas Weiskel indicates that the natural sublime issues from the preoedipal fear of being incorporated into an overwhelming maternal figure and from the correlative wish to be inundated (106). His argument implies that the gender anxieties underlying Poe's depiction of the maelstrom—the jet-black funnel of sweltering waters gleaming under the rays of an insistent moon—are the same as those that inform Norris's or Dreiser's visions of Niagara-like money flows. Marie Bonaparte emphasizes the maternal connotations of "A Descent into the Maelstrom"; she analyzes the story as a "tale of the mother" based on a "return-to-the-womb phantasy" (352). Bonaparte's argument is corroborated by Karen Horney, who indicates that female genitals can be symbolized by a whirlpool metaphor.[4] Horney regards this as evidence that the mysteries of motherhood constitute foci of anxieties no less potent than castration threats. In the logic of this psychoanalytical reading, Norris's speculators, like Poe's reckless fishermen, are struggling with the overwhelming power of a gigantic female entity, a mother figure that stirs fears of engulfment and loss of self.

Norris's gendered depiction of the scene of exchange is rooted in a tradition of representation in which the fear of the feminine serves to express anxieties over social, economic, and political chaos. Julia Kristeva contends that exorcising the figure of the archaic mother plays an important part in the rituals of fragilized patriarchal groups (92). For this argument, Kristeva draws on Mary Douglas's anthropological studies, which reveal that rituals use the human body "as a diagram of a social situation" (Douglas 115). Pollution rituals in patrilinear societies, Kristeva points out, consist precisely in evoking the body of the mother through abject, repellent symbols; this process, she contends, is meant to reaffirm religious prohibitions through exorcism (92). Neil Hertz, who analyzes texts related to the French revolution of 1848, contends similarly that political anxieties are often expressed in terms of sexual threats—particularly through the image of Medusa's head, the symbol that both signifies and exorcises castration anxieties (27).

Catherine Gallagher shows how psychoanalytical arguments like Kristeva's and Hertz's apply to the history of urban economics. She argues that Hertz's exclusive focus on castration anxieties envisages femininity only as the sign of an absence and of a lack. Like Kristeva, Gallagher believes, on the contrary, that the dread of the feminine proceeds from the fears of the mother's reproductive powers; when it is transposed to the political or economic arena, this emotion signifies the fear of the "possibility of seemingly disorganized reproduction (of children, of goods, of money, of value)" (55). Gallagher argues that, in nineteenth-century social reportage, threatening female characters—Gorgon-like costermongers, for instance—served as focus for both economic and gender anxieties: they embodied "the growth of an unnatural and irrational market economy" (56) that seemed to deny that "value inheres exclusively in the land and is passed from father to legitimate son" (56). Male hysteria, the gendered expression of the fear of social chaos, originates therefore in the apprehension of the "possible independence of urban life and its forms of wealth from the more traditionally organized countryside" (56).

Gallagher's argument provides an illuminating theoretical framework for the interpretation of the negative, threatening side of the naturalist gendering of the urban economy. She suggests that the fears raised by the city market originate in the subversion of the nexus between gender, property, and selfhood that structured life in agricultural societies. In this logic, landed aristocrats like the Frenchman de Tocqueville, whose writings Ghallagher analyzes, based their notions of property, inheritance, and identity on the assumption that "women's sexuality and reproductive capacities [must] remain proper" (56): "The assumed sexual propriety of women underlies both property relations and semiotics in the world Tocqueville inhabits, a world in which property is still acreage and the important self-representation is still the name of the father" (56). Gallagher's argument implies that the gender structures of the agrarian order were carried over into the urban realm, but could only survive in a fragilized form. This reasoning can be transposed to the analysis of Jeffersonian agrarianism, which stipulates that the yeoman's freedom and economic independence are based on the ownership and the proper husbanding of the land—a relationship to the fertile earth that reproduces the patriarchal configuration of the agrarian family. Nostalgia for this social order and for its gender arrangements crops up in Populist tracts, which describe agriculture as "the very foundation of all industries," or demand a "home and some portion of the earth from which to produce comforts" (qtd. in Palmer 18, 75). The Populist tendency to view the scene of exchange as parasitical or downright unnatural is therefore anchored in the fear that the urban market may be deprived of an intelligible principle of (re)production—that is, deprived of transparent economic mechanisms rooted in everyday experience; as it is, the city market threatens to sap the foundations of property and manhood, while it is nevertheless endowed with a chaotic and unpredictable power of proliferation.

The idea that the nineteenth-century urban sphere of exchange carried an aura of unnaturalness and gender disorder is corroborated from a different perspective by Carroll Smith-Rosenberg's analysis of mid-century anti-abortion movements. Smith-Rosenberg points to the existence of popular representations that depicted as castrating and feticidal monsters the affluent women who were suspected of having recourse to commercialized abortion. The logic of this discourse, she argues, raises the "unnatural and monstrous woman, lethal to men and babies alike" to the status of "metaphor for the commercialized city itself" (227). Gallagher's and Smith-Rosenberg's works indicate therefore that the fear of the social arrangements of the new cities leads to the elaboration of a gendered representation of the urban scene that conflates two opposite threats—sterility and wayward productivity.

Norris's text reworks the gender anxieties stirred by the commercial city in the ambivalent fashion that characterizes his brand of sublime economics. Norris's heavy emphasis on chaos, havoc, and loss—Jadwin's bankruptcy, Cressler's suicide—suggests that the novelist perceives the city along the same lines as the anti-abortion advocates described by Smith-Rosenberg: the urban market appears as lethal to men and basically sterile. The terrifying side of sublime economics raises the suspicion that the whirlwind of money and commodities may not be a productive force at all: on the contrary, it consumes the "pinch of human spawn" that dares to brave it (80). Yet, even though the fate of Norris's characters is tied to this disenchanted view of urban economics, the overall ideology developed by the text is not entirely hostile to the mechanisms of exchange. We have seen in *The Octopus* that the rhetoric of sublimity allowed Norris to convert incompatible elements into each other or to hold them in equilibrium within the text. Accordingly, alongside the nightmarish vistas of the dreaded maelstrom, the text also constructs a positive mode of apprehension of the sublime city markets.

Jadwin's campaign to corner the market constitutes the most conspicuous strategy by which the text aims to transcend the terror of the wheat maelstrom. This speculation deal embodies the fantasy of a retotalized economic traffic, which would be as open to human control as the pre-industrial simple market society. In this case, the mesmerizing energies of speculation stir in Curtis Jadwin the fantasy that the economy of the city can be captured and unified by means of brutal strength and will-power—and not by intuitive deciphering, as is the case in Dreiser. This desire to reconstruct a social totality is, of course, naive in that it assumes that the powers of the earth or the channels of the country's economy are a commodity that can be understood and possessed. The importance of this totalizing gesture resides in the fact that, though it inevitably fails, it is nevertheless attempted: the novel, following the logic of the failed sublime, needs to make visible in this fashion how far the productivity of the land exceeds the acquisitive powers of any single person.

Besides Jadwin's heroic enterprise, the text evokes the possibility of another, more fundamental type of pseudo-totalization: the promotion of the realm of exchange to the status of self-engendering arena of production. The idea that the chain of economic mediation can generate an economic surplus—through a process that Populist economics denounced, but could not properly theorize—is already implicit in the very image of the maelstrom: indeed, the dizzying vortex of speculation embodies the ability of the financial market to create value—in this case, a money surplus—without a referent in commodity production.

The avalanches of speculative gains are generated by means of the rapid cycle of transactions and by the unmotivated price fluctuations. By associating the productivity of the market to the gendered vision of agriculture, Norris's novel raises the capacity to yield this parasitical surplus to the status of a primal potency. The link between the world of the California ranchers and the chaos of the Board of Trade is of course the Wheat itself, which pours into the pits of the exchange and coils up into the eddies of the whirlpool: "There in the centre of the Nation . . . roared and rumbled the Pit. It was as if the Wheat, Nourisher of the Nations, as it rolled gigantic and majestic in a vast flood from West to East, here like a Niagara, finding its flow impeded, burst suddenly into the appalling fury of the Maëlstrom, into the chaotic spasm of a world force, a primeval energy, bloodbrother of the earthquake and the glacier" (80). On first inspection, this passage manifests the fear that the urban market checks the natural flow of the wheat and forces it to behave unnaturally; simultaneously, however, the presence amidst the spiral of speculation of this primal force, and of the titanic earth from which it issues, infuses Norris's portrayal of the scene of exchange with all the connotations of colossal fertility that characterized the gendered vision of agricultural work in *The Octopus*.

The ideological legitimation of the market is greatly facilitated by the decision to focus on wheat speculation, as opposed to stocks for instance. For, in Norris's world, the Wheat is both a substance born out of the legitimate intercourse of men and the earth, and on the other hand, a self-engendered primal force. As a product of the earth, the wheat lends economic legitimacy to the mechanisms that transform it into a commodity. The raw material of speculation, it motivates the value of the money for which it is exchanged even better than gold can guarantee the soundness of the currency. On the other hand, its conversion into money is naturalized by the fact that, as pictured by Norris, the wheat is sufficiently abstract to let itself be transformed into other forms of power. In this way, the capacity of the Wheat-as-primordial-force to "grow itself," as Norris puts it, can be grafted on to the urban sphere of production, which becomes therefore a self-engendered mechanism.

The fantasy of the self-engendered market corresponds to the dream of constructing what Constance Penley, drawing on the work of Michel Carrouges, has called a bachelor machine. Under this term, Penley refers to a "closed, self-sufficient system" characterized, among other things, by perpetual motion, electrification, voyeurism, masturbatory eroticism, and artificial birth (39).[5] Norris's urban economics resembles the bachelor machine paradigm because it pictures economic circulation as a closed system based on a sexualized technology. The arena of speculation, in its function as a feminine (re)productive machine, cements the relations between the men who have a share in its productivity. In Norris's economic vision, what allows men to master the reproduction of wealth in the city market is a sophisticated technology of exchange: besides its metaphorical origin in the maternal powers of the wheat maelstrom, wealth is generated by a semiotic and technological prowess; it proceeds from the mechanics of speculation, and is entirely dependent on new machines like the railroad, the telegraph, and mechanized agriculture. Also, this machine of (re)production constitutes a fit focus of voyeurism. The man-made vortex of exchange is set up as a sublime spectacle whose spectators are not only the host of shiftless men who hang around the brokerage firms, staring at the quotations with "their decaying senses hypnotised and soothed by the distant rumble of the Pit," but also the readers of Norris's sensationalist prose (83). Thus, the bachelor-machine hypothesis helps us describe a project of masculine empowerment of which the wealth-generating traffic is the symbolic stake: the terrifying (re)productive powers of the city are harnessed to serve the goals of men.

With its vision of the city as an apparatus of reproduction, Norris's novel anticipates by a few years the social theories of Fredric Clemson Howe and Simon Nelson Patten, which present an optimistic approach of the urban-industrial universe and are cognate to the bachelor machine paradigm. Howe's *The City, Hope of Democracy* (1905) defends city life against the anti-urban bias of the agrarian tradition, and against the view that city politics are inherently corrupt. Howe's essay delineates the project of an urban commonwealth where the stability and integrity of communal life is achieved through public ownership of all facilities. Howe's argument overlaps with Norris's economics in its depiction of the resources specific to city life. Howe argues that the urban scene should function as an artificial organism whose economic channels would mimic the fertilizing cycle of water, from sea to land and back again, or the circulation of the blood in the body. The concrete political program Howe has in mind is the establishment of a system that relies on taxes to create an equilibrium between social production and social distribution. This kind of well-regulated interdependence requires however a critical mass of population, and relies on a typically urban mechanism of production of wealth: "For the gathering together of mankind into close association, with its varied energies and activities creates a social treasure; a treasure whose magnitude we are now able to measure, and which treasure, if retaken by society, will enable all of the burdens which close association involves, to be borne without cost to the dwellers therein" (294). Thus, in Howe's vision, the specificity of urban economics consists in high population numbers and spatial concentration. "The crowding together of mankind" (294), instead of draining the wealth of the country as Populist economics implies, acts rather as a generative principle that creates resources unavailable in nature.

Howe's positive view of the concentration of populations finds a paradoxical echo in the claims of contemporary theoreticians of intensive agriculture. The writings of Prince Kropotkin—a Russian-born anarchist—and of his American disciple Bolton Hall were influential in Howe's time: Kropotkin is quoted explicitly in Upton Sinclair's *The Jungle*, and the basic principles of his work are central to the didactic program of Jack London's *The Valley of the Moon*. Kropotkin, unlike Howe, is not an apologist of urbanization as such; he reacts against the alienation induced by the division of labor, and sketches out a utopia made up of communities where agriculture would coexist with decentralized industries.

In Kropotkin's polity, people could work according to a system of "integration of labour"—sharing their time between the fields and the workshops (22). This scheme requires that agriculture be expanded to its full potential. Accordingly, Kropotkin provides a well-documented but quasi-fantastic picture of the crop productivity that can be achieved through intensive agriculture. What Kropotkin shares with Howe is the fact that his conception of production is radically anti-Malthusian, and that he dismisses overpopulation as a pseudo-problem: "We thus see that the over-population fallacy does not stand the very first attempt at submitting it to a closer examination. . . . We know that a crowded population is a necessary condition for permitting man to increase the productive powers of his labour. We know that highly productive labour is impossible so long as men are scattered, few in numbers, over wide territories, and are thus unable to combine together for the higher achievements of civilization" (137). Ironically, this defense of intensive farming could easily be mistaken for a plea for urbanization; this indicates that, at the turn of the century, some theoreticians of the city and of agriculture shared a common ideological response to the gathering of large concentrations of population. Their acceptance of the new masses was anchored in a belief that populations could thrive thanks to a principle of intensive production and exchange—mass economic generation, as it were. This ideological convergence is neatly paralleled in the oceanic sublime of naturalism, which uses gender tropes to express both natural and urban spectacles through the same imagery.

In Howe as in Kropotkin, the social treasure of urban conviviality and economic productivity is to be used for civic purposes; in Norris's capitalist-oriented discourse, however, the resources of the city work for the benefit of capitalists. This pro-market outlook finds its closest equivalent in Simon Nelson Patten's consistently anti-Malthusian plea in favor of urban exchange and consumption. Patten's theory of the surplus economy makes him an early apologist of consumerism, determined to establish the urban-industrial order as a self-sufficient, self-reproducing entity. Daniel Horowitz argues that Patten, under the surface of capitalistic self-confidence, belonged, together with Veblen and George Gunton, among those social scientists who sought to find a compromise between the outdated Puritan work ethic, and the new era of mass-production and leisure (see Horowitz 30). The moral problem faced by Patten, who had himself been educated under the old moralistic code, was the awareness that, under industrial conditions, working-class tasks could hardly be regarded as a source of artisan pride or as an anchoring ground of character. Therefore, taking stock of the wreck of the producers' ethos, Patten sought to define a leisure-based polity in which all classes could share, without for all that surrendering to the vulgarity of commercialism.

In *The New Basis of Civilization* (1907), Patten heralds the end of long centuries of economic scarcity. Industry and science, and especially scientific agriculture, Patten claims, have made it possible for humankind to outdistance "the pace of thousands of generations of his 'master'— nature" (15). In his argument, the overcoming of nature is the condition for the creation of an economic surplus, as "each gain upon nature adds to the quantity of goods to be consumed by society and lessens the labor necessary to produce them" (16). The erasure of the relationship to nature and the dwindling importance of labor easily leads to the construction of a self-activated economic cycle of conversions: "The surplus is not conserved as a permanent fund, but exists and grows only as it is perpetually transformed from goods to energy and from energy back to goods. Life, word and happiness are thus bound together and their measure is the surplus that vitalizes them" (26). In this process, one single substance reproduces itself over and over.

In bachelor-machine fashion, Patten's vision of an economic accelerator fueled by the creation of new wants is pictured as a substitute for feminine energies: the spending of commodities replaces the wasting of the "wealth of womanhood" (55) that characterized the old economic order. In literal terms, Patten means that, in the surplus economy, mothers no longer need to sacrifice the vital energies of a lifetime for the anguished nurturing and the economic support of their children. But at another level of reading, this results in the appropriation of the mother's reproductive power by what Pattens calls Capital; unlike in an economy that tolerates the pains of mothering, "Capital in its destruction reproduces itself and passes onward without the deterioration caused by pain" (55). The "superlative machine" (55) of Patten's surplus economy is therefore a self-contained and painless one; its relation to nature is ambivalent, in that it relies on Nature's "illimitable" resources (55), but submits them to constant scientific improvement. Thus, Patten's book projects the utopia of a society whose social contradictions are solved by an overflow of commodities, and whose origins are detached both from the process of industrial production and from nature.

Compared to Patten's utopia, Norris's celebration of the artificiality of the urban scene fails to achieve the sense of frictionlessness, closure, and self-sufficiency of stereotypical bachelor machines. In Norris, the portrayal of the self-engendering arena of exchange cannot escape the fear of transgression that originates in the subversion of the agrarian paradigm. This residue of ambivalence manifests itself in the uncanny connotation that clings to the maternal metaphorics of the urban market: the "primeval force" (80) of the maelstrom is characterized by means of tropes of abjection—it is a "tremendous cloaca" (79) and "the maw of a colossal sewer" (79). Through these references to excrement and pollution, Norris's text exorcizes the threatening dimension of feminine reproductivity, which the urban scene seeks to appropriate, but never manages to control.[6] The same unease underlies the use of half-human, half-animal myth figures—tropes that, according to Dorothy Dinnerstein, signal a human maladjustment toward animality and existing gender arrangements (2, 5). In *The Pit*, the urban domain is set in the shadow of "a monstrous sphinx with blind eyes" (421)—that is, the Board of Trade Building, which embodies the treacherous mysteries of speculation. These jarring notes express the suspicion that the arena of commerce is still tied to those social and economic processes—the production of value and commodities through human labor—that the mystifying spectacle of the city and the technology of exchange seek to supplant.

It is difficult, however, to discover in the unresolved ambivalence of Norris's failed sublime the foundation of a political critique of urban cap-

italism. More than in many other naturalist works, the sublime economics of *The Pit* define as natural a relation to the urban scene that places
isolated, fascinated observers—both characters and readers—against an
incommensurable spectacle. Thus, beyond the financial debacle that follows Jadwin's defeat at the hands of the colossal forces of reproduction,
one discerns the affirmation of the economic mechanisms that keep the
city in motion, however chaotically and ruthlessly. This is, I think, the
meaning of the last scene of the novel, where Laura Jadwin catches a last
glimpse of the "sombre mass," the "formidable façade" of the Board of
Trade Building silhouetted against the sky. The "monstrous Sphinx" (420–
21), silent and enigmatic, signifies the perpetuation of the economic mechanisms that it represents, regardless of the price in human suffering.

CHAPTER 8

Pastoralism Reconstructed:
Jack London's *The Valley of the Moon*

The gendered economics of the naturalist sublime, as it redefines urban landscapes, also modify the naturalist perception of the relation between the country and the city. In part 1, I pointed out that the oceanic imagery of the naturalist sublime tends to neutralize the distinction between urban and pastoral world. This literary strategy, I believe, marks the progressive dominance of urbanization and industrialization over the American landscape. Jack London's *The Valley of the Moon* is a text that registers with great intensity the surrender of American farmers to the economic logic of the metropolis. It is also a rare case of a naturalist novel that advocates the flight from the city to the life on the farm. Unlike a traditional frontier narrative, however, London's novel cannot afford to praise the virtues of the American virgin land; its agenda consists rather in finding a compromise between the city and the country—a program that requires the redefinition of domestic ideology and of work-based models of manhood. Ironically, the utopia delineated by this narrative of the return to the land looks, from our point of view, like a blueprint for the home-centered lifestyle of suburbia.

The narrative of *The Valley of the Moon* is structured as a *Bildungsroman*, retracing the itinerary of two protagonists—Saxon Brown and Billy

Roberts—who realize that "folks wasn't made to live in cities" (89). Disgusted with Oakland, the pair decide to tramp across California until they find the perfect plot of land that will allow them to recover their dignity and self-sufficiency. On the road, they encounter characters with very varied lifestyles—from industrial farmers to bohemian communities—who help them define the potentialities open to a young couple who have set their mind on reclaiming the heritage of the American farmer. Unlike most naturalist works, the character's quest is fulfilled at the end of the story: the young couple find their dream farm in the Sonoma Valley—the Valley of the Moon.

London's narrative is anchored in theories of male supremacy and in a quasi-mystical discourse of Anglo-Saxonism. In the logic of the text, these two ideological configurations are directly relevant to the analysis of urban and rural conditions. What drives Saxon and Billy away from Oakland is economic exploitation, strike riots, and immigrants—Irish, "Dagoes and Japs and such" (22). Immigrants are sharply characterized as a source of random social unrest; if a brawl breaks out at a Bricklayers' ball, it can only be because "the Celtic blood was up" (27). This murderous violence ends up contaminating Billy, who commits a completely unprovoked assault on his own lodger, and is therefore sent to jail. Saxon suffers a miscarriage as a result. She then starts dreaming of the golden age when people "had not lived in cities nor been vexed with labor unions and employers' associations" and when "they shot or raised their own meat, grew their own vegetables, were their own blacksmiths and carpenters, made their own shoes . . ." (178). She manages to convince her husband to look for government land, away from a racially contaminated city where life supposedly cannot bloom.

Nativist themes like those uttered in *The Valley of the Moon* were, according to John Higham, a political obsession for London. Higham writes that, after the California nativist Homer Lea had laid down the principles of the doctrine of the Yellow Peril, it "remained . . . for [London] to translate this creed into a frontal assault on the new immigration and to disseminate it far and wide" (172). To Higham, London is a typical representative of the populist nativism that appeared on the West Coast, where Asian immigration was perceived as a threat. These doctrines were characterized by feelings of racial defeat: by the early twentieth century, Higham argues, "Anglo-Saxon nationalism, bereft of the exhilarating prospect of continued overseas expansion, was reverting to the defensive" (173). This sense of racial entrenchment led to an obsessive ideological attack on ethnic groups that had settled in the United States.

Racial defensiveness is indeed central to *The Valley of the Moon:* London's celebration of the Saxon stock against the "squat, ungainly and swarthy" (102) Italians and Chinese constitutes a response to fears of proletarianization that are expressed in yearnings for an ethnically homogeneous yeoman polity. In the new economic environment of *The Valley of the Moon,* where trusts dictate their policies to the state legislatures, the "real Americans" (155) of the urban proletariat like to compare themselves to "the last of the Mohegans" (155). The pride they derive from their racial heritage is rooted in the fact that their parents or grandparents took part in the "great hegira of the land-hungry Anglo-Saxons" (50), who crossed the plains in covered wagons and fought the Indians. In the context of urban civilization, these pioneers and their offspring are portrayed as a secret aristocracy, a disseminated brotherhood, rather than as a solid ethnic community. This impression of semi-clandestinity is generated in the text by the fact that all the people Billy and Saxon meet on the road, and who stand ready to provide them with valuable advice, magically turn out to be members of the fraternity of the old settlers. Yet an important number of these characters enjoy a lower social status than their ancestors. Saxon Brown, Billy's future wife, perfectly embodies this situation of social decline: the glorious past of her family is symbolized by a mahogany chest of drawers that was carried by her parents over the Atlantic, then across the plains. One of the drawers contains poems written by Saxon's mother, a poet of some renown, whom Saxon imagines in the shape of a gutsy naturalist amazon, but who could nevertheless master a poetic idiom inaccessible to her working-class daughter.

In spite of their dreams of a prestigious racial past, Saxon and Billy remain urban savages whose dream of escape is fashioned by urban culture. The image London's heroine has formed of her Saxon ancestry, for instance, is based partly on the oral history of her mother's tales, but also on "copies of paintings and old wood engravings from the magazines of a generation and more before" (102) in which Saxon discovers "half-naked, huge-muscled and fair-haired" Germanic warriors, landing on a beach to fight the Celtic "skin-clad savages" (102). Far from being a bedrock of authenticity, racial identity is mediated through the mirror of popular magazines, and it is immediately adapted to the contemporary context of ethnic strife in the city. In an even more caricatural way, Billy's and Saxon's pastoral dream turns out to be a motion picture fantasy. It is during a nickelodeon show that Saxon surrenders to the attraction of country life: a pastoral romance set on a midwestern farm completely captures the young woman's imagination, not for the sake of the love story, but for the sight of "the chickens," "the warm wall of the barn," and "the sleepy horse with its ever recurrent whisk of tail" (280).

The movie theater epiphany indicates that what the two protagonists will find on the road is not fundamentally different from their urban experiences. The continuity is noticeable in two respects: on the one hand, the California countryside turns out to be full of immigrants; on the other, rural communities are, like cities, structured by a pattern of gendered economics that empowers women at the expense of men. The evolution of Billy's sense of manhood is the chief index through which this hegemony of the feminized urban scene is made visible. Saxon initiates the two protagonists' quest for farming land mostly to help her husband regain his self-respect. Yet Billy's situation at the end of the text, though financially much more favorable, still raises questions about the possibility of male empowerment in a city-dominated context. The paradoxical fragility of Billy is due to the fact that his physical might is not a decisive asset in the city. When Saxon meets him for the first time, she thinks he is "one of those rare individuals that radiate muscular grace through the ungraceful man-garments of civilization" (15). Yet since "civilization" (15) cannot be phased off, the sculptural Billy is in danger of being relegated to the status of a *"boy, a great big man-boy"* (15), whose main distinction is to be "a dream of a dancer" (16). Billy's powerlessness is painfully exposed during the teamsters' strike. The conflict turns him into a bitter, even physically aggressive, unemployed worker; meanwhile Saxon, favored by the workings of the gendered market, manages to make money by selling handmade lace underwear, of all things.

Because Billy constantly flaunts an impressive but economically inefficient virility, his personality is ruled by the logic of what Amy Kaplan calls "the spectacle of masculinity" ("Romancing" 665). In an argument cognate to Judith Butler's theory of gender performativity,[1] Kaplan points out that many turn-of-the-century texts depict men engaged in staged exploits rather than in actual work, conquest, or violence. The focus of Kaplan's analysis is American imperialism; yet her argument can easily be transposed to Jack London's novel of late-nineteenth-century pastoralism: for Kaplan, the evolution of manhood is indeed tied to changes in men's relationship to the land. In this logic, the pastoral vision of America allowed the male body to claim an organic link to an ever-growing territory ("Romancing" 665). Yet, after the closing of the frontier, the expanding continent was replaced by a disembodied empire, relying more on export markets than on territorial annexation. In Kaplan's account, it is the loss of this link to a well-defined territory that induced imperial manhood to express itself in heavily mediatized spectacles, on the model of Theodore Roosevelt's war exploits (665). Likewise, I believe that the naturalist depiction of urban life similarly suggests that there is little anchorage to be found for men in an economic structure modeled as an unstable and unreadable body. In such a context, masculinity is reduced to the reenactment of its former self, and male power is bypassed by women like Saxon, who enjoy a direct affinity with the gendered economy.

The novel examines in turns several modes of social insertion that might alleviate Billy's disempowerment. This involves marking out a subject position that renders Saxon's libidinal and economic proficiency less threatening to her husband. For that purpose, the protagonists must redefine the boundaries of the domestic and the public sphere in ways that counteract the sexualized economy of consumption, without however enacting an unworkable patriarchal backlash. The solution promoted by London's novel is the sexually fulfilling marriage: Saxon's desire must be allowed to express itself—within the bounds of domestic space, that is. The mentor who initiates Saxon to this arrangement is Mercedes Higgins. This trickster figure is a neighbor of Saxon's and Billy's who enjoys the reputation of being a local witch. Mercedes's field of expertise is the science of seducing men into durable relationships. To Saxon, her theories on the art of seduction constitute a bona fide sex education curriculum, worded in the "solemn" and "magnificent" accents of the sublime: "Saxon listened, in a maze, to what almost seemed a wild farrago, save that the phrases were fraught with dim, mysterious significance. She caught glimmerings of profounds [*sic*] inexpressible and unthinkable that hinted connotations lawless and terrible. . . . She trembled with fear, suffered qualms of nausea, thought sometimes that she would faint, so madly reeled her brain; yet she could not tear herself away" (144). The awe-inspiring energies evoked by Mercedes should, of course, be tapped with the proper restraint. For instance, Mercedes's veritable obsession with the marketable value of fine underwear—pieces of clothing she enthusiastically calls "the pretties! the dainties! the flimsies!" (135)—exceeds Billy's sense of propriety. London's text stipulates that the area reserved for sexuality—even in its seductive, fetishistic form—should be expanded, yet also insulated from market forces.[2] Accordingly, Saxon's decorative flimsies will be hand-made, hand-washed, and withdrawn from public circulation. The proper locale for such a home economy, the text suggests, is a farm in the country.

Unfortunately, Billy discovers that the city-wise economy of his native Oakland also shapes the modern farmer's relationship to the land. In its didactic thrust, the novel stigmatizes the unthinkable "stupidity of the old-fashioned farmers" (340) who stick to holdings with "too much land, too little farmed" (329); against such waste, the text voices an enthusiastic plea for intensive farming—an agriculture of artificially cultivated proliferation whose principles of reproduction are as artificial as the libidinal configuration of the urban scene. To London, intensive agriculture represents the ideological compromise that may heal the trauma of the closing of the frontier. This signifies that Billy must give up his outdated virile fantasy that "we Americans just gotta have room," that it is essential "to look at a hilltop an' know it's my land, and know it's my land down the other side an' up the next hilltop" (318). Against Billy's nostalgic view of frontier manhood, London quotes Bolton Hall, the author of *A Little Land and a Living*. Bolton Hall's essay—an Americanized version of Kropotkin's theories—closely parallels London's in that it starts out from a negative vision of the city, directly inspired by the American pastoral tradition: "The tendency of population to flock to the already congested cities," Hall writes, "is a menace to the prosperity of America" (65). Yet, for all his rhetoric of self-sufficient rural manhood, Hall sketches out a vision of modern agriculture so beholden to big city markets that it downplays the importance of the fertility of the land: "Don't be deluded by five-acre plots on easy terms, even if the soil is fertile, *where there is no market*; the farther you go from a good market the less the acre is worth" (37, emphasis added). The good land, according to Bolton Hall, is radically different from Billy's pastoral utopia; it is at bottom "any place where one can put fertilizers"; most suitable of all would be to "get a long lease near a growing city and with good trolley or railroad connections" (89).

The virtues of this urban-oriented agriculture are impressed on the two protagonists when they discover a Portuguese-run farm. In this scene, they become aware of the farming miracle that allows immigrants who were "hatched in the Azores" to "start accounts in banks" (310). More puzzling to the protagonists, these newcomers are working the land that used to belong to unsuccessful Anglos. One reason for this success is racial: Americans, a bystander contends, "ain't got the *sabe*, or the knack, or something or other—they weren't wised up to farming," whereas "the Porchugeeze is natural-born farmers" who do not hesitate to put "the whole blame family" to work (310, 311). More impressive than this ethnically based intuitive superiority is, however, the immigrants' obvious technical expertise: on the Portuguese farm, "not an inch is wasted" (311): "Where we got one thin crop, they get four fat crops. An' look at the way they crowd it—currants between the tree rows, beans between the currant rows . . . an' rows of beans along the end of the tree rows" (311). This system of forced reproduction where every inch of soil is "workin' over time" (311) not only generates vegetables and fruit, but also money, as the value of the land has been multiplied more than ten-fold since it was bought from the Americans. Intensive farming, Portuguese-fashion, is therefore homological to the urban sphere: it exploits the principle of multiplication of value by overcrowding described by F. C. Howe and S. N. Patten, and it requires the presence of immigrants.

As impressive as it is, Portuguese intensive farming remains tinged with a connotation of alien mysteriousness, and cannot therefore serve as a straightforward model for the two protagonists. Much more alluring is Mrs. Mortimer's market-wise system of farming. Mortimer, the second major trickster adjuvant of the novel, is a widow who had to retrain herself from her position as a librarian into her new status as a highly successful commercial farmer. The result is, as Saxon sees it, a domain characterized by "neatness, efficiency, and intensive cultivation with a vengeance" (331). Compared to the Portuguese farm, whose principle of reproduction is essentially biological, Mortimer's economy is much more speculative. What first attracts the young woman to the widow's farm is the fact that the vegetable patches are bordered with flower-beds. This, she learns from Mortimer, is an advertising trick: "The flowers caught your eyes, . . . and that's the very reason they were planted with the vegetables—to catch eyes" (333). Thus, Mrs. Mortimer turned her "little place into a show place," and built a network of personal relationships with customers and retailers that allowed her to become not only a well-known local figure, but also a brand name. Anything sold under the Mortimer brand fetches a higher price than any other product of comparable quality. Mortimer's is therefore an agriculture of seduction, which uses all the semiotic mechanisms of the spectacle of the city market.

Despite her irreproachable genteel credentials, there is a risk that Mrs. Mortimer's speculative farming should appear a little too mercenary to the two heroes. Billy, who clings to the dream of a boundless horse ranch, thinks that Mrs. Mortimer's ways are "just a trick" (334), though indeed a paying one. The visit to the widow's cottage puts some of those fears to rest, however. It is the first time that Saxon enters a middle-class home, and she is intensely interested to hear that Mrs. Mortimer did a lot of interior decoration "with her own hands" (339). This reference to an economy of feminine handicrafts recalls Saxon's own attitude to her embroidered underwear: both Mortimer's produce and Saxon's flimsies are meant for seduction, and they both partake of the mysteries of reproduction. In this way, another link is established between the gender arrangements of the city market and a markedly feminine mode of making the land thrive. Billy's male instincts are ruffled, of course: he is not willing to enter a business whose public relations duties would probably involve "tradin' on [his] wife's looks" (343). Mrs. Mortimer's tutelage will eventually allay those fears. The young people's new neighbor, Mr. Hale, complements Mrs. Mortimer's contribution by offering Saxon and Billy free access to his library on scientific farming. In this way, Billy hears of the possibility of intensive horse raising, and momentarily sheds his dream of the big ranch. At the end of the novel, pointing at their vegetable patch, he can proudly proclaim that even Portuguese immigrants "ain't got nothin' on us when it comes to intensive farming" (517).

In an ironical light, it would be possible to interpret the compromise Billy and Saxon have to settle for as an allegory of the founding of suburbia: their moderate-size farm is situated halfway between city and country; though it is pictured as a pastoral paradise, it enjoys an easy access to the railroad and the urban markets—features that Bolton Hall deems essential to prosperity. Kirk Jeffrey has described the compulsion of nineteenth-century Americans, traumatized by the rise of urbanization, to develop a cult of the rural home: in this view, the family must serve as a pastoral retreat from the dog-eat-dog world of the market (25). The projects developed by both Hall and by London, in spite of the authors' pioneer bluster, are roughly similar to this middle-class utopia. Hall describes the "modern farm-house" (43) in terms that are distinctly suburban: the new home is endowed "with its labor-saving appliances, its piano, its books and magazines" (43). In London's version of this petit-bourgeois utopia, the gender tensions that have strained the relations between Billy and Saxon can find a resolution of sorts: when they have become successful entrepreneurs, Saxon and Billy reach a stage where they can exchange checks between each other, since even Saxon is granted some degree of economic independence. Though the discourse of male supremacy is never disowned and Saxon still washes her flimsies by hand for Billy's pleasure, they come to the understanding that, in their business life at least, their prosperity was due to teamwork.

The novel could close on this image of financial success, brought about by a combination of feminine reproductive wisdom and scientific expertise. Yet London rounds off his extremely heterogeneous narrative in an atmosphere of romance. It is hardly surprising that, once settled on the land, away from the devouring city, London would want his heroine to become pregnant again. But beyond that, the novel attempts to tie up the loose ends of Billy's work-gender status. Billy had so far enjoyed the position of a show-tent cowboy, living off the resources of a farm run according to the principles of a feminine crop-raising method. Eventually, however, his dream of the large range is also fulfilled, against the momentum of the narrative: he is allowed to buy the neighboring farm, which has long been neglected by the ignorant old-school American farmers. The pastoral dream that started the two protagonists on the road seems therefore complete—at least to a certain extent. For by buying the farm with its beautifully picturesque canyon, Billy also acquires a hidden clay pit, which will be worth a fortune to the town's brickyards. Thus, the Edenic setting of the North California valley is defaced by the white scar of the clay, which lies ready to be baked into the bricks that build the cities from which Saxon and Billy were trying to escape.

≈꒾ PART 3

*The Sociology of
the Naturalist Sublime*

The "Common Lot" of 1890s and 1900s Realism: Middle-Class Responses to the Metropolis

The system of gendered economics described so far constitutes the groundwork of the naturalist sublime—the backdrop that the novels take for granted at all stages of their depiction of the city. The present section analyzes the social bonds constructed by means of this sublime discourse. To start with, I approach the literary sociology of naturalism from a contrastive angle: the texts discussed in the present chapter—most of them by Chicago novelists H. B. Fuller and Robert Herrick—perpetuate the tradition of realist discourse beyond Howells, into the 1890s and 1900s; as such, they resist the urge to represent the city in sublime terms. Fuller and Herrick, rather than attempting to provide a panoramic view of urban economics, are intent on registering the eroding influence of the metropolis on the specific environment of middle- and upper-class families—professionals, typically. Middle-class domesticity is, of course, an issue in naturalist texts as well: Dreiser deals with it in the account of Hurstwood's decline, and so does Norris in the narratives of bankruptcies in *The Pit*. But in the latter cases, the pessimistic appraisal of urban life is mitigated by the belief that the sublime forces of the city may work, for some characters at least, as a vitalizing source of power. On the contrary, in Fuller's *The Cliff-Dwellers* (1893) and *With the Pro-*

cession (1895), or Herrick's *The Common Lot* (1904) and *The Web of Life* (1900), the occasional intrusion of the rhetoric of terror merely points to the presence of economic or ethnic threats outside the characters' rounds of life. Instead of elaborating a romance sociology on the basis of these parasitical sublime tropes, turn-of-the-century realism addresses the crisis of urbanization by creating family-centered narratives tailored to the new cultural needs. A major priority for Herrick's and Fuller's fiction was indeed the exploration of the social and emotional adjustments required to restore a modicum of stability—an acceptable share in what Herrick calls the "common lot" (*Common*)—to middle-class characters destabilized by the metamorphoses of the American scene.

Jane Addams's Domestic Paradigm of Urban Space

I wish to introduce the issues of 1890s realism by first discussing Jane Addams's settlement work, which displays deep affinities with the project of city fiction. In order to fight urban poverty and social fragmentation, Addams advocated the creation within immigrant neighborhoods of settlements where social workers could work and find accommodation. Settlements were meant to help reconstitute an extended family in the city. This knowable community, must, Addams believes, make it possible to establish cross-class networks of personal relationships, thus mending a broken social fabric.[1] In *Twenty Years at Hull-House*—Addams's autobiographical account of her settlement work—the author states that, to be realized, her ideals need "the mere foothold of a house, easily accessible, ample in space, hospitable and tolerant in spirit, situated in the midst of the large foreign colonies which so easily isolate themselves in American cities" (76). Addams expected this new space of interaction "to make social intercourse express the growing sense of the economic unity of society" (76). The settlement stands therefore as an enlarged domestic sphere—similar to the utopia of conviviality recreated by characters of Howells's *A Hazard of New Fortunes*.

The project of social reconciliation that takes place in the privileged area of the settlement attempts to break down all the social barriers—class, gender, ethnicity—that render city life apocalyptic in Jane Addams's eyes. Among these various fields of action, however, Addams's most conspicuous success resides in the healing of generational gaps within immigrant families. One of the main contributions of Addams's social science is precisely to have made visible to middle-class readers the fact that urban life induces tensions between first-generation immigrants and their offspring—an issue central to the fiction of early immigrant writers like Abraham Cahan or Anzia Yezierska. Addams's reflections on "Immigrants and Their Children" reveal that members of the second generation have disowned their parents' traditions in favor of the culture of the American metropolis (181). Addams's project assumes that, by reconnecting this severed cultural and generational bond, social workers can dramatically improve the lot of the foreign populations that have settled in the city.

The motherly and neighborly model of human relations Addams elaborates for the sake of this healing process transposes the legacy of the pastoral tradition to the urban context. According to Addams, urban immigrant families must cope with the fact that the new generation, lured by American popular entertainment, has turned its back on its cultural inheritance, without developing rituals of their own. Faced with this situation, Addams goes to work like a family therapist with a strong pastoral bias. Her goal—in direct application of the general program of Hull-House—is to bridge the "chasm . . . yawning at the feet of each generation" (172), and to have the second generation respect their parents again; the assumption that underlies this statement is that a semblance of preindustrial, rural conviviality can be brought back to life in the neutral space of the settlement. Characteristically, it is with the older generation that the educational strategies of Hull-House score their most obvious success: Addams hopes "to reveal the humbler immigrant parent to their own children" (172–73) and to free the parents from the "tutelage in which all Americans including their own children, are so apt to hold them" (174).

Among the features that Addams's politics of the knowable community shares with urban realism—the family-centered scope, the nostalgia for the pastoral world, the anticonsumerist ethos—I want to emphasize the importance the social worker grants to the dialectic of generations. While the rhetoric of sublimity in naturalist fiction tends to devitalize historical narrative, both Addams's sociology and the family-centered realistic fiction of the 1890s and 1900s can avail themselves of a very concrete medium for the representation of historical change: in these texts, the anxieties that accompany the transition from the producer's ethic to the corporate economy of consumption are dramatized through generational narratives. Economic change in American realism is perceived as an aspect of a painful handing over of family traditions. Also, both Addams and the realist novelists represent the origins of the urban population through the realistic categories of historical change, individual agency, family, and neighborhood communities. I

point out in chapter 10 that this realist handling of origins differs starkly from the naturalist practice of representing a character's past through
a discourse of atavism.

Embattled Families: Phillips's, Fuller's, and Herrick's Urban Fiction

The generational narratives that Addams sees at work in immigrant communities are central to the narrative economy of turn-of-the-century realism. In this corpus, family narratives are used in order to articulate the
writer's sense that prosperity in post–Civil War America has been obtained
at the cost of economic inequality and moral corruption. One schematic
example of this narrative pattern appears in David Graham Phillips's *The
Second Generation* (1906), where the son of a hard-working industrialist is
in danger of surrendering to the ways of the leisure class, and of losing
thereby any capacity for running the family business. Here, as in other
works of the period, the aspirations of the generation that comes of age
are viewed with apprehension. Under the pressure of destabilizing patterns
of upper-class consumerism, a son's career choice, or, as in Howells's *The
Rise of Silas Lapham* (1885), a daughter's marriage prospects, are events
fraught with moral and economic peril. The realist text is obsessed with
the thought that, in the turn-of-the-century context, there is, literally and
figuratively, an inheritance to be squandered. In *The Second Generation* and
in Robert Herrick's *The Common Lot*, two novels in which the inheritance
motif plays a predominant part, this legacy is explicitly associated with the
values of the work ethic and small-town spirit, which are superseded by
leisure and greed in the new society.

Phillips's *The Second Generation* is exceptional in its eagerness to make
the younger generation shoulder the blame for the development of conspicuous consumption. In other novels, the betrayal of the middle-class
work ethic and of domestic values is perpetrated by the seniors—be they
greedy fathers, who have betrayed the legacy of the Lincoln republic,
or ambitious women, who set the pace of conspicuous consumption. In
Herrick's *The Web of Life*, for instance, the influential Dr. Fredrick H.
Lindsay, a market-wise physician catering to the upper-classes, and
Colonel Hitchcock, a Civil War veteran who has made a fortune in business, embody the middle-class surrender to the immorality of excessive
wealth. Fuller's *With the Procession* fustigates David Marshall, an old-style
merchant for remaining so stultifyingly dedicated to his business that he
finds himself totally helpless to prevent his family from embracing the

new fashion of easy spending. Sinclair's *The Metropolis* (1907) shows how upper-class Civil War veterans have betrayed the political and economic interests of their fellow soldiers by amassing a fortune in financial speculation. In this novel, Judge Ellis tries to lure Allan Montague, a young midwestern lawyer, into sharing the spoils of economic corruption. The world Montague is invited to join is one where the seduction of consumption acts as a feminine, unmanning menace. Society women in *The Metropolis*, *With the Procession*, and *The Common Lot* are upper-class temptresses who set the pace of upper-class fashion, and fire the ambition of younger people, thus wrecking their career or domestic life. In Fuller's *The Cliff-Dwellers*, Mrs. Ingles, a wealthy arbiter of tastes, is depicted as a ghostly presence who, without even appearing in the text, wreaks havoc with the lives of those characters who try to emulate her.

In their attempt to manage the crisis of urbanization, Fuller's and Herrick's novels rewrite sentimental plots along pessimistic lines. This appropriation of sentimental literature is definitional of realism: Alfred Habegger argues that American realist novels established their claims to realistic verisimilitude by giving a real-life twist to conventions borrowed from domestic fiction—to its character-types, for instance: "The book *is* realistic if it gives individual features to the standard character-types and creates a plausible causal sequence departing from the scenarios they are often found in" (ix). Realism in the nineties applies this strategy with a vengeance. Habegger remarks that the novel as a genre is "bound up with sex and courtship" (viii) and that, accordingly, domestic fiction of the 1850s and onward always includes "a final scene allowing the union of a man and a woman" (viii). Such romance endings would, however, be inappropriate in Fuller's and Herrick's fiction. If the new metropolis is suffused with a sense of ethical declension, it becomes awkward to use matrimony as a mode of narrative closure. Thus, Fuller's *The Cliff-Dwellers* and *With the Procession*, as well as Herrick's *The Common Lot* and *The Web of Life*, pay lip service to the sentimental convention insofar as they do end with the union of the two main characters, temporarily reaffirming the middle-class social order. Yet the sentimental plot of these texts is stripped of its halo of happiness, and is replaced by the acceptance of a disenchanted, sensible marriage. This unsentimental vision of a reformed family is the result of an ideological compromise. On the one hand, the transmission of the moral and political legacy of the American experience requires that the bonds of matrimony be secured against all social and economic odds. On the other hand, realist verisimilitude dictates that the novelists should give vent to their sense of being trapped in a time of restricted possibilities; accordingly, their pessimism is channeled through the literary choice of presenting realist couples deprived of glamor or emotional fulfilment.

Fuller's *The Cliff-Dwellers* shows the sentimental claims of marriage to be closely entangled with the realities of business. In this text, as in Herrick's *The Web of Life*, the simultaneous inadequacy and inevitability of the sentimental model leads the author to resort to a double marriage plot. *The Cliff-Dwellers* presents a single building—the Clifton—as a microcosm of Chicago. The novel contains a numerous cast, which covers a wide range of middle- and upper-class types and occupations—from the scion of a rich family only perfunctorily interested in business activities to the dishonest real-estate agent or the socially ambitious stenographer. The story focuses on George Ogden, a middle-class young man with an Eastern background, and on his relations to the Brainard family. The elder Brainard is a Howellsian millionaire—tyrannical, stubborn, deprived of genteel graces; his lack of social sensitiveness jeopardizes the life of his children. George, unwilling to become a submissive son-in-law dominated by his wealthy wife's family, first refrains from proposing to Abbie Brainard, and marries Jessie Bradley instead—a young woman with the appearance of sound middle-class common sense. Unfortunately, Jessie turns out to cherish impracticable social ambitions fueled by the influence of acquaintances much wealthier than herself; predictably, she does not prove to be overfond of children. Jessie's extravagances and the dishonesty of the agent who manages the Ogden estate soon drive George to the point of embezzling Brainard, his employer. George's dramatic downfall, as well as the deadly generational conflicts that devastate the Brainard household, do not seem to allow of anything but a tragic ending. Yet this is a story of survival, at least for the main protagonist: the narrative manages to dispose of George's wife by having her die shortly after the death of her first child. George, no longer a young man, is then free to marry Abbie, whose good looks have faded and who has been brought down to the social level of her husband because of her tragic family history.

Herrick's *The Common Lot* relies both on the device of the marriage of reduced expectations and on the motif of the endangered legacy. Herrick is less cynical than Fuller about what is being bequeathed to the younger generation of Americans. In the beginning of this work, the death of Power Jackson, a midwestern self-made man, raises the possibility that a worthy form of moral idealism might be passing away. As a testimony to the spirit of the industrious elders, Jackson plans to devote his fortune to the establishment of an industrial school. The narrative centers on Jackson's nephew, Francis Jackson Hart, a young architect who has spent a few years in Paris and who cannot stand the sights of Chicago. At first Francis regards Jackson's will as a personal insult—an unjust trick that deprives him of the money with which he would have financed a career abroad. With limited financial means, and soon married to a young woman as penniless as himself, Francis resolves to make the most of his Beaux Art training by embarking on lucrative architectural schemes. His social aspirations are molded by the example of Mrs. Phillips, a typical upper-class temptress whose flashy lifestyle represents all that Francis's wife Helen dislikes.

Francis's surrender to the seduction of the leisure-class results in aesthetic and moral corruption. Francis receives the commission to design the Power Jackson school, but his project is flashy and derivative. Moreover, he is obliged to strike a deal with Graves, a contractor whom he knows to be dishonest. Helen is appalled by Francis's enthusiastic acceptance of a professional life characterized by dog-eat-dog competition and shady arrangements. The architect's moral conscience is reawakened when a hotel that he built in complete disregard of safety rules is destroyed in a deadly fire. The building had been offered to Francis by Graves as a lucrative perk for his collaboration in the Jackson school commission. Thoroughly shaken, Francis becomes reconciled with Helen's ethos of professional dedication. The novel closes with the inauguration of the Jackson school, a project whose moral and artistic significance has been thoroughly betrayed. Well aware of this, the reunited Francis and Helen are ready to live up to the egalitarian ethos of Power Jackson by accepting to spend their life among the middling lot—a social status that Francis so far vehemently despised.

An important literary dimension of stories of sensible matrimony resides in the fact that the perpetuation of the family cell, in addition to playing a central part in the construction of middle-class morality, is inextricably linked to the very possibility of writing: in these novels, history and narrative are articulated through the sequence of generations, so that the text needs the continuous chain of birth and inheritance to perpetuate itself. In this context, investigating proletarianization and immigrant life would hamper the realist novelist's ability to depict the reproduction of middle-class family life: it might indeed drag his or her fictions into areas of the urban field so destabilizing that any form of domesticity becomes meaningless. Thus, realist novelists limit their scope of analysis to middle-class life, even if the gain in narrative consistency thus achieved comes at the price of a loss of epistemological depth. The sensible marriages of Fuller's and Herrick's novels act therefore as a strategy of containment, similar in function to the rhetoric of sublimity. Indeed, while naturalists, when they feel their analytical acumen giving ground, switch to the rhetorical fireworks of the sublime, realists produce narratives that end with a strained ideological compromise; instead of a histrionic movement outward, the realistic text offers a disillusioned and sometimes satirical gesture of entrenchment.

Domestic Ideology and Individualistic Rebellion in Herrick's *The Web of Life*

Though the defensive, even conservative, impulse of Fuller's and Herrick's fiction is unmistakable, the realists' decision to represent the crisis of urbanization from the vantage point of endangered households endows the domestic ideal with a marginally oppositional value. Social historians describe the nuclear family as a historical phenomenon well circumscribed in time, which appeared in the beginning of the nineteenth century and fulfilled the economic needs of the emergent middle-class. Mary Ryan retraces the development of domestic life from the early-nineteenth-century corporate home economy of agrarianism to the post–Civil War urban-industrial family. Ryan argues that the new social configuration was characterized by the withdrawal of the family from the domain of economic production, and by the introduction of the strict separation between the male sphere of production and the female sphere of consumption, child-rearing, and culture (231).

Ryan's account indicates that the realist novelists' distrust of the new economic sphere was determined by the new household structure: she remarks that the sphere of domesticity, once its boundaries had been defined, modified the perception of the sections of social life outside itself. When the ideal of privacy achieved the status of a sacrosanct value, the public sphere "was construed as some mysterious, impersonal web of forces existing beyond the cottage gate" (234): "To be in a public place was to be in a crowd of strangers, adrift in the anarchy of the streets. Middle-class urbanites would beat a hasty retreat from this alien public world" (234). It is precisely from this alienated, fragmented crowd that the characters of realist fiction are recoiling. That the separation of the sphere exacerbated the rejection of the big city is corroborated by the declarations of religious figures who denounced the perversion of urban life and held up the domestic ideal as a refuge from the chaos of the streets. Kirk Jeffrey argues that the writings of the Reverend John Todd or of Catherine and Harriet Beecher Stowe popularized the conception that the family was a locus of spiritual regeneration whose protective power was grounded in the fact that it was either literally or figuratively a pastoral retreat (Jeffrey 26).

In this movement toward the privatization of everyday life, there was, however, a utopian impulse that goes beyond the mere celebration of the home. Nancy Cott, in *The Bonds of Womanhood,* has pointed out that the concepts of womanhood and sisterhood elaborated within the framework of domestic ideology played an important part in the development of nineteenth-century feminism. Likewise, Mary Ryan claims that the separation of the male and the female realm did not really involve a confinement to private space: "a sphere," Ryan argues, "is not a home," because women's activities encompassed a whole network of associative life (186).

Eli Zaretsky suggests that Cott's and Ryan's reasoning can be extended to men's activities as well. Zaretsky emphasizes the liberating potential inherent in the cultivation of personal relationships within a capitalist social context (14, 55). In his view, the separation of family life, which derived from the generalization of the wage labor system, laid the foundations for the development of subjectivity, that is, of "a separate sphere of personal life, seemingly divorced from the mode of production" (14). Zaretsky believes that individuals whose subjectivity and public life are dissociated can be impelled by their sense of alienation to alter the conditions that brought their social and psychological discontents into existence. He points out that the protest against the sense of fragmentation induced by proletarianized social relations is often worded in the name of bourgeois individualism. These forms of individuality can, however, threaten capitalist hegemony (55). In this perspective, the rebellious potential of modernist art, its search for originality and uniqueness, is rooted in an individualist outlook that was mediated through the initial anchoring ground of personal life—the family, that is (42).

Zaretsky's historical view is particularly relevant to Fuller and Herrick because, in their works, a centrifugal protest against competitive careerism is voiced through a defense of family life—the only institution that seems worth saving. Among these texts, Robert Herrick's *The Web of Life* presents an unusually radical and complex picture of middle-class alienation. In this work, the internal and external pressures bearing on middle-class professionals, as well as the utopian retreat they can hope for, are depicted with a bitterness that almost wrenches the text away from the conventions of realism.

The Web of Life centers around the figure of Sommers, a young surgeon looking for a suitable social position in 1890s Chicago. Sommers is repelled by the decadent luxury of the new upper-classes, but equally wary of the industrial proletariat, who have just declared the Pullman strike. The surgeon decides to seek his happiness beyond the conventions of society, in an out-of-wedlock affair with a woman slightly below his own class. His lover, Alves Preston, is a schoolteacher whom he meets when he saves her drunken husband from bullet wounds. Unmindful of the possible scandal, Sommers leaves his well-paid job and resolves to share her lower-middle-class round of life. The couple move to the makeshift lodgings of a pavilion left over from the World's Fair—a place that serves as a paradoxical locale for a pastoral romance at the periphery of the metropolis. Yet, as the Pullman strike reaches its climax, Sommers becomes an asocial reader of eccentric social theories and Alves grows uneasy about the sacrifices he had to make for her sake; worse still, she comes to face blackmail threats from a woman who claims Alves hired Sommers to put her husband to sleep. She then decides to take her own life by skating to the brink of the huge ice floes that cover Lake Michigan. After his plebeian lover has thus conveniently been disposed of, Sommers experiences an epiphany: as corrupt and chaotic as the city may be, it constitutes the web of life to which he shall return. Accordingly, the surgeon surrenders to the entreaties of Louise Hitchcock, the bright and beautiful daughter of an industrialist of the Civil War generation; Louise lures Sommers back to his class by offering him the prospect of a sensible marriage that will not turn the couple into upper-class parasites.

What distinguishes *The Web of Life* from the other texts by Fuller and Herrick discussed in this chapter is, first, the change in narrative scope that follows from its emphasis on downward mobility. Instead of having to be saved from the moral corruption of social climbing, the hero is rescued from a fling into proletarianization. The incursions into social domains below or beyond the perimeter of upper- or middle-class rituals confer to the narrative a degree of openness and flexibility that contrasts with the sense of confinement that characterizes drawing-room realism. The novel is indeed remarkable for its sensitivity to urban landscapes and for the originality with which it makes urban geography serve its narrative ends. With an imaginativeness equaled only in Upton Sinclair, it portrays Chicago as a city half-formed, patchy, animated with a vitality that spends itself in channels that were never tailored to concerted human purposes. Characteristic of Herrick's spatial metaphorics is the description of Washington Avenue, a thoroughfare that seems to have been "drawn on the map by a ruler, without regard to habitations" (65). Sommers reflects that the prestigious avenue, which resurfaces in faraway proletarian areas where one would least expect to find it, could stretch infinitely across the prairie "into Indiana, to the Ohio River,—to the Gulf for all he knew" (65). As a symbol of the whole city, it accommodates within its abstract emptiness neighborhoods of all social levels, scattered along vacant stretches of land held together only by the network of ghostly, screeching electric cars.

The historical import of Herrick's metaphorical landscapes manifests itself most consistently in the apocalyptic descriptions of the ruins of the White City, the buildings of the Chicago World's Fair. In spite of his pessimism, Herrick does not present the "wreck of the fair" (56) as the expression of a cultural project that is inherently flawed:[2] when the fair's buildings are set ablaze by the Pullman strikers, Sommers reflects to Alves that in this devastation, "beauty [is] eating beauty" (173). Before the blaze, Sommers had regularly visited the site of the fair for the repose and meditative atmosphere that surrounded the ruins of the Spanish convent, or the wings of the Art Building. The latter seemed "to stand guard against the improprieties of civilization" (56), represented quite conspicuously by the wasted acres of the sprawling city around the site of the fair.

There is, however, a shade of ambiguity in Herrick's description: as the ruin of a stunted American utopia, the wreck of the fair cannot remain immune to the corruption that defeated the values that it was supposed to embody. Given the historical context of the end of the century, it is only in a perverted form that the dream of culture evoked by the Art Building can possibly unfold: what Sommers sees on the deserted fields is therefore not only the hieratic architecture of a civilized world, but also the "rotting buildings" of a "play-city" (57), reduced to futility by the pressure of the sterile metropolis that surrounds it. As this description rises to a cosmic perspective, it opposes the "marvellous clarified atmosphere of the sky, like iridescent gauze, showering a thousand harmonies of metallic colors," to "the illimitable, tawdry sweep of defaced earth" of the city on the prairie (57). This implies that the fair has failed in its function of cultural mediator: Herrick's city remains torn apart between unattainable ideals and a human world that drags nature itself into its own degeneration. There is no space here for what, in his discussion of agrarianism, Leo Marx calls a "middle landscape" (97)—an intermediate realm of action where human agency could mend the ills of urbanization. It is quite logical then that the White City should regain its grandeur only in an apocalypse of fire.

The urban idyll of Sommers and Alves represents a major attempt at transcending the nightmare scenario embodied in the burning of the fair buildings. There is a remarkable note of optimism in Herrick's decision to make his characters move from a lower-middle-class boarding house to the ticket-booth of the World's Fair. This gesture manifests the hope that the grandiose cultural project of the World's Fair can be salvaged, at least in the context of a relationship of authentic personal love. The building itself, shaped like "a little stucco Grecian temple" with imitation bronze doors, is not immune to the cultural ambiguity that characterizes the larger fair itself—the intimation that utopian aspirations are mixed with inauthenticity. But in this case, it is the positive potential of the simulacrum that predominates—its appeal to a wider, richer horizon of culture: the temple appears as a "strange little product of some western architect's remembering pencil," which "brought an air of distant shores and times, standing here in the waste of the prairie, above the bright blue waters of the lake" (265). In such a passage, the text holds up the possibility that a perfect community of two people can be established in the interstices of the social fabric, by appropriating and even revitalizing the cultural artifacts of the larger group.

In this realist text, reality must, however, soon enough catch up with romance. Alves is the voice of common sense and conformity on this occasion; because of her background and her failed marriage, she knows that class barriers cannot be crossed or disregarded at will: "She saw with sudden clearness what she had done to this man she loved. She had taken him from his proper position in the world; she had forced him to push his theories of revolt beyond sane limits. . . . Worse yet, she had soiled the reverences of his nature. What was she but a soiled thing! The tenderness of his first passion had sprung amid the rank growth of her past with its solid little drama" (303–4). While the outcome of the novel vindicates Alves's sentimental perception of class boundaries, it remains ambiguous about Sommers's rebellion, whose value is strangely left unquestioned. To Alves, the fact that Sommers develops "strange ideas about money getting" (277) is a clear sign that his alienation from society has reached a critical point. Sommers argues for instance that "the physician should receive the very minimum of pay possible for his existence" because "in waging his battle with mysterious nature, he only unfits himself by seeking gain" (277). While this radicalism might signify that Sommers is losing his mind, his statements are presented in neutral essay fashion, and are eventually disproved only by the surgeon's surrender to the presumably corrupt social system.

By suggesting that the values of authentic subjectivity cannot be reconciled with middle-class norms of professional and family life, Herrick precipitates a narrative crisis that cannot be solved through the sensible-marriage device alone. Thus, the conclusion of the commonsense marriage between Sommers and Louise Hitchcock at the end of the story requires that the narrative strands of the novel first be tied up by means of the more spectacular tactics of the rhetoric of sublimity. The ice field covering Lake Michigan, over which Alves resolves to skate to her death, represents the center of sublime dread; strewn across black water that "gurgle[s] treacherously," rent by "snakelike, oozing crack[s]" (296), the ice floes resonate with loud uncanny voices. Herrick ventures the hypothesis that the "savage, tranquil, immense" field of ice embodies the indifferent face of nature (297). Yet in this narrative context, it is more logical to assume that this vision of nature, like the debased earth that surrounds the grounds of the World's Fair, is carved in the semblance of the huge city, which is always visible from the frozen surface of the lake. The icy sea, towards whose "limitless bosom" (305) Alves feels irresistibly drawn, exerts the same kind of hypnotic fascination as Dreiser's Broadway crowds or Norris's wheat pit. Like the mystifying naturalist city, the shrieking and groaning fields of ice move at the whims of hidden stirrings, "in obedience to the undercurrents, the impact from distant northernly winds" (307).

Shortly before Alves throws herself into the water, the allegorical vision veers toward a dialectical conversion: Alves views the frozen immensity as "the true conception of life—one vast, ever darkening sphere filled with threatening voices, where she and others wandered in sorrow, in regret, in disappointment, and, also, in joy" (308). The reminiscence of the perfection of her passion for Sommers in the midst of this desolation marks an essential turning point, because the passage is ultimately meant to introduce an idea of sacrifice and redemption. What has to be parted with is the dream of absolute fulfillment in a love relationship, or as Zaretsky puts it, the idea of "human relations, and human beings, as an end in themselves" (57). Sommers, musing over his lover's death, accomplishes the sacrifice by deciding that "the human modicum of joy" (315) of an average marriage could never have satisfied "the deep thirst of love in her heart" (315). Thus, convinced that "he had given the best he had" (315) to meet the demands of a relationship that could find no place in the society of their time, Sommers turns back towards the task of carving for himself the middling place that befits his social obligations.

The scenario of social reintegration reaps immediate rewards from this descent into the terrors of the urban sublime. No sooner has Sommers carried Alves's body back to the World's Fair toll-booth than he decides that he has come to "the end of his little personal battle with the world . . . the end of revolt" (315). What makes that resolution credible is a shift from the dark, uncanny rhetoric through which Alves's suicide is conveyed to a more serene variety of biological sublime, which literally revitalizes the social relations and values that the first part of the novel had so efficiently discredited. Thus, after Alves's death, Sommers find redemption in a new form of ecstatic community: "He should return to that web of life from which [Alves and himself] had striven to extricate themselves. She bade him go back to that fretwork, unsolvable world of little and great, of domineering and incompetent wills, of the powerful rich struggling blindly to dominate and the weak and poor struggling blindly to keep their lives: the vast webs of petty greeds and blind efforts" (315–16). Through this reconciliation with "the commoner uses of life" (315), the social contradictions that prodded the protagonist to individualistic dissent seem to be miraculously neutralized: they acquire the enigmatic significance of "the mysterious web of life" that people weave "for ends no human mind could know" (348). In practical terms, however, this shift toward mystical vitalism makes the defense of middle-class marriage and conviviality an excessively demanding business, accessible to mystics alone. In this, *The Web of Life* highlights the fragility of the communities defined by the family plots of urban realist fiction. Motifs such as the historical inheritance, the passage of generations, and the characters' reconciliation to sensible matrimony make up a form of discourse that does not find its coherence on the basis of its own narrative codes.

Naturalist Gothic:
Population Economics and
Urban Genealogies

Gothic Economics in Jack London's *The People of the Abyss*

While discussing Fuller and Herrick, I have focused on the internal causes of the instability of the realist world: speculation, conspicuous consumption, as well as the competitiveness of professional careers. At this
point, I wish to turn to the analysis of the naturalist representation of
the urban population—a presence that, according to realist texts, threatens middle-class America from outside. The discussion of Howells's *A
Hazard of New Fortunes* has revealed that realist fiction rejects the urban-
industrial proletariat beyond the periphery of its narrative scope. Among
Chicago realists, there are some interesting attempts to resist this literary tendency to exclude and demonize non-genteel populations: in Herrick's *The Web of Life*, a middle-class doctor and an upper-class young
woman can still elbow their way, shaken but relatively safe, through hostile cohorts of Pullman strikers who are wrecking train cars. For the protagonist of Herrick's novel, it is preposterous to brand anarchists as "a
kind of Asiatic plague that might break out at any time" (154–55); strikers are no less brutish than the economically depraved upper-classes.
However, the general drift of realist and naturalist texts is more accu-

rately reflected in passages of H. B. Fuller's *With the Procession*, where the author depicts the new immigrant working-classes as a *"camorra"* of "steerage-rats" haunting the business quarters of the middle classes, or dragging young Anglo-Saxons into sex scandals (*Procession* 134, 133). This racist caricaturing, reserved for secondary characters in realist fiction, is characteristic of what I wish to call naturalist gothic—the grotesque representation of populations in naturalism.

June Howard has described the historical context that led to the naturalist obsession with the working classes, and that therefore underlies the development of naturalist gothic. Howard, like Robert Herrick, emphasizes the importance of the railroad strikes as a precipitating factor in the change of middle-class attitudes toward labor. For her, the 1877 strike played the same part as the 1848 revolution in France: it turned the American bourgeoisie into a conservative force that from then on could view the lower classes only as a potential source of disorder (76). Against liberal readings of turn-of-the-century fiction, Howard writes that the fear of class warfare "must be recognized as a powerful element of the ideology of the period," and is also "part of the material worked by naturalism" (77): late-nineteenth- and early-twentieth-century novels often uncritically reproduce or even expand the class discourse developed during the crisis of the 1890s, and prove particularly receptive to nativist thematics. Howard's description of the naturalist representation of the working class revolves around the naturalist image of the proletarian brute. Drawing on Hayden White's studies of the cultural stereotype of the wild man, as well as on Melvyn Dubofsky's analyses of working-class stereotypes, she argues that naturalist fiction consistently equates the working class with savagery, racial difference, and atavism (78, 86). In this logic, naturalism uses a process of metaphorical conversion that transcodes the class divisions of the industrial world—a relatively new phenomenon in the United States—into a form of radical, racially connoted otherness. This strategy, Howard concludes, validates a scientifically based form of social control: by picturing the proletarian brute as an alien object exposed to the gaze of middle-class observers, naturalist novels construct a structure of feeling that makes possible the development of a form of middle-class social science—sociology, criminal anthropology, and eugenics. The purpose of these disciplines will be to explore and to contain otherness in the social field.

In the present argument, I want to point out that the figure of the brute is part of a discourse whose field of relevance is broader than the transcoding of class as biological atavism. A channel of expression for the middle-class fear of urban life, naturalist gothic sets up a paranoid structure of feelings that establishes complex linkages between city economics, the origins of populations, and the strategies by which the energies of the masses can be channeled for political ends. First, in an analysis of Jack London's documentary essay *The People of the Abyss* (1903), I argue that the very features of proletarian brutes in naturalist gothic are determined by the gendered economics that inform the novelist's representation of production; the affinity between economics and biology that Jack London takes for granted constitutes the basis of a vitalist system of population management. I then go on to show that this discourse of vital energies is meant to map two main fields of experience—a genealogical and a political one. In this chapter, I examine how the gothic contributes to the depiction of the biological and ethnic past of naturalist characters; in chapter 11 I argue that the gothic provides the tropes for a discourse of hypnosis and suggestion, through which naturalist novels delineate the methods by which the political containment of uncanny urban dwellers can be effected.

Jack London's *The People of the Abyss* (1903) is a nonfiction investigation of the slums of the London East End. This muckraking project, modeled on the mysteries of the city, is meant to bring to the eyes of middle-class audiences the frightening realities of the English underclass. In this, the text has a cautionary value: Jack London contends that the urban horrors unveiled in his East End documentary are not symptomatic of a social pathology that affects Europe exclusively: the abysmal poverty of the Old World capital represents the future of the American metropolis, or, more accurately, its contemporary hidden side. Through its very subject, London's text is rife with sensationalistic tableaux; its most acutely gothic passage, which will be my main object here, appears in the "Vision of the Night" chapter; in this dream-like vision, the author tells of a nightmarish trip among subhuman "creatures of prey," "gorillas," or "gutter-wolves" (103). London uses grotesque descriptions of the city's "breed[s] of city savages" (104) as illustrations for a political argument reminiscent of H. G. Wells's *The Time Machine:* he stigmatizes the capitalists for creating the conditions that led to the development of a "new species" of degenerates (104).

In terms of genre, *The People of the Abyss* is strikingly heterogeneous, even by naturalist standards. On the one hand, London's survey of the East End is tied to the conventions of social science realism—from case studies to statistical charts; yet the text is also organized according to a device whose literariness is heavily foregrounded: the metaphor of a descent into hell.

Within this framework, Jack London's horror visions are distinctly recognizable from their immediate textual environment: the stylistic breaks induced by the gothic are arguably the most representative manifestation of the generic dialogization of naturalist fiction. Indeed, any discussion of naturalist gothic necessitates an analysis of the strategic use of generic discontinuities. Generic shifts, particularly from realism toward the gothic, constitute in themselves a rhetorical device—a sublimity speech act: the reader's momentary loss of generic bearings can be cultivated as a necessary element in the economy of the novel—as is systematically the case in fantastic literature, for instance.[1] In naturalist works, the shock tactics of generic discontinuities are used to generate an epistemological threshold effect: they mark out the boundaries beyond which documentary exploration cannot reach. In this sense, their function is similar to that of the oceanic sublime: by substituting for the realistic gaze a visionary discourse of terror, incursions into the gothic genre precipitate what Thomas Weiskel calls an "intuition of depth" (23).

In Jack London's "Vision of the Night" chapter, the gothic intuition of depth yields the realization that the urban class system contains beings that outreach the powers of discourse. The passage is preceded by the account of one of the narrator's visits through the slums. The itinerary is at first described in full documentary detail, including a string of street names. Then, the realistic approach is abruptly abandoned: "It is rather hard to tell a tithe of what I saw. Much of it is untellable. But in a general way I may say that I saw a nightmare, a fearful slime that quickened the pavement with life, a mess of unmentionable obscenity that put into eclipse the 'nightly horror' of Piccadilly and the Strand" (163). This gothic spectacle precipitates an expansion of the gaze worthy of the oceanic sublime: Dreiser and Norris's oceanic idiom, I have argued, signifies the magnitude of the urban scene by picturing it as a boundless expanse. By comparison, the sublime features of the gothic genre are grounded in effects of depth and intensity; they are rooted in a fascination with physical deformity, horror, and hidden recesses of experience. Rhetorically, the discourse of the grotesque—with its allusions to the "fearful slime," the "twisted monstrosities," or the "creatures of prey" of the urban crowd—is sublime because it systematically relies on hyperbole. Hyperbolical caricature has, in this case, the effect of an open-ended comparison: it is as if the author's discourse, seized with vertigo, were unable to catch up with the intensity of the vision it was meant to record; the author is therefore reduced to designating the unmentionable object through enumerations of the most extreme—yet still insufficient—terms available.

Part of the dread stirred by naturalist urban novels issues from the fact that, in naturalist gothic, the discourse of gendered economics express-es itself allegorically, through a display of libidinal monsters. The rep-resentation of urban economics in the semblance of sexual processes implies indeed that the repressed tensions of the city must resurface in the shape of biological dysfunctionings. In Norris's *The Pit*, the focus of reproductive perversion was the vortex of speculation, which dragged the whole city into economic chaos. In Jack London's urban gothic, the city's teratological economy comes to light in grotesque animal allegories: the paradoxes and the pathology of the metropolis are literally inscribed on the bodies of the "gorillas" and the "gutter-wolves" of the London East End: "Their bodies were small, ill-shaped, and squat. There were no swelling muscles, no abundant thews and wide-spreading shoulders. They exhibited, rather, an elemental economy of nature, such as the cave-men must have exhibited. But there was strength in those meagre bod-ies, the ferocious, primordial strength to clutch and gripe and tear and rend. When they spring upon their human prey they are known even to bend the victim backward and double its body till the back is broken" (163). London's urban savages are both pitifully weak and inexplicably strong; in spite of their debility, they have a capacity for unpredictable acts of violence whose viciousness is literally supernatural. As such, their vital make-up resembles the paradoxically fertile and barren economics of Norris's Chicago, where speculators go bankrupt amidst overflowing floods of wheat. Thus, by peopling their novels with crowds of libidinal monsters, naturalist novelists create within their texts a site where the anxieties generated by urban economics may be embodied in the guise of fascinating horror.

The biological perversion of the East End population takes, in Lon-don's account, the shape of oedipal and preoedipal threats, which the text brings to light by means of successive leaps into horror. In the first para-graphs of the chapter, the mobs of city savages form a bachelors' crowd that rules the street: these are male monsters on the prowl—"a new spe-cies" (164) with predatory stares and threatening hands. In spite of the differences in social class, these urban savages are reminiscent of the alienated men who drift around Norris's Board of Exchange: in London as in Norris, the city belongs to a crowd of men that are both unnatu-rally powerful—proletarians can break people in two, speculators control the apparatus of exchange—and powerless in their alienation. Yet, once London has established this atmosphere of male aggression, he completely reverses his perspective. In the kind of non sequitur that the gothic discourse makes possible, the vision of oedipal dread is abruptly rewritten into preoedipal terms:

> But [the male predators] were not the only beasts that ranged the menagerie. They were only here and there, lurking in dark courts and passing like grey shadows along the walls; but the women from whose rotten loins they spring were everywhere. They whined insolently, and in maudlin tones begged me for pennies and worse. They held carouse in every boozing ken, slatternly, unkempt, bleary-eyed, and tousled, leering and gibbering, overspilling with foulness and corruption, and, gone in debauch, sprawling across benches and bars, unspeakably repulsive, fearful to look upon. (164)

The reversal of perspective introduced by this spectacle of abject femininity marks a new epistemological threshold: in an allegory within the allegory, the apparition of the repulsive women discloses the underlying truth of the bachelor crowd—the predominance of perverse feminine power in the city. Thus, by virtue of a narrative logic that goes by concentric circles of revelations, we understand that the whole East End, and the larger city beyond, could rest on a biological infrastructure embodied in the figures of foulsome inebriate females with "rotten loins" (164).

Catherine Gallagher and Mark Seltzer have emphasized how central the figure of the uncontrollable working-class breeder was to the late-nineteenth-century representation of city life (Gallagher 55; Seltzer 96):[2] literary and sociological explorations of the underclass inevitably converge toward the figure of the slum mother, whose grotesque physical presence, Seltzer writes, "provides . . . a visual and corporeal model of the social" (100).[3] In Jack London, monstrous working-class mothers are paradigmatic of the urban economy because, as reproducing bodies, they are the origin of a citywide process of unregulated biological exchange: their degenerative vital fluids are free to circulate across boundaries of class and race. Before London himself, the principles of this socio-economics of abjection had been laid out in the writings of social reformers influenced by eugenics. This was, for instance, the drift of Josiah Strong's *Our Country*, a book in which the author warned Americans about the biological perils of urbanization. In his argument, Strong quotes "The Bitter Cry of Outcast London"—an English social study that heavily draws on the rhetoric of abjection. The British pamphlet conjures up visions of "'pestilential human rookeries'"—secluded spaces "'swarming with vermin'" and saturated with "intolerable" stenches (qtd. in Strong 130): "'To get into [the tenements], you have to penetrate courts reeking with poisonous and malodorous gases, arising from accumulations of sewage and refuse scattered in all directions, and often flowing beneath your feet'" (qtd. in Strong 130). In this environment, Strong indicates, sanitary inspectors may stumble into slum cellars containing "a father, mother, three children and four pigs" (131). What comes out of this form of sociology is the image of a city engaged in a process of animal reproduction that allows organic gases and body fluids to cross even the boundaries of species.

In his handling of the rhetoric of eugenics, London is peculiarly apt at sketching out how the city's biological traffic runs from one locale to another—from the heart of the slums to respectable working-class families, or to the plane of larger population flows. When it constructs this chain of contagion, London's text makes expert use of the rhetoric of sublimity: it assumes indeed that a barely representable hidden world—biological degeneration, in this case—lurks behind the surfaces of everyday life. In the segments of his essay where realist discourse predominates, London depicts embattled families that try to keep up their standards of respectability in the East End context. Johnny Upright, for instance, the private detective who helps the narrator in his investigations, is the head of a fairly affluent working-class household; Upright's two daughters are described coming back from church, still wearing their Sunday dresses. The narrator discerns in them the "delicate prettiness which characterizes the Cockney lasses" (17). Yet in the East End, this form of beauty "is no more than a promise with no grip on time, and doomed to fade quickly away like the color of the sky" (17). The threat that hangs over the two girls is the degenerative population traffic that affects the whole English racial stock: "Year by year," London writes, "rural England pours in a flood of vigorous strong life" into the city; however, this stock "not only does not renew itself, but perishes by the third generation" (28). The impact of this process is delineated a few pages later, in the portrait of the narrator's landlady: although a "woman of the finest grade of the English working class, with numerous evidences of refinement," the landlady is nevertheless "being slowly engulfed by [the] noisome and rotten tide of humanity" of the East End (21).

According to London's multilayered chart of the East End, the biological traffic that wreaks havoc with working-class domesticity is ultimately rooted in another, equally sinister sublime undercurrent—conspicuous wealth and financial speculation. London argues indeed that the

average capitalist, "who sees and thinks life in terms of share and cou-
pons" is responsible for the existence of the "hordes of beastly wretch-
edness and inarticulate misery" (98). In this logic, capitalist exploitation
is the antithesis of the healthy vital outlook of those "who [see] and
[think] life in terms of manhood and womanhood" (98): capitalism makes
"a beast of [the worker], and of his seed through the generations, by the
artful and spidery manipulaton of industry and politics" (98). It is in this
passage, where a traffic in human seed is equated with flows of money,
that London makes visible the pattern of overdetermination that informs
his gothic discourse: biology interfaces with economics and expresses it
metaphorically; by bringing to light the libidinal horrors of the East End,
London holds up a distorting mirror, which represents allegorically the
pathology of the very system of economic exploitation that created the
East End slums. In this grotesque version of the gendered economy, the
moral degeneracy of capitalism and the degeneracy of the flesh can be
subsumed under one identical heading: "the progeny of prostitution" is
literally identified with "the prostitution of labor" (165).

Realist and Darwinian Stories of Origins in Norris's *McTeague*

Atavistic regression is a constant undertone in the biological economics
of Jack London's *The People of the Abyss*: the "hordes of beastly wretch-
edness" of the East End (98) are peopled with degenerate "cave-men"
that can be unfavorably constrasted with the equally atavistic, though
supposedly more glamorous, Nietzschean figure of the "great blonde
beasts" (98).[4] In these instances, London, like other naturalists, represents instinctual perversion through Darwinian tropes of primitivism.
The naturalist appropriation of Darwinian discourse has traditionally
been read within a problematic of determinism and free will; the atavistic figures in that case are grotesque embodiments of the instinctual
background that restricts the characters' freedom.[5] In neo-historicist
readings, the naturalist reliance on evolutionary theories has been described as an ideological strategy in the representation of class and race:
novelists, in this perspective, align themselves on the agenda of eugenics researchers who, as Donald K. Pickens puts it, "merely projected their
[own] class prejudices as objective laws of civilization and nature" (4).
Scientists and novelists alike depicted non-genteel characters as evolutionary throwbacks, stuck halfway on the ladder of human development.

In these pages, I wish to read the atavistic components of naturalist gothic as a genealogical discourse tailored to the epistemological needs of the urban world. In this interpretation, the figure of the "abysmal brute," to take up Jack London's formula (*Abysmal* 3), is overdetermined in that it condenses two sets of cultural anxieties: besides its role as an allegorical representation of the underclasses, it provides the novelists with a literary tool for the exploration of the origins of all urban populations, in their relation both to the technological environment of the city and to nature. Naturalist novels acknowledge indeed that the development of cities has rendered problematic the issue of origins—personal or anthropological. The coexistence of heterocultural populations, the harnessing of nature for urban needs, and the social marginalization of small-town life make it difficult to maintain the continuities on which narratives of origins are based. Some turn-of-the-century works handle this genealogical anxiety by sticking to the discourse of the knowable community. Later in this chapter, I point out that Abraham Cahan's depiction of the New York ghetto and Charles Waddell Chesnutt's stories of small-town life do not emulate the discourse of naturalist atavism, and represent genealogical otherness through a mixture of realism and utopian romance. On the contrary, Émile Zola, Frank Norris, Jack London, as well as urban reformers like Jacob Riis and H. M. Boies, borrow from Darwinian theories of atavism that, once they are transposed to literature, portray the hidden urban past in the grotesque colors of the gothic.

Genealogical anxiety on a cosmic scale is strikingly illustrated in the opening chapters of Theodore Dreiser's *The Financier*. There, the protagonist, young Frank Cowperwood, watches in utter fascination a week-long struggle between a lobster and a defenseless squid, which is methodically sliced up by its patient predator. This primeval scene of power is presented as a sublime dramatization of the survival of the fittest, with a clear genealogical import: the fight itself follows an account of Cowperwood's spells of metaphysical questionings—"How did all these people get into the world? . . . Who started things anyhow?" (7)—where we learn that the young hero cannot accept the story of Adam and Eve as a credible tale of origins. The lobster epiphany puts this questioning to rest. The spectacle of the lobster snipping at the waxy body of its prey reveals to Cowperwood that real power originates in a distant atavistic realm; the scene also raises the tantalizing prospect that a character like the future financier could appropriate these energies for his own purposes.

The depiction of the semi-cannibalistic fight between archaic sea creatures adds to Dreiser's novel an element of generic heterogeneity characteristic of naturalist gothic. Dreiser's text is paradigmatic of naturalism in that it develops its genealogical discourse on two planes: the
Darwinian vignettes—the initial lobster scene as well as, at the end of
the novel, a one-page appendix about a killer fish with a chameleon-like
"power of simulation" (447)—compete with a detailed realistic account
of the financier's family history. Likewise, the economics of Cowperwood's world are viewed from contrasted angles—through a scrupulous
literary account of financial transactions and, on the other hand, through
a romance depiction of grotesque predators of the depths. I believe that,
in naturalist fiction or Darwinian social science, these two discourses are
complementary from a dialogic perspective: the realist genealogical idiom satisfies itself with reconstructing the history of social relations by
tracing the succession of generations, marriage, and inheritance. This
realist strategy is, I have pointed out, central to the generational thematics of realist novels and to Jane Addams's urban sociology. On the other
hand, the naturalist discourse of origins is an idiom of sublimity that
explains the origins of contemporary individuals by invoking stretches
of evolutionary time that are by definition unrepresentable. Instead of
attempting to elucidate everyday experience in terms of proximate phe-
nonena, it elaborates interpretations that promote distant and uncanny
forces to the status of foundations of social life. In this configuration, the
sublime past is made to express allegorically the truth of the commonsense present: it interprets the contemporary world, as it were.

The interplay of realist and naturalist genealogies in turn-of-the-century texts has been described by Mark Seltzer, who argues that the "mutation" from realism to naturalism involves a thematic shift "from inheritance to heredity, from progress (as evolution) to recapitulation (as
devolution), from histories of marriage and adultery to case histories
of bodies, sexualities, and populations" (140). Seltzer implies thereby
that there is a basic continuity between the two discourses—that even
when it focuses on nonrealistic brutes and freaks, the naturalist novel
"maps in high relief" the narrative and thematic features of realism
(140). In the following discussion of Frank Norris's *McTeague*, I wish
to nuance Seltzer's argument by indicating that the Darwinian genealogies of naturalism do not simply reproduce on a larger scale the logic
of the kinship-based stories of realist fiction: instead, they play the part
of a metaphorical substitute for the realist idiom when the latter proves
to be unequal to the task of accounting for class and ethnic otherness.

Thus, while the protagonists of H. B. Fuller's and David Graham Phillips's novels worry over the prospects of the generation that directly follows or precedes them, characters in naturalist fiction are preoccupied with their prehistoric forebears. In this, they share the situation of Henry Adams, who, in his autobiography, expresses the puzzlement that a nineteenth-century human being like himself—especially one with the prestigious kinship credentials of the New England Adamses—must from then on include uncanny shellfish fossils in his genealogical tree (230). Atavistic figures like Adams's shellfish obey, however, different norms of family decorum or literary verisimilitude than their realist counterparts; in the overall economy of the text, they can enter patterns of overdetermination in which realist characters do not fit.

Frank Norris's *McTeague* qualifies as a genealogical narrative in two respects: because it investigates the evolutionary ancestry of its main protagonist and because it provides a metaphorical exploration of the origins of the California economy. The novel chronicles the descent toward savagery of a San Francisco dentist who never enjoyed a secure hold on the basics of civilized behavior in the first place. McTeague's reversion to his primitive origins is precipitated by sexual jealousy and by irrational greed. Sexual rivalry opposes the dentist to his rival, Marcus Schouler, for the love of Trina Sieppe, the daughter of Swiss-German immigrants. McTeague wins Trina's hand; yet the jealous Marcus uses his political influence to have the dentist sued for practicing without a license. From then on, Trina's and McTeague's marriage degenerates: Trina obsessively hoards her own savings, refusing to share them with her jobless husband. For this, the dentist murders her. McTeague then runs away with Trina's gold to the desert, where he is hunted by the police and by Schouler. The novel ends in Death Valley, with the vision of the dentist, marooned in a sea of burning sand, exhausted, handcuffed to the body of Marcus, whom he has just pummeled to death.

The emotional impact of the genealogical discourse of McTeague consists in an ability to reveal abysses of primitive violence below the surface of urban everyday life.[6] Surprisingly perhaps, Norris's masterpiece of naturalist gothic devotes a lot of energy to establishing a realistic representation of neighborhood life. In the opening chapter of the novel, for instance, the hero is shown indulging in one of his few pastimes— casting a flâneur's glance at the street beneath his "Dental Parlors" (4): "It was one of those cross streets peculiar to Western cities, situated in the heart of the residence quarter, but occupied by small tradespeople who lived in the rooms above their shops. There were corner drug stores with huge jars of red, yellow, and green liquids in their windows, very brave and gay; stationers' stores, where illustrated weeklies were tacked upon bulletin boards; barber shops with cigar stands in their vestibules" (5). It would be difficult to surpass the commonplace orderliness of this cityscape; the long description, which itemizes the activities that fit each period of the day, is exclusively geared toward customs and rituals. As a result, the petit-bourgeois neighborhood evinces a small-town feeling that is rarely encountered in the novels of the naturalist sublime. Norris's protagonists are, of course, grotesque in appearance and behavior, but the narrative premises of *McTeague*—a marriage that fails because of the spouses' inability to control their passions, a friendship that turns to hatred because of sexual and economic jealousy, a tale of professional failure—are domestic in nature, and differ thereby from the titanic ventures of *The Pit* or *The Octopus*.

Under its innocuous surface, however, Norris's San Francisco is made up of a population of aliens—immigrants, of course, and also of people who are strangers to each other and to themselves; characters like these are irreducible to a realist aesthetic that prizes familiarity and knowable communities; Norris portrays them therefore by intertwining local color and the gothic. In its opposition to realism, Norris's defamiliarizing method of characterization is reminiscent of the contrast that Coleridge and Wordsworth established between their respective poetic methods: the novelist seeks to make the commonplace surface of urban life supernatural, while realist novelists like Howells—or social workers like Jane Addams—attempt to render the threatening otherness of the metropolis familiar. As in Jack London's naturalist gothic, *McTeague*'s world is uncanny because it exhibits a mismatch between the primitive behavior of the characters and, on the other hand, the hollow social rituals that mark them out as inhabitants of a modern city. In the expository passage, the narrator, in alienated fascination, scans McTeague's physique and itemizes the weekly schedule of his few moments of entertainment—among which the inflexible succession of the "six lugubrious airs" (2) the "young giant" (3) plays on his concertina; the uncanniness evoked by these dehumanizing catalogs is sharply highlighted by the narrator's constant awareness of the threatening physique of the dentist: McTeague has "immense limbs," a salient jaw "like that of the carnivora," and "hands . . . strong as vises" (3).

The dissonance between primitive impulses and cultural habits manifests itself in part through a comedy of social mimicry. It is as if the people of Polk Street hadn't yet had time to interiorize their petit-bourgeois roles, and felt ambivalent about the markers of their own social ascension. Marriage may be "the—the foundation of society" (156), as one character stammeringly puts it, but it remains so unfamiliar a ritual that Mr. Sieppe, Trina's father, heavily perspiring, feels compelled to lead his daughter through the ceremony by scrupulously stepping on the chalk marks he has drawn on the floor beforehand. No wonder then that McTeague and Trina should suspect that there is "a certain inadequateness about the ceremony" (165). The ineffectuality of domestic rituals is epitomized in the plight of the Sieppe household—the perfect embodiment of the work ethic. Mr. Sieppe tries to keep his family under a system of military discipline that proves ultimately pointless; he can as little prevent his son "Owgooste" (96) from defecating in his pants at the Music Hall as he can control the vagaries of an economy that will eventually drive him to emigrate to New Zealand. McTeague, the chief victim of this grotesque satire of domestic and social arrangements, remains intimidated by the bric-a-brac of his own household, even though it is composed of harmless items such as chromos of a little boy and a little girl dressed up as old people, and carrying captions that read "I'm Grandpa" and "I'm Grandma" (157). Because of the alienated gaze from which McTeague's universe is viewed, the elements that at first sight make up the commonplace surface of neighborliness can be turned out to be defamiliarizing and grotesque. Behind this atmosphere of cultural malaise lies the suspicion that characters themselves are little more than animals in city clothes—both social automata and biological freaks whose reversion to the primitive state remains a threatening possibility throughout: when the jealous Marcus Schouler fights McTeague over Trina, he tears off his opponent's ear with his bare teeth.

Against the idiom of urban local color, Norris plays off two types of romance discourses of origins—Darwinian atavism and, on the other hand, the discourse of gold, through which the author charts an economic genealogy of California. In his suggestive reading of *McTeague*, Walter Benn Michaels has shown that Norris's bizarre thematics of gold fetishism and avarice rework the cultural anxieties that underlay the gold standard controversies of the end of the century. Michaels's interpretation has a genealogical import in that it analyzes the link between nature and the money economy. Michaels mentions for instance that the nineteenth-century controversies about the gold standard were phrased in evolutionary terms: goldbugs believed in the evolutionary primacy of gold; they contended that gold, which they considered to be inherently valuable, had been preferred over other metallic currencies by a process of evolutionary selection. By the same logic, their tracts were haunted by the specter of a reversion to a moneyless society, "but one remove from barbarism" (145).

The present reading assumes that, in Norris's genealogical approach to the monetary economy, gold plays a similar part as wheat does in *The Octopus* or human seed in Jack London's *The People of the Abyss:* it is a material symbol exchanged according to a sublime economic cycle. Here, however, I want to focus on the fact that it also circulates from the past to the present: in its genealogical dimension, the "virgin metal" subsumes a chain of economic transformation that coincides with the history of the Gold state, from ore extraction—embodied in McTeague's early career as a miner—to consumption, represented in the medical practice of the San Francisco dentist, who fills city dwellers' teeth with gold.

The ability of gold to serve as central symbol in Norris's diachronic narrative is due to the fact that gold straddles the line between artificiality and nature, value and material; as Walter Benn Michaels puts it, gold is "a natural object (metal) that looks like an artificial one (money)" (157). Thus, gold may serve as a symbolic hub for contradictory stories of origins: the same material can embody both McTeague's domestication and degeneration; it can articulate housemaid Maria Macapa's nostalgic idea that the golden age of society is lost; or it can express the novel's eventual suggestion that culture and savagery are closely interwoven.

In this light, McTeague's eventual return to the gold-filled California wilderness cannot entirely be regarded as an escape from urban culture. As in *The Octopus,* the sublimity speech acts of Norris's discourse of gold blur the nature/culture dichotomy: their hyperboles create rhetorical contexts where human technology and landscapes are both dissociated and uncannily interpenetrated. This paradoxical bond is illustrated in the sublime descriptions of mining at the end of the text: McTeague reaches an "untamed" region, whose "primeval forces" (379) emit an "incessant and muffled roar" that evokes the breathing of an "infinitely great monster alive, palpitating" (388). The uncanny sound is, however, not in itself a product of nature: it is the tumult "which disengages itself from all vast bodies, from oceans, from cities, from forests, from sleeping armies" (388).[7] From a genealogical perspective, this passage implies that the wilderness—this "vast unconquered brute of the Pliocene Epoch" (380)—does not hark back to a more remote evolutionary stage than do technological incongruities like mining machines—the "insatiable monster[s], gnashing the rocks to powder with [their] long iron teeth" (380).

Logically, the blurring of evolutionary boundaries effected by Norris's gold economics should conflict with the novelist's Darwinian discourse. In this, naturalist fiction further complicates a model of evolutionary temporality whose scientific formulation was already paradoxical. Henry Adams reveals in his *Education* that, in Norris's time, the evolutionary debate was characterized by the victory of the uniformitarian paradigm over catastrophism. Uniformitarians, unlike their opponents, denied the existence of abrupt discontinuities in geological and biological history (*Education* 927–28). Adams, himself seduced by catastrophism, manifests his amazement at the levity by which his friend, geologist Charles Lyell, endorses the uniformitarian orthodoxy (928). In view of this controversy, it appears that *McTeague*, like other naturalist texts, freely mixes catastrophist and uniformitarian themes. McTeague's story is catastrophist in its intimation that its characters can abruptly revert to savagery. However, the discourse of gold, which conflates past and present, adds an uncanny element of uniformitarianism to this picture of threatening atavism: it suggests that the catastrophic reversals occur not in the course of a genuine natural history, but in a timeless present.

In this paradoxical way, the apparently incompatible premises of Darwinian primitivism and the gold economy are made to contribute to one single social allegory: the representation of California as an economic system stuck in the stasis of primitive infancy. The thematics of infancy is here signified in gender terms: the keynote of gendered economics in *McTeague* is indeed the oral stage of sexuality—the libidinal configuration of infants, which revolves around ingestion, incorporation, suction, and cannibalism. The gold-mining apparatus, for example, is depicted as an insatiable baby clinging to an inexhaustible mother: "Its enormous maw fed night and day with the carboys' loads, gorged itself with gravel, and spat out the gold, grinding the rocks between its jaws, glutted, as it were, with the very entrails of the earth" (380). Orality, Freud argues, seems to be "harking back to the early animal forms of life" (*Three Essays* 337). In this view, the California economy, with its "monstrous gluttony" for gold, belongs on the bottom rung of the evolutionary history of mankind. What Norris's gold thematics adds to this evolutionary paradigm is, however, the idea that the novel's oral discourse is not meant to depict the initial moment of a historical sequence, followed by other stages of economic development: any illusion that there is such a time continuum is bound to be undercut by the logic of gold, which short-circuits temporal scales. As a result, degeneration—McTeague's surrender to cannibalistic urges—is not really a journey into time, but rather an ongoing process of the urban economy, in which industrialism and savagery coexist in a paradoxical bind.

Atavism and the Construction of Ethnic Otherness

Norris's *McTeague*, as it juggles with temporal dichotomies, defines the genealogical configuration used by most naturalist writers for the representation of class, gender, and ethnic otherness. The two realms of naturalist time—atavistic past, familiar present—are, according to this paradigm, connected by mysterious, indeed catastrophic continuities. Through these twists in the temporal fabric, the evolutionary past interferes with the lives of modern subjects, bringing about unexpected genealogical encounters. The genealogical epiphany, we will see below, is a motif that naturalist novelists share with turn-of-the-century realist African-American or immigrant writers like Charles Waddell Chesnutt and Abraham Cahan, who use this device for the sake of nostalgic romance or comedy. In naturalism, however, these moments of recognition are consistently uncanny because they allegorize the confrontation with forms of otherness that, in the context of the city, are viewed as radically undecipherable and threatening.

By reading the evolutionary discourse of naturalism along these lines, I imply that writers turned to Darwinian science precisely because it provided the gothic imagery that would give a perceptible literary shape to the fear of class and cultural heterogeneity in the city.[8] This appropriation of Darwinism was the more convenient as the evolutionary or hereditarian disciplines that provided the theoretical backbone for naturalist fiction—for Émile Zola's *Rougon Macquart* cycle, in particular—viewed atavism and evolution in a pessimistic light. In chapter 13 I will show that a few novelists—Dreiser, London—use their own invocations to the primitive as a source of empowerment; yet most other writers and scientists—Norris, Zola and the late-nineteenth-century neo-Darwinists—fault evolutionary mechanisms for linking humankind to a noxious ancestry: in this logic, the impact of prehistoric ancestors on modern populations manifests itself as degeneration—the regressive process that affects characters like Norris's McTeague and his rival Schouler. We will see that naturalist texts attempt to counterbalance degeneration by elaborating a discourse of Anglo-Saxon manhood, thus defining a psychological profile supposedly immune to the contagion of alien racial, gender, or class influences.

The evolutionary validation for the fear of degeneration was articulated in the writings of German biologist August Weismann, the initiator of neo-Darwinism. In the 1880s, Weismann developed his theory of the germ plasm according to which the "determinants of heredity were forever sealed from the effects of experience" (qtd. in Bannister 138); culture could therefore not influence evolution for the good of humankind. In his history of American social Darwinism, Robert Bannister underscores that Weismann's theory deeply disturbed American evolutionists like John Fiske, who had so far followed the optimistic legacy of Lamarck and Spencer.[9] Weismann's views made it problematic to wed Darwinism with an ideology of progress: they reduced evolution to a bestial scuffle; biological selection, English Darwinist Thomas Huxley claimed, should, in this light, be combated "with ethics" (Bannister 143). In the same vein, Philadelphia penologist H. M. Boies argued that the immeasurable expanses of evolutionary time were as likely to breed "all the inherited rottenness and corruption of the ages" as to nurture racial strength (290).

Neo-Darwinian pessimism influenced the development of eugenics— a discipline initiated in Britain by Sir Francis R. Galton and in the United States by Charles Benedict Davenport and the Eugenics Records Office (see Haller 8, 63). Eugenics postulates that, in the absence of a spontaneous dynamic toward human progress, it is advisable to straighten the course of biological evolution by scientific intervention. Donald K. Pickens indicates, however, that this new scientific activism was motivated by the most anti-democratic tendencies of the Progressive reform movement. "Eugenists appeared as progressives in their use of 'science' in reform matters," Pickens writes, "and yet, worried about the growth of democracy in an urban and industrial America, they merely projected their class prejudices as objective laws of civilization and nature" (4). Their overt concern consisted indeed in improving what they called the racial stock and with preserving the Anglo-Saxon work ethic.

Mark H. Haller indicates that the most publicized achievement of eugenics in the United States was New York merchant Richard Dugdale's scientific genealogies of criminality (21). In 1874, Dugdale, while visiting a New York prison, discovered that six members of one single family had been jailed at the same time. Dugdale, Haller explains, charted the genealogy of this notorious brood, whom he chose to call the Jukes: "In five to six generations of the family, Dugdale unearthed 709 Jukes or persons married to Jukes, of whom eighteen had kept brothels, 128 had been prostitutes, over 200 had been on relief, and over seventy-six had been convicted criminals" (Haller 22). The founder of this dynasty, Dugdale mentioned, was a woman, whom he labeled "Margaret, the Mother of Criminals" (Haller 22); her offspring cost the public more than a million dollars in relief and judicial expenses. Eugenic studies of this kind spread the fear of degeneration in that they described criminal impulses both as an ancestral legacy and as a menace that trickles down to the present—as a stigma of poverty and a citywide peril. According to this logic of genealogical contamination, the Jukes act as substitute ancestors—dystopian ones, that is—of the whole New York population.

Hereditarian discourse, as it is articulated in Dugdale's writings, led Zola and his American counterparts to elaborate models of psycho-social characterization relying on narratives of atavistic resurgence and doubling: protagonists in these allegorical plots are confronted with embodiments of their own prehistorical instincts.[10] In Zola's stock market novel *L'Argent*, for instance, the genealogical encounter occurs when Saccard, a reckless speculator, learns through a blackmail scheme that he has fathered an illegitimate son. Little Victor is a grotesque likeness of Saccard; his very physique lays bare the ancestral pollution that lurks behind the urbane countenance of his progenitor. While the father discreetly squanders the fortunes of the Paris aristocracy, the son indulges in the immorality and sexual violence that Zola associates with urban working-class life. In the United States, atavistic allegories were a staple of Jack London's fiction: his Alaskan stories—*White Fang, The Call of the Wild*—focus on animals and humans that explore their atavistic roots. More explicitly still, London's short novel *Before Adam* is narrated by a self-described "freak of heredity" whose dreams are invaded by his Neanderthal ancestor, aptly named "Big-Tooth" (2); the protagonist—a timid "city child"—finds himself waging his own forefather's wars against Cro-Magnon warriors (2). An ironical variant of this device appears in London's "South of the Slot" (1914), where the novelist depicts the double life of Freddie Drummond, a sexually repressed sociologist. Drummond is split between his role as a Darwinian ideologue for the wealthy, and, on the other hand, the working-class persona he adopts for his field trips "south of the slot" (817)—beyond the dividing line that separates middle-class San Francisco from the proletarian brutes. In this socialist tale, the hero's working-class persona—Bill Totts, a virile union-man whose sweetheart is "graceful and sinewy as a panther" (824)—ends up smothering the conservative Drummond altogether.

June Howard pointedly argues that the terror and fascination of ata-vism can be read as the symptom of a fear of proletarianization: it re-writes allegorically the anxieties of sections of the middle classes that "passionately defend their narrow footholds of economic security," and secretly dread to be dragged down to the status of supposedly abject working-class Others (95). Though proletarianization is indeed central to atavistic fears, I believe also that class anxieties do not fully account for the ideological impact of naturalist genealogies. The examples of Jack London's Freddie Drummond and Frank Norris's McTeague suggest that naturalist atavism functions by activating a mechanism of overdetermi-nation: it weaves together several psycho-social parameters—class, gen-der, ethnicity—within the make-up of single protagonists. Thus, in "South of the Slot," Bill Totts—Drummond's double—is the more fas-cinating an embodiment of the working class as he boasts a libido fu-eled by "the weltering muck and mess of lower and monstrous organic things" (824). Likewise, the savagery of Norris's characters in *McTeague* is made doubly mysterious by the fact that it is imbricated in the elusive gold economy. It is this overlayering procedure that allows the novels to construct the atmosphere of overall uncanniness that characterizes city populations—thus persuading their readers that social others are not simply different, but in fact unfathomably so. In this line of reading, atavism does not appear as the product of class divisions exclusively, but as the emanation of an open-ended urban scene that makes the eerily polysemic discourse of origins possible.

The textual devices by which naturalist discourse constructs its pat-terns of genealogical overdetermination can best be brought to light by contrasting naturalist atavism with what might pass as its realistic coun-terpart: stories of the forgotten past by African-American and immigrant writers—in my sample, Charles W. Chesnutt and Abraham Cahan. I have so far described sublime genealogies as the antithesis of the generation-oriented narratives of genteel or local-color realism, which have no use for gothic devices like atavistic doubles. The situation of minority writ-ers—poised between North and South, Europe and the United States, the ghetto and Anglo society—reveals however the possibility of anoth-er type of story of origins, linked to a different mode of articulating class and ethnic difference. Quasi-ancestral figures do appear in these large-ly realistic texts, but they are not emanations of a totally unexplainable realm. Instead, they are the object of what I wish to call genealogical epiphanies: a character's sudden insight into his or her own ancestry.

What is revealed in those moments is the all-too-real resurgence of a past legacy that the protagonists attempt to repress.

The memories that catch up with Mr. Ryder, the protagonist of Charles W. Chesnutt's "The Wife of His Youth" (1899), concern his life under slavery. Ryder heads the Blue Veins society, a cultural circle for the colored elite, open to mulattoes exclusively. When the story starts, the prosperous middle-aged bachelor is completing the preparations for a ball, where he plans to propose to Mrs. Dixon, a widow younger and whiter than himself. He is interrupted by the arrival of a "very black" old woman, named Lisa Jane, who seeks the eminent citizen's assistance in order to find her husband, Sam Taylor. The latter, a young mulatto she had married when a slave (10), had disappeared during the confusion of the Civil War, twenty-five years before. Ryder is visibly startled at being shown Taylor's photograph. Once alone, he stands before his mirror "gazing thoughtfully at the reflection of his own face" (17). At the ball itself, Ryder holds a speech about devotion and faithfulness, using Lisa Jane's story as a parable. He then discloses that he is Sam Taylor himself, and that Lisa Jane is "the wife of his youth." A rather shiftless young man before emancipation, Ryder had gone North after the war and developed into his present prosperous self. Struck by Lisa Jane's devotion, he gives up his engagement to Mrs. Dixon, and resumes his union to the old woman, even if the terms of the former slave marriage are no longer legally binding.

In Jack London's stories of atavism, genealogical encounters are fraught with gothic fear; Chesnutt's tale, however, carries a milder strain of romance. There is of necessity something dreamlike in the irruption of a person coming from what is in the logic of the story a parallel world. Accordingly, Lisa Jane's entry is surrounded with portents of dream and magic—genuine or ironical. Before she arrives, Ryder is reading Tennyson's comically inappropriate "Dream of Fair Women" (8). Once Lisa Jane stands in front of him, she looks "like a bit of the plantation life, summoned up from the past by the wave of a magician's wand" (10). Likewise, in "Cicely's Dream," another of Chesnutt's stories of the color line, premonitory visions play a crucial part as mediating agents between two worlds. Young Cicely, a black North Carolina farmhand, learns in a "delightful dream" (134) that she will make a discovery essential to her future happiness. Soon after, she finds a wounded man lying in the wood, suffering from post-traumatic amnesia. The man, whom Cicely calls John, could pass as either white or black. Cicely falls in love with him, and takes care of his re-education. Yet, when he retrieves his memory, he turns out to be a white man, Captain Arthur Carey from Massachussets. Throughout, Cicely had lived in dread of this negative genealogical epiphany: as a reader of omens, she knew that "some dreams [go] by contraries" (135).

As narrative devices, Chesnutt's genealogical epiphanies activate a dynamic that goes from dreamlike romance toward demystificatory realism. In Chesnutt's "The Wife of His Youth," the resurgence of the antebellum world—Lisa's memories of slavery, her southern dialect—has a ring of authenticity that brings in sharp relief the social ambitions of middle-class protagonists who feel "more white than black" (1). In broader allegorical terms, the confrontation of past and present makes visible the double consciousness that affects blacks after slavery and keeps them toggling between parallel, unequal worlds. The demystificatory gesture initiated by the genealogical encounter carries a comic potential: Chesnutt exploits the comedy that can be derived from characters who ape manners borrowed from a dominant group, and who fail to acknowledge that they thereby reinscribe an ethnic boundary within their own community.

With their interweaving of oneiric and realistic elements, stories of the color line appear as ironical variants of the romance. Fredric Jameson argues that the nineteenth-century texts influenced by the romance juxtapose the magic and the commonplace (*Political* 144). He contends that this form of literary heterogeneity is the product of "transitional moments" in history—periods characterized by the "uneven development" of modes of production (148, 141). In this view, the romance is an ideological response to a historical situation where "an organic social order" is in the process of being displaced "by nascent capitalism," while still "coexisting with the latter" (148). Accordingly, what lies behind the discontinuities of Chesnutt's stories is the unequal contrast between the agrarian South and the urban North—two worlds that the stories rewrite respectively as a site of romance and as a down-to-earth realm of money making and social competition. In this logic, the North/South geographical dichotomy is overdetermined in that it comes to signify also class and ethnic difference: poor Southern blacks are, in Chesnutt's stories, opposed to affluent Northern mulattoes.

Jameson's model brings out the similarities that link stories of the color line to immigrant fiction: genealogical epiphanies in each tradition originate in an encounter between, schematically, the mode of production of the country (or of the small town) and, on the other hand, the city. Jewish ghetto novelist Abraham Cahan handles this issue from a realist angle, submitting to scrupulous demystification the accents of romance evoked by the confrontation of Old and New worlds. Cahan's *Yekl, A Tale of the Ghetto* (1896) narrates the failed reunion of Jake, a young Jewish garment worker, and his wife and son Gitl and Yosselé, who come from the Russian village of Povodye. The story is set in the East Side ghetto—a world of workshops, popular leisure, and streets teeming with "panting, chattering . . . multitudes" (30). In this context Jake appears as a carefree young man who flaunts such newly acquired American mannerisms as an expertise in baseball and boxing. After work, Jake leads "a general life of gallantry" (52): at Professor Peltner's dancing school, he meets women friends—Mamie and Fanny, who are unaware of the fact that he has a wife and child in Russia. Yet Jake soon finds himself "in the grip of his past" (50). As genealogical narratives go, his life in Povodye with Gitl and Yosselé now appears to him as "a dream" (59) or "a charming tale which he was willing neither to banish from his memory nor able to reconcile with the actualities of his American present" (55). At the death of his father, however, he resolves to buy transatlantic tickets for his family. In Ellis Island, Gitl is "overcome with a feeling akin to awe" (76) when she beholds her husband, now a "stylish young man" dressed and shaved as only noblemen do in Povodye. Jake however, sees in Gitl a "dowdyish little greenhorn" (75) wearing a "wig of pitch-black hue" (71) that, with her dark complexion, lends her "resemblance to a squaw" (72). The spouses are so dissimilar that the customs officer doubts whether they are "actually man and wife" (73). In spite of harrowing efforts, Gitl never becomes Americanized enough to suit Jake's taste, so that the story ends in divorce. Following the pattern of the marriage of reduced expectation, Gitl remarries a more orthodox, older man. Jake ends up reluctantly marrying Mamie, the more cynical and money-minded of the young man's girlfriends.

In *Yekl*, genealogical anxiety and its concomitant romance motifs manifest themselves both in the grotesque pairing of Gitl and Yekl, and in the cultural duality that affects each protagonist. Gitl's befuddlement on landing in New York is, characteristically, due to her inability to make two separate beings—"her own Yekl and Jake the stranger"—merge into "one undivided being" (87). Likewise, characters in the ghetto have two names—Yekl/Jake; Yosselé/Joey—testifying to Old and New World allegiances. In this context, sartorial transformations act as quasi-magical devices by which characters hope to toggle between their split-off selves. When Gitl lets one of her neighbors—her fairy-tale adjuvant, as it were—dress her up New York style, she beholds in the mirror a face that strikes her "as unfamiliar and forbidding" (143); however, "the change please[s] her as much as it startle[s] her" (143). Neither this sartorial metamorphosis nor even a love potion will, unfortunately, secure Jake's affections. Yet, through these superstitious gestures, Gitl manages to *"oysgreen"* herself—to shed part of her Old World persona—and to marry Mr. Bernstein (104).

Cahan handles the romance twists of Yekl and Gitl's story with the deliberate irony of a narrator well-acquainted with the shortcomings and assets of the two realms of experience described in his text: both the Old World and the New are, depending on the characters' perspective, endowed with exaggerated appeal or uncanniness. Whereas Jake discovers that the dreamlike world of Povodye can still affect him in New York, Gitl, like Norris's McTeague, feels surrounded by household appliances that seem to stare at her "contemptuously" and "haughtily" (90). Overall, either form of magic cancels the other. Ironical demystification is possible here, as it is in Chesnutt and Hopkins, because the story charts the genealogical interactions of characters hailing from knowable communities: though dreamlike in its remoteness, the Old World or agrarian past remains a sufficiently familiar world; likewise, the urban present of these tales—a neighborhood or a well-structured community—works according to rituals whose pretensions can be debunked.

The discourse of naturalism can understandably not hold on to the configuration of the knowable community that informs Chesnutt's and Cahan's ironical genealogies. In hereditarian science the pastoral past appears as an unattainable social anchorage invoked for nostalgic or reactionary purposes. For instance, prison reformer H. M. Boies, in his *Prisoners and Paupers*, justifies his commitment to eugenic reform by invoking the primacy of rural domesticity, which alone can safeguard "the privacy and completeness of . . . domestic relations" (95). Boies's program of reproductive regulations works at cross-purposes with his ideology of small-town rootedness, however, since it necessitates a massive intervention by urban-based experts. Likewise, Jacob Riis's investigations of New York immigrants indicate that the representation of urban ethnicity through naturalist discourse subverts the logic of knowable space. *How the Other Half Lives*, Riis's account of tenement life, adheres to the realist epistemology of the familiar world in that it represents the slums as an aggregate of small towns, described in chapters entitled "Chinatown" or "Jewtown," for instance (77, 85). The representation of race implied thereby is highly compartmentalized: Riis tries to reduce the otherness of immigrants by anchoring them geographicaly—by streets and neighborhoods—and by characterizing them through catalogs of xenophobic clichés—Jews can be recognized from "their unmistakable physiognomy" (84), Bohemians have no propensity for crime, and so on. This territorial logic is epitomized in Riis's statement that his survey produces "a map of the city, colored to designate nationalities" (20)—a map that, by his own admission turns out out to be a "crazy quilt" (22).

However, we have seen in Howells's *A Hazard of New Fortunes* that the spectacle of the New York tenements tends to defeat attempts at classificatory containment: in Howells, the protagonist never managed to interpret ethnic diversity in terms of his own experience. In *How the Other Half Lives*, the failure to bring immigrant life within the realm of the familiar is noticeable in Riis's description of Chinatown: Asians are "monstrous" and "cat-like" pagans, Riis contends, because they spread the poison of the "accursed" opium pipe (80), enticing to their perdition "girls hardly yet grown to womanhood" (80); in this traffic, Chinese laundries serve as "outposts of Chinatown . . . scattered all over the city, as the outer thread of the spider's web that holds its prey fast" (80). Here, Riis adopts the tropes of contagion we have encountered in Jack London's naturalist gothic: by implying that the whole of New York is crisscrossed by hidden continuities and secret channels, eluding the authority of white men, he constructs for the Chinese an ethnic profile fueled by racial, sexual, and economic paranoia.

The uncanny connotations of Riis's portrayal of the Chinese are produced by means of a mechanics of open-ended overdetermination. In this context, overdetermination amounts to a system of genealogical *mise-en-abyme:* markers of ethnicity signify sexual perversion, which in turn signify an uncanny economic power, which is itself rooted in an unrepresentable urban field. Thus, the unfamiliar features of urban dwellers are not the expression of a hidden knowable world, as was the case in Chesnutt and Cahan, but are synecdoches of the more elusive otherness that naturalist texts attribute to the urban sphere as a whole. This type of characterization, which is central to the racial discourse of naturalism, endows protagonists with what I wish to call genealogical auras—sets of markers pointing to obscure ethnic, class, or gender affiliations. The genealogical aura, in my definition, performs similar ideological functions as atavism without being tied to explicit allegorical signifiers: its meaning is not necessarily embodied in prehistoric ancestors, Old World doubles, or underclass grotesques like Dugdale's Jukes clan. This textual device presupposes that, in a society deprived of genealogical legibility, individuals may find themselves linked across class and ethnic barriers by degenerative hereditarian chains. In this, the ethnic prejudices expressed by genealogical auras are a sign of distrust toward all aspects of the city's relations of interdependence.

The view that ethnic difference is anchored in an uncanny citywide field informs *The Valley of the Moon*, the novel in which Jack London most clearly articulates his nativist discourse: this narrative is structured as a sequence of positive or negative genealogical epiphanies, in which the protagonists, Saxon and Billy, encounter fellow Anglo-Saxons or enigmatic immigrants. We have seen that Saxon and Billy feel threatened by Portuguese immigrants, Adriatic Slavs, or Chinese-American farmers primarily because of the latter's higher economic performance and better knowledge of agriculture. Still, London's racial discourse backs this economic explanation with a less positivistic argument: when it comes to raising crops, the Portuguese have got "the sabe" (310), just as the Adriatic Slavs "have a way with apples" (364). How the Chinese manage to have an intimate knowledge both of crops and of the market "is beyond me," confesses a bedazzled commission merchant to Billy (424). In these lines, economic fears are transcoded into the nativist motif of the inscrutable Oriental: the Chinese are, first, attributed an intuitive affinity with two mysterious areas of sublime economics—the commodity market and agriculture; then, the novel rewrites this economic skill as a stigma of racial difference, thus fleshing out their genealogical aura. The ambivalence of the text is absolute in this case: the skills of the Chinese would pass as providential intuition if they were held by the Anglos; in Dreiser, they represent the very formula of Carrie Meeber's ascension. Yet, when embodied in the successful Chinese, they can only evoke the mysterious side of urban economics.

Anglo-Saxon manhood is for London and Norris the antidote to ethnic otherness. I have indicated how important the assertion of Anglo-Saxonism was in *The Valley of the Moon*, where the two protagonists' quest is motivated by the desire to reclaim the male American yeoman's lifestyle against the pressure of immigration. In the present discussion of genealogies, I wish to untangle the complex pattern of overdetermination by which Norris's wheat novel *The Octopus* defines both Anglo-Saxon and non-white identities: ethnicity in Norris's text is constructed against the background of a polity dominated by insurrectional mobs, economic speculation, and overcivilization; it is therefore fleshed out by the sublime discourse Norris uses for the representation of the powers of nature, of economic forces, and of primitivistic violence.[11]

In *The Octopus*, Anglo-Saxon men are supposed to exorcize from their own behavior psychological traits that are otherwise embodied in chaotic political crowds. Norris's novel depicts masses in terms that, I indicate in chapter 11, fit a naturalist crowd sociology based on hypnosis. Crowds, in this logic, are abjectly submissive and, conversely, prone to irrational primitive aggression. This characterization, which fulfills the paradoxical logic of naturalist gothic, is illustrated through animal allegories: on the one hand, the weakness of mobs is signified in a sheep-gathering scene and a jack-rabbit chase. There, Norris associates the formation of crowds with a regressive process of disindividuation, experienced as a loss of masculinity. The sheep, when herded together, are "no longer an aggregate of individuals" but "a . . . slowly moving mass, huge, without form" (31). Likewise, as a mass, the rabbits lose "all wildness, all fear of man" (502). Their revolting powerlessness expresses itself in olfactory form, through the "warm, ammoniacal odour of the thousands of crowding bodies" (31). The activist component of the mass, on the other hand, is the "human animal . . . with bared teeth and upraised claw" (272) that manifests itself in the political wrath of Norris's ranchers. We should however not mistake the "hideous squealing of the tormented brute" (272) for a proper masculine antidote to gregariousness: manhood in *The Octopus* is embodied in figures of self-control. The ranchers' rebelliousness offers, on the contrary, a spectacle of degeneration: it is an expression of disenfranchised masculinity driven to hysteria. Thus, the crowd carries a form of gender perversion in which aggression is vented in the language of weakness.

The instinctual disorder of the crowd is, for Norris, a characteristic of non-whites. The text needs to frame mass behavior in such racial terms because its Anglo-Saxon characters—the California ranchers—are themselves political insurgents. Thus, Norris's construction of ethnicity provides the strategy of containment that stipulates how far the farmers' political resistance may go. This ideological gesture is allegorized in caricatural terms in the jack-rabbit chase, where the Anglo-Saxon farmers do most of the hunting, but leave Mexicans and Mediterranean immigrants in charge of a slaughter from which even dogs shy away. By attributing the actual killing to "the hot, degenerated blood of Portuguese, Mexican, and mixed Spaniard" (502), Norris's Anglo-Saxonism covers up the genealogical continuity that links the Anglo-Saxon "People" to the violent impulses mobilized in their own political protest: in their actions against the trusts, the farmers appear indeed as a growling "awakened brute" (273).

Besides the political crowd, the capitalist corporation constitutes the other sublime body that threatens to engulf Anglo-Saxon manhood. The planetary lure of the trust is made explicit in a passage where Magnus Derrick and his son Harran watch in fascination the ticker tape announcing the latest fluctuations of the Chicago wheat pits. "At such moments," Norris writes, the farmers "no longer felt their individuality. The ranch became merely the part of an enormous whole, a unit in the vast agglomeration of wheat land the whole world round, feeling the effects of causes thousands of miles distant" (54). In these lines, Norris uses the sublimity speech acts that, I pointed out previously, make all large economic forces depicted in his text mutually translatable: the dread of the immense land is made identical to the fear of the trust—and, in a further allegorical echo, to the peril of industrial crowds.

Behind the novel's allegorical evocation of the trust lurks the fear that the farmers might not be able to preserve their masculine autonomy toward a sublime entity with which they experience deep-seated affinities. Norris's text exorcizes these anxieties by creating a character who condenses different facets of overcivilization—gender ambiguity, acquiescence to market capitalism—and who can simultaneously be branded as un-Anglo-Saxon. This scapegoat is Lyman Derrick, the renegade son of Magnus Derrick, the ranchers' leader. Lyman is a corrupt attorney who ends up selling out to the cause of the railroad. He is depicted as a "well-dressed, city-bred young man" (439)—a feminized mother's child who "had inherited from [his mother] a distaste for agriculture and a tendency toward a profession" (74). The mother's influence endowed Lyman with an unmanly "talent for intrigue"(74), illustrated in his predilection for "caucuses, compromises and expedients" (75). Lyman's departure from Norris's notion of Anglo-Saxon masculinity is, in a crude derogatory gesture, signified by the fact that the attorney has a slightly swarthy complexion—a "dago face," as one of the irate farmers puts it (447). His dark skin tone grants Lyman Derrick a genealogical aura that makes him as suspiciously alien as the economic forces he embodies. As such, it marks him out from other Anglo-Saxons—his father, the poet Presley, the engineer Annixter—who negotiate the lure of the trust with more dignity.

The mechanism of overdetermination that makes the surprisingly racist portrayal of Lyman Derrick possible presupposes that the farmers' economic universe is a network of semi-magical connections, where all energies interface. Only thus is it possible to sketch out, as Norris does,

subtle correspondences between Lyman's swarthy complexion, the Anglo-Saxon shape of Magnus Derrick's nose, the Mexicans' lust for killing, the crowds of jack-rabbits, and the proliferation of the Wheat, channeled through planetary markets. The paranoid belief that any sign of
ethnic otherness resonates with all other mysterious aspects of the urban world is, I wish to argue, the specific contribution of naturalist gothic
to late-nineteenth-century racialism and nativism. The defensive character of this reactionary political idiom is visible in the fact that, as it
denounces the uncanny traits of urban populations, it promotes a back-
ward-looking nostalgia—yearnings for a simpler small-town world, for
frontier manhood. It is as such a form of discourse that could be appropriated for what James T. Patterson has called the "narrow visions" of
Progressivism—the "nativist, self-interested side" of pre–World War I
discourse (61).

The Politics of
Hypnotic Persuasion

Mesmeric Crowds: Le Bon's *The Group Mind* and London's *The Iron Heel*

With their sensationalist imagery and their calls for class and ethnic paranoia, the genealogies of urban gothic corroborate the idea that naturalism cannot transcend the fascination and terror of the city: it can only support a failed variety of the sublime that keeps readers and writers locked in powerless ambivalence toward the urban spectacle. Yet the naturalist failure to depict the full depth and scope of city life cannot accurately be assessed without factoring in aspects of turn-of-the-century fiction that strive against the image of observers paralyzed by dread. The naturalist sublime follows indeed the pattern set by Dreiser in *Sister Carrie*, where the city proves fatal for one character but beneficial for another. Likewise, Mark Seltzer, commenting on Norris, argues that the confrontation with the degenerated naturalist brute can trigger a dialectic of revitalization (38). I wish to show therefore that, alongside the narratives of degeneration, it is necessary to describe naturalist stories of regeneration in which the experience of gothic fear leads, tentatively, to empowerment. We will see that these stories find their field of application in the portrayal of politics and art.

In the present chapter, I wish to examine the narratives of regeneration that focus on the interaction of crowds and political leaders. There is in late-nineteenth- and early-twentieth-century American fiction a corpus of texts—from Henry James's *The Bostonians* to pre–World War I socialist novels—that elaborate what might be called a politics of the mesmeric voice. Drawing on the turn-of-the-century interest in hypnosis, these works suggest that the energies of urban masses can be channeled by the charismatic power of individuals with quasi-superhuman oratorical gifts. It is difficult for post–World War II readers not to notice in these naturalist eulogies of superhuman orators the disagreeable ring of totalitarian politics; in this reading, naturalism, by its emphasis on political charisma, contributes to a form of totalitarian discourse that views alienated masses as amenable only to forcible control; the discourse of oratory constitutes therefore another proto-fascistic feature of the genre, on a par with Norris's and London's nativism, primitivism, and male supremacy. Though I acknowledge the relevance of this view, I believe also that the naturalist thematics of charisma was mobilized for too many dissimilar projects to be subsumed exclusively as a totalitarian feature. It would indeed be difficult in this case to determine why Henry James portrayed political charisma as inimical to genteel culture, or why Jack London, Hamlin Garland, and Upton Sinclair made the politics of charisma the main vehicle for populist, Progressivist, or socialist fiction.

The existence of hypnotic phenomena—suggestion, fascination, animal magnetism, or even spiritism—is seldom thematized in naturalist fiction—much less so than the superman doctrine, for instance. What Dreiser calls the "mesmeric operation of super-intelligible forces" seems to be taken for granted to such an extent that it needs no elucidation (*Carrie* Pennsylvania 78). Yet naturalist novels hold very high stakes in the deployment of a psychology of suggestion. Acknowledging the presence of unconscious impulses in personal or social life, the novelists elaborate a mechanism that enables strong individualities to influence others at a distance, and that also ensures the transferrability of psychological magnetism and instinctual currents.

Hypnotic fascination in naturalism is activated when characters or narrators are confronted with spectacles—the crowd, typically—that evoke the untotalizable urban scene. In Stephen Crane's *Maggie, A Girl of the Streets*, the heroine's brother Jimmie, a tough young teamster, falls "into a sort of trance of observation" (15) when he gets caught among the "multitude of drivers" (15) in the New York traffic; in these moments, he "fix[es] his eyes on a high and distant object" (15) and orders his horses to plough through the hordes of "pestering flies" below (15). Likewise, in Frank Norris's *The Pit*, mesmeric paralysis overcomes men who face the chaos of the Board of Trade. The urban mass arouses these feelings because, in its very graphic presence, it constitutes an object that simultaneously symbolizes the recovered totality of social life and the impossibility of piecing together its freakish, fascinating components. As a deceptively retotalizable field, the multitude both lulls the self into hypnotic torpor and fosters the illusion that the fragmentation of the urban experience could still be resolved by the intermission of the unusual power of mesmeric personalities. In this fantasy of control, naturalist mesmerism acts as an exacerbated avatar of the *flâneur*'s gaze, as Walter Benjamin describes it. Benjamin portrays the mass as a "phantasmagoria"—a spectacle for detached, "estranged" *flâneurs*, sensitive to the narcotic pull of the urban scene (*Reflections* 156). In a more activist variant of this stance, the naturalist discourse of mesmerism expresses the utopian aspiration that the mesmeric intensities of the throng might be appropriated and rerouted for the observer's own purposes.

⁂

Turn-of-the-century psychologists and sociologists concurred with naturalist novelists in arguing that hypnosis constitutes the driving force in the psychology of the urban masses. For this part of my argument, I discuss two theorists of hypnosis—Gustave Le Bon and Sigmund Freud—in parallel with two turn-of-the-century novels—Jack London's *The Iron Heel* (1908) and Henry James's *The Bostonians* (1886)—whose treatment of mesmeric phenomena closely overlaps with Le Bon and Freud. I mean to show thereby that the naturalist discourse of mesmerism develops along two axes: Le Bon and London, for instance, provide sensationalistic accounts of the hypnotic intensities of the crowd without clearly indicating how these energies can be organized; James and Freud, on the other hand, analyze the hierarchical mechanisms that allow charismatic leaders to rise out of the crowd and take control over their constituencies.

In his *The Crowd: A Study of the Popular Mind* (1895), French sociologist Gustave Le Bon developed a brand of mass psychology whose tropes and ideological assumptions converge with the discourse of French or American fiction. Like the naturalist novelists, Le Bon attempts to define the form of leadership that can stand up to oceanic multitudes. Reflecting on the political violence of the French Revolution, he stigma-

tizes the dangers of what he calls "the era of crowds" (14)—presumably
the rise of the turn-of-the-century labor movement. His argument starts
off from the realization—familiar to sociologists—that "under certain
given circumstances . . . an agglomeration of men presents new characteristics very different from those of the individuals composing it" (23).
From this premise, he elaborates a typology of group behavior in which
the crowd is portrayed as essentially regressive from a psychological and
an evolutionary point of view: individuals in the crowd are lowered to
the status of "women, savages, and children" (36); they descend "several rungs in the ladder of civilization" (32), live in a realm of wish fulfillment, and forsake any sense of individuality and moral inhibitions.

Le Bon interprets the fusional character of the crowd as a hypnotic
phenomenon that can only be counteracted by a stronger force of suggestion. The crowd's regression is due to the fact that members of the
group fall into a state of trance that leaves them powerless with regard
to those who wish to manipulate their unconscious desires. The author
offers several near-synonymic terms for this hypnotic energy: magnetic
influence, paralysis of the brain, fascination, suggestibility, and contagion
(31). By organizing his argument around the concept of contagion—the
spontaneous tendency of the mass to hypnotize itself—Le Bon confers
to his vision of the crowd the oceanic aura that is predominant in American naturalism: the multitude is pictured as an overwhelming field of
magnetic influences; hypnosis arises mostly *from* the crowd, so that no
one is immune to its delocalized magnetism. However, against the prospect of "being devoured" (102) by these mesmeric multitudes, Le Bon
underlines the necessity of grooming new leaders—heroes who, like
Napoleon, are "unconscious psychologists, possessed of an instinctive
and often very sure knowledge of the characters of crowds" (19). The
defining characteristic of the leader is what Le Bon calls "prestige"—the
ability to feed on the hypnotic power of the crowd and thereby to mes-
merize it into subjection. Prestige is the foundation of what he calls "the
mysterious power" (62) of crowd persuasion—political oratory. Through
their mastery of language, Le Bon claims, political speakers can "cause
the birth in the minds of crowds of the most formidable tempests, which
in turn they are capable of stilling" (62). Mass politics in this perspective amounts to an efficient management of the mesmeric word.

The dialectic of urban masses and their leaders theorized by Le Bon
is strikingly portrayed in Jack London's *The Iron Heel* (1908). This novel of political anticipation provides a pessimistic appraisal of the future
of the class struggle in America. Its protagonists, Ernest Everhard and

his wife Avis, are agents of a socialist underground, the Brotherhood of Man. As such, they are struggling against the Iron Heel—a capitalist dictatorship that is taking over the American republic.[1] In London's narrative, Ernest and Avis rise to the status of quasi-superhuman guerilla fighters by struggling against fascistic militias and facing the fury of oceanic crowds. The high point of Avis's political education is indeed the scene where she witnesses a failed rebellion of thousands of grotesque Chicago slum dwellers.

Like Le Bon's treatise, *The Iron Heel* singles out political oratory and the spectacle of human mobs as objects of mesmeric fascination. The seduction of oratory is embodied in the figure of Ernest, an ex-horseshoer turned Marxist philosopher/activist. Ernest is "an intellectual swashbuckler" (337) who once served as a "soap-box orator" (338) and has developed into a socialist lecturer intent on shaking middle-class audiences out of their complacency. Like most of London's working-class protagonists, Ernest is endowed with "bulging muscles and [a] prize fighter's throat" (337). Suitably, Avis, initially a genteel professor's daughter, is seduced not only by Ernest's leftist political ideas but more pointedly by the "clarion-call" (327) or the "war note in his voice" (339), which feeds on his conspicuous physical strength. Ernest's oratorical "masterfulness," Avis reveals, "delighted . . . and terrified" her, so that her "fancies roved wantonly until [she] found [herself] considering him as a lover, as a husband" (339). Shortly after Avis meets Ernest, the young woman lies awake at night "listening in memory to the sound of his voice" (339). This characterization, whose sublime imagery blends political and erotic appeal, is epitomized in Avis's confession that she "longed to see [Ernest] master men in discussion" (339).

Described in those terms, Ernest's oratorical prestige is based on conflicting psychological resources. On the one hand, Ernest fulfills the rationalistic legacy of Marxian socialism: he is "a born expositor and a teacher," and is graced with "a certain clear way of stating the abstruse in simple language" (338). Yet he is also a Nietzschean "blond beast . . . aflame with democracy" (326), that is a "superman" (326) protagonist whose paradoxical charisma is altogether too violent to serve the pure light of understanding. Avis pointedly remarks that "no ready-made suit of clothes ever could fit Ernest's body" (325). Likewise, the libidinal energies that radiate from Ernest's "heavy shoulder development" (325) threaten to burst the rational framework of London's didactic narrative: they align him with darker, gothic powers. Small wonder then that Ernest, when he addresses the ultra-conservative Philomath club, should deliver a "terrible diatribe" (375) that fails to win his upper-class hearers over to socialism; rather, his words awaken in them the "snarl" of the brute (339)—"the growl of the pack, mouthed by the pack, and mouthed in all unconsciousness" (376). In the vocabulary of naturalist genealogies outlined above, we might conclude that Ernest's fascinating oratory, supported by his awesome physicality, speaks to the most regressive recesses of his audience's genealogical aura.

Overall, the primitivistic tropes that construct Ernest's power create uncanny rhetorical associations between elements that the narrative should logically keep distinct: on the one hand the socialist revolutionary is depicted in the same terms as the social Darwinian capitalists and on the other he is associated with the most threateningly mesmeric body depicted in the text—the urban crowd itself. The latter link is an indirect one, established through rhetorical similarities rather than narrative confrontation: Ernest is never actually shown addressing urban masses—only smaller groups of militants or political adversaries; he does not take part in the Chicago insurrection. Even so, the paradigm of militancy embodied in his absent figure is linked to the Chicago crowd in ways that question the very possibility of proletarian leadership: the mob elicits the same gothic intensities as those that, in Ernest's profile, seem antithetical to his professed socialist program. The grotesque nature of the Chicago slum dwellers is advertised in the fact that the insurrection scene takes place in a chapter named "The People of the Abyss," which metafictionally recalls London's East End documentary by the same title. Accordingly, the Chicago crowds are depicted by means of tropes of degeneracy similar to those used by the author for the characterization of Old World poverty. The mob is an "awful river" made up of "the refuse and the scum of life" (*Iron* 535). It exhibits the impossible conflation of physical menace and debilitation that characterizes London's working-class grotesques: the "demoniacal horde" (*Iron* 535) brings together fiendlike "apes and tigers, anaemic consumptives and great hairy beasts of burden, wan faces from which vampire society had sucked the juice of life . . . festering youth and festering age" (535). The questions raised by this characterization are therefore whether any form of prestige can transcend the entropy of the mass and whether leaders can escape being tainted by the mob's abjection.

London's adventure tale is, however, not meant fully to explore this political contradiction. Instead, the novel patches up its discourse of leadership by articulating Avis's confrontation with the Chicago insurgents in the guise of a narrative of regeneration. The heroine, feeding on the mesmeric energies of the mass, achieves a semblance of empowerment. During these riot scenes, Avis acts as an undercover agent wearing the uniform of the Iron Heel militias, so that she is not expected to side with the rioters. Her trajectory through the insurrectional turmoil oscillates between the terror of being "overborne by the crowd" (535), spells of intense activity, and moments of hypnotic fascination when she feels supported by an entranced feeling of immunity. At one point, Avis and Hartman, one of her fellow secret agents, made conspicuous by their middle-class attire, are attacked by an old woman "in fantastic rags," wielding a hatchet in one of her "yellow talon[s]" (536). Avis imagines she is being "torn to pieces" (537) and faints; Hartman is killed in the fray. The aggression seems, however, to find an ambiguous compensation when the heroine, coming to her senses, realizes that the crowd is trampling what she knows is a woman's body—possibly her old aggressor. A mysterious bond is therefore established between the dying woman and Avis herself, as if the protagonist recognized in the sacrificial victim's death the fatal outcome that she has provisionally been spared. From then on, Avis enjoys the feeling of invulnerability of a hypnotized subject. Barely noticing that she is now helped forward by another revolutionary, Garthwaite, her attention is fastened on a fascinating spectacle: "In front of me I could see the moving back of a man's coat. It had been slit from top to bottom along the centre seam, and it pulsed rhythmically, the slit opening and closing regularly with every leap of the wearer. This phenomenon fascinated me for a time" (537). The hypnotic torn coat, soon lost from sight, exerts a mesmerizing power disproportionate to its seemingly anecdotal status. Its importance consists in establishing the existence and efficiency of hypnotic influence itself: the coat bears Avis along through the human flood, as efficiently as Garthwaite's careful guidance. Both the mesmeric garment and Avis's male partner are manifestations of the supportive aura that allows the heroine to survive several brushes with death. At the end of the slaughter, Avis comes across as a romance character who has been graced with magical invincibility: reflecting on the terrible day, she says: "It is all a dream, now, as I look back on it" (538).

Avis's ability to be both detached from and intimate with mob violence marks her first step in the dynamic that leads her from helpless hypnotic fascination to a configuration of the gaze that mingles fascinated detachment with the aspiration toward an activist will-to-power. The degree of mastery she can hope for is made visible in the passage where she experiences a mystical illumination that defines her relationship to the "fascinating spectacle of dread" (535):

And now a strange thing happened to me. A transformation came over me. The fear of death, for myself and for others, left me. I was strangely exalted, another being in another life. Nothing mattered. The Cause for this one time was lost, but the Cause would be here to-morrow, the same Cause, ever fresh and ever burning. And thereafter, in the orgy of the horror that raged through the succeeding hours, I was able to take a calm interest. Death meant nothing, life meant nothing. I was an interested spectator of events, and, sometimes swept on by the rush, was myself a curious participant. For my mind had leaped to a star-cool altitude and grasped a passionless transvaluation of values. Had it not done this, I know that I should have died. (536)

These lines depict the self-absorbed ecstasy of a character who blends the paradoxical traits of the revolutionary and the *flâneur*. The contradictions inherent in this stance appear in the fact that Avis flaunts a mystical detachment that is not borne out by her actual behavior. What passes for detachment from London's or Avis's points of view is the constant effort to negotiate the mesmeric attraction that drags the heroine into the crowd, and, insofar as she absorbs this hypnotic power herself, that helps her rise above the mass, to a "star-cool altitude" (539). Avis's spectatorial fascination is therefore not simply a sign of her surrender to the "awful river" of insurgents "that filled the street" (535) or to the city's deterministic forces; it is a subject position constructed by dint of constant work and fueled by the hope that social others, however overwhelming, could still be reduced to a detached observer's control.

Avis's dream of social mastery conflates two closely related ideological agendas—Nietzschean will-to-power politics and social-science positivism—each of which associated with its own model of leadership. When Avis describes herself as "an interested spectator of events" (536), her detachment is comparable to the paralysis that, June Howard argues, affects turn-of-the-century social science reformers when they survey urban poverty (111). In Howard's logic, these feelings of impotence, camouflaged under a pose of scientific neutrality, lead up to the implementation of a political agenda. In French naturalism, Zola himself emphasizes the connection between scientific observation and activism: in "The Experimental Novel," the French novelist contends that the experimental method requires that observation be followed by commitment to reform—by the desire "to be master of good and evil" (177).[2] In this logic, the practice of writing cements a coalition of scientists and politicians: novelists must become "experimental moralists," whose "practical sociology" is oriented toward social engineering

(177).³ Avis fits this social identity because, even as she casts a cool narrator's eye on the Chicago massacre, she imagines how this debased environment can be reshaped along socialist lines.

Alongside the call for objective spectatorship, Avis's description of her trance foregrounds Nietzschean concepts—the "transvaluation of values" (536) and the eternal return of the same. The "transvaluation"—or, according to Nietzsche's current translator, the "revaluation" (*Twilight* 31)—designates the ethical transcendence that places the Free Spirit beyond good and evil. It matters little here that London borrows these terms indiscriminately, that Nietzsche, unlike Avis, does not associate the transvaluation with detachment:⁴ this technical discourse is meant mostly to signify the narrator's rise to the plane of philosophy itself. As she utters these slogans, Avis takes on the ready-made persona of the artistically oriented tyrants, who, French philosopher Albert Camus argues, fitted Nietzsche's ideal of the Free Spirit (66). Her epiphany embodies therefore a fantasy coalition of writers and politicians, all devoted to elitist aestheticism.

In flaunting these Nietzschean credentials, London emulates pre–World War I intellectuals like Theodore Dreiser and H. L. Mencken, who felt they were witnessing momentous social changes, controllable only by exceptional personalities. For the socialist Jack London, the Nietzschean figures of the Free Spirit and the Superman hold up the promise of acceding to spiritual and instinctual realms beyond the bounds both of genteel morality and of the working class. As such, they give London the constant privilege of merging with and distancing himself from the object of his literary descriptions. In *The Iron Heel*, this flexible subject position is illustrated in Avis's dreamlike ability to switch at a moment's notice between her persona as a scientific revolutionary and as a distanced philosopher. In darker terms, the same ambivalence underlies the fact that she feels as little empathy toward the Chicago slum dwellers as would the middle-class reformers described by Howard. To the heroine, these lumpen proletarians are the unredeemable offspring of a diseased system of exploitation. Thus, it is almost logical to see her contemplating the "orgy of horror" from a standpoint beyond life and death, at the side of the professional killers of the Iron Heel.⁵

Ultimately, the narrative logic of *The Iron Heel* corroborates the fact that Avis's distanced subject position, be it modeled as hypnotic charisma or Nietzschean elitism, is bound to leave unresolved the issue of political empowerment. Two-thirds into the text, Ernest recedes to the margins of the story and leaves the political field to Avis, thus introducing into London's dystopian text the pathos of the absent leader. Meanwhile, Avis, though a remarkably resourceful fighter, fails to acquire through her regeneration the one skill that would enthrone her as a proper mob leader: there is no evidence that she develops the power of sublime oratory.

The Construction of the Charismatic Voice in Freud's Paradigm of Hypnosis and James's *The Bostonians*

As political activists, Ernest and Avis Everhard are caught in a double bind: they are either barely equal to the task of controlling a polity of sublime illegibility, or, if too efficient, are suspected of carrying a demonic power. Le Bon's model of crowd management proves in fact inadequate to address this paradox of leadership. Freud, commenting on Le Bon, remarks that the Frenchman's concept of hypnotic prestige cannot account for the dominance of leaders: by characterizing prestige as a free-floating substance immanent to the group, Le Bon portrays leaders who are on the same footing as the crowd to which they owe their quasi-miraculous power (*Group* 13, 21). Naturalist political novels, on the contrary, need to show that charismatic talent can be constructed, exchanged, and appropriated according to predictable rules, not by the whims of a quasi-mystical principle.

The model of mesmeric influence that fits the naturalist accounts of the construction of charismatic leadership was elaborated, shortly after the naturalist decades, in Freud's *Group Psychology and the Analysis of the Ego* (1921). Group formation in Freud obeys the hierarchical family scenarios of psychoanalysis. In this view, leaders are libidinal objects of identification, whose status is transcendent to the group. Their dominance is justified not by mysterious prestige but by the fact that they occupy a well-defined subject position—they stand in the slot of the paternal superego, an instance that, in *Group Psychology*, Freud still calls the "ego-ideal" (42). By portraying the leader as a superego figure, Freud submits the crowd, which is gendered feminine in Le Bon, to the structuring presence of a dominant father figure. What the psychoanalyst needs to explain, however, is how the individual ego can accept hypnotists and crowd leaders as parental figures: he must elaborate a model of the ego that makes provisions for substitutions of the figure of authority. This mechanism, which Freud calls introjection, is possible because the "ego-ideal" is an abstract paternal instance, which derives its compelling power from "the influence of superior powers, and above all, of parents" (42).

Defined in these inclusive terms, the ego-ideal can function as a site within the ego itself whose slot can be filled by different entities, provided they are cloaked in the haze of respect and dread associated with parental figures.[6] In the case of hypnosis and group formation, an external authority figure is introjected: when a person is overwhelmed by the power of a mesmerist, it means that, for that individual, "the hypnotist has stepped into the place of the ego-ideal" (46). In group formation proper, a much larger number of people introject the same object—the figure of the leader.

Freud's model of the superego provides a telling framework of interpretation for Henry James's *The Bostonians* (1886), which depicts a power struggle among several authority figures for the control of a young oratrix's voice. Verena Tarrant, James's protagonist, displays a talent for eloquence that is considered inspirational by the feminist and radical audiences whose political agenda she helps propagate. She is the paradoxical offspring of a misalliance between Adeline Greenstreet, the daughter of a Bostonian abolitionist family, and Selah Tarrant, a mesmeric healer whom one character depicts as "cunning, vulgar, [and] ignoble" (82). The chief contenders for the possession of her gift are Olive Chancellor, a young Bostonian devoted to the feminist cause, and, on the other hand, Olive's cousin Basil Ransom, the scion of Mississippi slave owners. Because of these two characters' rivalry, Verena finds herself entangled in a narrative where political and sentimental interests are closely interwoven. Olive is in love with Verena, and wants to keep her within the feminist fold. Basil lusts after her, and longs to turn her into an icon of southern womanhood; in this guise, her politically dangerous power would no longer serve the forces of reform, while Basil himself could develop into a charismatic propagandist for reactionary causes. Besides Olive and Basil, Verena is pursued by Mathias Pardon, a newspaperman who wants to manage her career, and by Henry Burrage, a sentimental suitor. Henry wants to offer the young woman social prominence and affluence without requiring her to shed her feminist propagandizing. Verena turns down Henry on Olive's insistence, later to find herself subjugated by Basil's entreaties. The ending of James's novel is worthy of a cynical *Bildungsroman*, in which the heroine's mentors develop her gift the better to enslave her: Basil's victory, instead of leading up to a sentimental resolution, points forward to a future of inevitable tears.

Verena's voice is a prized asset because it represents a force that can change power relations both in the private and in the public sphere. Of course, because of the class affiliation of its characters and author, *The*

Bostonians stands at some distance from the naturalist texts that deal directly with the problematic of proletarian masses. Yet James's story represents as social disturbances of the most threatening magnitude any development in the public world that affects the boundaries of genteel domesticity. The novel gives voice to anxieties over the new shape of public space by linking the management of crowds with the regulation of gender: James, like Freud, indicates that hypnosis is the libidinal channel that links an individual's sexual behavior to the vagaries of civic entities like the city's multitudes. In the novel, the political activists that cultivate mesmerism are typecast as "witches and wizards, mediums and spirit-rappers" (37), manipulated by "roaring radicals," "female Jacobins," and "nihilists" (37); cultural chaos in Boston is plotted by hordes of "long-haired men and short-haired women" (94). In this, the novel depicts a situation comparable to what Ann Douglas describes in *The Feminization of American Culture:*[7] a society where intellectual channels like the ministry and literature have slipped into the hands of what James calls a "herd of vociferating women" (75). Conversely, Lynn Wardley argues that the fear of feminization in *The Bostonians* is closely linked to anxieties about urbanization at large. Wardley points out that, in two of his essays, James "associates the sound of women in public life with the various aliens, the proliferating newspapers, and the burgeoning urban crowd" (640). Wardley's description of the affinity of women's voices with urban space circumscribes both the attraction and the danger of Verena's power: at her best, Verena manages to reduce "into a single sentient personality" (*Bostonians* 265) a polity that seems to elude such synthesis. To the male characters of the novel, however, the echo of women's voices in the public sphere betokens a loss of hegemony: "Now embodied, now disembodied," Wardley writes, "voices carry into public spaces where they are all too easily altered" (639).

A channel that mediates between the familiar world of domesticity and the disquieting expanses of the public scene must of necessity be endowed with a paradoxical form of verisimilitude. Accordingly, Verena's voice is portrayed from opposite epistemological perspectives—a mechanistic and a spiritualist one. Robert C. Fuller underlines the importance of the positivist/spiritualist dichotomy in turn-of-the-century debates about mesmerism. He contends that Europeans like Charcot, Breuer, and Freud favored a mechanistic model of the phenomenon, while Americans chose from the very beginning to interpret Anton Mesmer's legacy along mystical lines: they claimed that, through hypnosis, "an individual's 'inner source of feeling' somehow opens the finite mind to transpersonal domains" (211–12). Fuller's dichotomy is highly productive for James's novel, provided we do not overemphasize its geographical logic. From what precedes, it appears that Freud qualifies indeed as a mechanist, but that the European Le Bon fits in many respects the spiritualist mould. The complexity of *The Bostonians*, I wish to argue, resides in the fact that it plays off these two approaches against each other: Verena's power is now taken apart, now regarded as a source of mystery; it straddles therefore the boundary of realistic debunking and naturalist gothic.

The positivistic analysis of suggestion is the stuff of James's satire. The mechanics of spiritualistic inspiration are, in this light, quite down-to-earth: during Dr. Tarrant's spiritual séances, the mesmerist's wife may for instance be required to lend her husband some all-too-material assistance if tables fail to "rise from the ground" and sofas will not "float through the air" (95). Likewise, the mesmeric rapport is activated by crude gesticulations: Verena's repellent father imposes his "long, lean hands" upon the young woman's head in order to "start her up" (81, 78). Overall, James's comedy of demystification fulfills Freud's description of substitutions within the superego: it pictures the coaching of Verena's voice as a ludicrous game of permutations, where a set of mentors—the young woman's parents, Olive Chancellor, Basil himself, or newspapermen like Mathias Pardon—are vying to make the young woman express their own ideological concerns through her miraculous medium. This mechanistic satire debunks the Tarrants' claim that Verena is the channel of an external, spiritual force: when they assert that Verena acts at the bidding of "some power outside" that seems to "flow through her" (80), the Tarrants are trying to hide the fact that their daughter might be a mere parrot, regurgitating the "patches of remembered eloquence" she learned from the "nostrum mongers" who manage her (84, 94).

There are, however, limits to comic demystification in *The Bostonians*: mystical mesmerism is only satirized in those moments when it is associated with feminism. The text can indeed not allow its comic discourse to trivialize a power that Basil wants to capture for his own empowerment. James's narrative must therefore lead us to accept the existence of an otherworldly gift in a realistic environment. This management of mystery and realism fulfills Jameson's description of the thematics of magic in the romance: medieval romances, Jameson indicates, use magic in order to allegorize the confrontation with evil (*Political* 119). The struggle is waged, however, in moral and epistemological ambiguity: good and evil in these texts are not anchored in individuals but delocalized through the channels of white and black magic; the white knight of romance is hard to tell from its black counterpart (131). Later secular avatars of the romance, Jameson indicates, could not handle the supernatural and therefore found substitutes for magic; nineteenth-century novels, for instance, rewrite the elements of magic "as charismatic forces that radiate outward from historic individuals" (131).

In *The Bostonians*, the substantiality of magical power, as well as its ambiguities, are inscribed in the heroine's physique—the concrete manifestation of her charisma. Doctor Prance, a skeptical woman physician, on observing Verena for the first time, is struck by the fact that her mesmeric fascination proceeds from an uncanny mixture of unhealthy ethereality and unbridled vitality: "The value of [Verena's] performance was yet to be proved, but she was certainly very pale, white as women who have that shade of red hair; they look as if their blood had gone into it. There was, however, something rich in the fairness of this young lady; she was strong and supple, there was colour in her lips and eyes, and her tresses, gathered into a complicated coil, seemed to glow with the brightness of her nature" (82). Because Verena displays such an "an odd mixture of elements" (82), her narrative itinerary consists in a process of disambiguation: through a dialectic between sentimentalism and gothic romance, the text separates out the white magic of her inspirational oratory from its darker, disquieting components. Throughout, Verena's "fantastic fairness" (229) remains the guarantee of her inspired voice, in the double sense that it constitutes its visible expression and also its shield: the text needs to reemphasize Verena's beauty almost obsessively, because her striking physique allows the young woman to remain an unusual charismatic figure under the easily recognizable garb of a sentimental heroine. In this way, in spite of the hundreds of pages of fierce attacks against the political values Verena stands for, the young woman is not reduced to the status of a loathsome puppet—like her father is—or to the condition of sexless freak, like her friend Olive.

By having Verena's beauty serve as signifier of her gift, James makes hypnotic influence literally a matter of embodiment and disembodiment. The novel, in its play with ambiguities, suggests that charisma is both tied to Verena and, enigmatically, not hers to control. The young woman's mentors are at first only too eager to believe that she is the sole repository of her spiritual inspiration. In this case, Verena is indeed a figure beyond kinship and class; her charismatic power is immune to the social blemish that affects the daughter of a mesmeric healer of "inexpressibly low" extraction. Olive, who literally buys off the young woman from her trashy parents, believes that Verena is an "incalculable" phenomenon, one of those geniuses created "fresh from the hand of Omnipotence" (133): "It was notorious that great beauties, great geniuses . . . take their own times and places for coming into the world . . . holding from far-off ancestors, or even, perhaps, straight from the divine generosity, much more than from their ugly or stupid progenitors" (132). This mystical expropriation from kinship and class is later echoed in Basil Ransom's outcry that, regardless of where Verena comes from, she is "outside and above all vulgarizing influences" (330).

Once the novel has established that Verena could be extruded from her abject family on legitimate social and aesthetic grounds, it sets up what we might call a traffic in mesmeric power, according to which Verena's gift is entrusted to her several mentors. The farcical scramble among the contestants for Verena's voice—newspaperman Matthias Pardon suggests, for instance, that he and Olive "should run Miss Verena together" (156)—may create the mistaken impression that her power can be exchanged indiscriminately, as Freud's model of hypnosis suggests. The solidity of embodiment is, however, as much a problem for Verena's mentors as the fluidity of disembodiment. The young oratrix is both hypnotizer and hypnotized; she possesses something that others can control, but not reproduce. As such, the relationship that ties her to her mentors cannot be one of complete domination—at least until Basil tears her away from her public career. Olive and Basil will therefore try to graft their authority onto this irreplaceable channel of power in a relationship that oscillates between complementarity and ventriloquism.

Olive is the only mentor whose relationship to Verena initiates a reciprocal "partnership of . . . two minds" (169), likely to enrich the young woman's gift. Their spiritual marriage offers the powerful image of a perfectly reconstituted body—"an organic whole," as Olive puts it (169)—made up of the intense, well-educated, but plain and awkward Olive, and of the beautiful charismatic speaker. This friendship, Olive believes, will allow Verena to develop a "magical voice" (170). It represents indeed a mode of circulation of the charismatic voice that neutralizes the contradictions of disembodiment and embodiment: the union of two intimate friends, it protects Verena against dilution of her precious gift among the urban crowds, and it renders the distinct sensibilities that it brings together productive in their differences.

Basil's capture of Verena's voice requires that the young woman's connection to Olive be severed. This new uprooting of Verena's gift would, however, not be narratively credible if it were motivated exclusively on accounts of Basil's suitability as a love choice. The southerner embodies embattled American manhood, with a revanchist edge. In contrast with Henry Burrage, he fails to meet the standards of sentimental marriage-ability not only because of his poor financial prospects, but also because his southern chivalry conceals a cynical attitude toward matrimony. In order to reverse these unfavorable odds, the text throws a suspicion of lesbianism over the intense friendship that binds Olive and Verena. Eve Kosofsky Sedgwick remarks how difficult it is to make visible James's references to homosexuality, because, in James as in other Victorian novelists, homosexuality remains "unspeakable"; it is referred to only as a "secret" or a "singularity" (*Epistemology* 203). Accordingly, in *The Bostonians*, the image of a lesbian Olive is simultaneously evoked and obscured through evasive language and prurient innuendoes: referring to Olive's sexual identity, Basis wonders, "what sex [is] it, great heaven?" (324). More insidiously, the motives attributed to Olive for buying off Verena from her parents—commitment to feminism, friendship, personal ambition—never quite manage to account for the possessiveness of her love for the young oratrix. The element that definitively throws a shadow of opprobrium on the whole relationship is the account of Olive's bargaining with the Tarrants. In an uncanny instance of self-censorship, the narrator claims that the transaction had "some curious features," but that he has been "forbidden to do more than mention the most striking of these" (176).

Beyond the homophobic attacks, Basil's only asset in the love contest is a dark mesmeric appeal that counterbalances Verena's more utopian form of inspiration. The young man has spellbinding eyes, "dark, deep, and glowing" (36); his head is fit "to be seen above the level of the crowd . . . or even on a bronze medal" (36). Mrs. Birdseye, an old feminist activist, in a gesture of ironical misrecognition, discerns in him the mark of a "genius" (59), as well as the potential to become a leader for the cause of reform (272). In his courtship of Verena, the seductive potential of the Mississippian proves to have the value of a mesmeric "spell" (322), which allows him to cloak "monstrous opinions" in the delightful ring of his "sweet, distinct voice" (322). That this power can take coercive, even violent forms is shown in the scene where Verena relinquishes her former allegiances. Surprised at seeing her feminist convictions crumble, Verena feels that "it must be a magical touch that could bring about such a cataclysm" (375). At the end of the scene, the transfer of power is figured symbolically by Verena's realization that the "wizard's wand" (375) she held in her pocket has been spirited away by her lover's spell. More ominous still, *The Bostonians* takes for granted the existence of a brutal world of instincts underlying the rituals of seduction. This violence creeps into the text in the indirect description of a boating trip with Basil from which Verena returns physically unscathed, but shattered, "crushed and humbled" (399). Olive interprets her friend's mood as "a kind of shame, shame for her weakness, her swift surrender" to Basil's call (399). Verena herself wishes "to keep the darkness" over an incident, which could be interpreted as rape.

When the novel closes, Basil has won the contest of mesmeric influence: Verena's gift is about to be bottled up in the private sphere where it poses no danger to patriarchy. This ending is, however, plagued with dissonances; throughout the text, the narrative interest is tied to Basil's strenuous path of seduction; yet the novel does not seriously attempt to make Verena's confinement desirable. Basil's prophecy that she "won't sing in the Music Hall" (393) but rather for his private pleasure compares poorly with the glowing descriptions of her public oratory. Conversely, the beginnings of Basil's life as an author of reactionary tracts promise only a modest form of empowerment, as does the barely sketched possibility that Olive might become a speaker of her own. Lynn Wardley resolves this lack of narrative closure by pointing out that, contrary to what the novel might suggest, James's essays do not advocate the return of cultivated women to the domestic sphere (640): in the age of incorporation and urbanization, the novelist indicates that the reproduction of culture should be performed by women in public institutions. In this logic, the dissonant ending is satirical, as it makes fun of the absurdity of Basil's domestic ideal. Still, I think that the text makes us feel a sense of loss at Verena's humiliation that exceeds anything a satirical ending could inspire. I believe therefore that James develops through his discourse of mesmerism what we might call a dystopia of desire: with the detachment of cynicism, we are invited to witness a purposeless play of forces, in which the feminists' ambitions are countered by Basil's ruthless power of seduction.

Shadow Communities of Oratory and Romance

When *The Bostonians* alludes to Verena's power of uniting audiences by means of her mesmeric speeches, the text implies that the function of oratory is community building. James handles this thematics negatively, of course. Instead of celebrating the unanimistic entity thus created, he chronicles a retreat to the micropolitics of domestic patriarchy; conversely, his novel envisages crowds only in terms of lack and unaccountable excess: public space in *The Bostonians*, Lynn Wardley points out, echoes with the voices of presumably weak, though unnaturally empowered women (640). However, regardless of James's commitment to genteel patriarchy, his analysis of the new American public sphere defines the issues with which populist and socialist novelists like Hamlin Garland, Upton Sinclair, Charlotte Teller, and Arthur Bullard have to grapple when they depict communities of oratory. In particular, James expresses through his anti-feminist rhetoric the insight that the turn-of-the-century city is a phantomlike community in absentia; his decision to endow public space, crowds, and mass culture with stereotypically feminine attributes like uncanniness and instability betokens a generalized anxiety toward the city's social bonds. The urban field—particularly the areas beyond the horizon of middle-class observers—are in this logic not amenable to control, and can therefore not be made present within literary discourse.

In *The Bostonians*, as in later naturalist novels, uncanny oratory is a tool of political pseudo-totalization in that it mediates between the visible features of urban life and what we might call the shadow communities of the sublime city. To borrow Jacques Derrida's terminology, we may argue that the mesmeric voice performs on a social level a management of presence and absence. The post-structuralist philosopher contends that the construction of meaning in language is dependent on mechanisms of representation that presuppose absence—the absence of the object of discourse, of the speaker, of the moment of utterance (*"Speech"* 54, 65, 68, 76, 85). In this perspective, hypnotic speech is supported by the most candid of all voices: unlike everyday language, it lays no claim to self-presence; Le Bon's and Freud's paradigms reveal indeed that the mesmeric voice owes its uncanny power to its relation to an absent exteriority—a fascinating source beyond the speaker him- or herself. In *The Bostonians*, for instance, the play of embodiment and disembodiment that characterizes the circulation of Verena's gift—the fact that her voice is never fully anchored in her body nor totally disseminated—makes visible the intermingling of presence and non-presence that Derrida calls "the process of death at work in signs" (*"Speech"* 40).[8] This *différance* within inspirational oratory is, I think, the more detectable if speech is shaped by the heterocultural urban-industrial field—if the charismatic politician must, as Upton Sinclair puts it, "speak with the voice of the millions who are voiceless" (359). In a Bakhtinian perspective, the otherness in language that Derrida calls death is therefore the evidence of the dialogization of discourse, the trace in a given voice of shadow communities and their alien idioms.

Representing shadow communities can, however, not be carried out within the bounds of realist discourse. By developing a thematics of hidden constituencies, the texts tip over into romance and sublime ambivalence; they elaborate what Jameson would call a politics of white or black magic, depending on whether the totalizing image of the city they conjure up is a utopian or a dystopian one. Benjamin's essay "The Storyteller," a text whose relevance to naturalism I emphasized in chapter 4, indicates what white magic amounts to in the field of political oratory. The German critic's storytellers derive their charismatic appeal from the fact that, through their craft, they help the members of their community integrate otherness within their own tradition. The storyteller, Benjamin writes, weaves "into the fabric of real life" experiences that are literally or metaphorically distant—anecdotes from faraway countries, or, more typically, death itself (*Illuminations* 86–87). The social practice depicted by Benjamin is tied to the context of knowable communities—to groups of pre-industrial craftsmen and merchants. The "incomparable aura" (109) of traditional tales—their mysterious synthesis of availability and distance—is indeed the creation of storytellers who have the opportunity to be "rooted in the people" (101). Thus, it is as if the shadow community evoked by the pre-industrial storyteller were the total horizon of the knowable group itself, reconstituting in its collective memory a tradition that no radical otherness should threaten.

Compared to Benjamin's storytellers, orators in city novels must be endowed with what might be called a surrogate or a prosthetic aura: they must acquire sublime, larger-than-life inspirational powers commensurate to an absent, disembodied polity. Oratory of this kind seems to come, as Henry James puts it, "from behind the scenes of the world" (*Bostonians* 84). It carries an aura of black magic because it reveals to knowable groups their connections with social others, or, even more pessimistically, because it shows the impossibility of federating within one voice the fragments of the industrial city. By the same token, mesmeric speakers who serve as channels for such defamiliarizing social epiphanies cannot lay claim to the status of rooted, organic representatives of their constituencies. Accordingly, narratives of oratory are, like James's *The Bostonians*, propelled by a dialectic of suspicion and disambiguation: characters must figure out whether the charismatic figure is an agent of good or evil.

The corpus for the present discussion of communities of oratory includes Hamlin Garland's populist novel *A Spoil of Office* (1897), as well

as three socialist texts—Upton Sinclair's *The Jungle* (1906), Charlotte
Teller's *The Cage* (1907), and Arthur Bullard's *Comrade Yetta* (1913). In
these works, sublime oratory divides thematically into two branches,
devoted to making visible, respectively, shadow communities of a political and of a reproductive type. The former narratives—Sinclair's and
Garland's works—aim at establishing their political utopia by means of
cultural or political channels. On the other hand, texts that rely on the
reproductive sublime present charismatic figures that act as heralds of a
vitalist cosmos linking present-day society to a virtual community of
ancestors and descendents. Each form of discourse can coexist and over-
lap within the same texts. In the reading of Sinclair's *The Jungle*, for instance, I privilege the cultural and political dimension of the problematic of retotalization. In Teller and Bullard, whose works are devoted for
the most part to union militancy, I point out how paeans to the reproductive community can be used as an alternative—usually a conservative
one—to the project of political reform.

A Spoil of Office

Hamlin Garland's *A Spoil of Office* (1897) is the only text in my corpus
that, like Benjamin's nostalgic evocation of storytellers, celebrates an organic form of charismatic power. Against the prospect of seeing the political voice dissipated throughout the urban polity, Garland utters the hope
that grassroots political movements of the American midwest may still
bring forth inspirational speakers whose power remains tied to the local
group. The community of oratory portrayed in *A Spoil of Office* is the Farmers Alliance—the driving force of the Populist movement in the 1890s. The
novel starts out from the recognition that, as Henry Nash Smith puts it,
there is a "yawning gap between agrarian theory and the actual circumstances of the West after the Civil War" (192). The Jeffersonian myth of
the American bountiful garden has given way to economic inequality and
to the corruption of post–Civil War sectional politics. In his effort to dra-
matize the struggle to uphold the egalitarianism of the Jeffersonian republic, Garland turns the whole midwestern world into a field of political
education and legal contention. The novel provides a glowing account of
the utopian aspirations that led midwestern farmers to join the Grange, a
pre-Populist farmers' association, then the more radical Alliance. In the
novel, oratory, steeped in midwestern republican traditions, constitutes the
main inspiring force for the agrarian militants.

The education of Talcott Bradley, a midwestern farmhand craving for
culture and for a role in politics, is the central issue of *A Spoil of Office*.

Bradley goes to college, is elected to county and state offices, spends a season in Washington as a Democratic congressman, and ends up as a speaker for the Alliance. His two most influential mentors are Ida Wilbur and Judge Brown; the former is a feminist reformer who speaks for the Grange and later for the Alliance; the latter initiates Bradley into the rituals of politics. Of all role models, Ida Wilbur is most impressive: in the initial chapters of the novel, her address to a Grange meeting fires up Bradley's longing for culture and politics; later, she introduces the protagonist to Populism. Her marriage to Bradley at the end of the narrative reveals that, in this text, political awakening runs parallel with sentimental romance.

Public speaking in Garland is the offshoot of what Lawrence Goodwyn, in his history of Populism, calls a movement culture—namely the associative rituals and the set of shared values that support a democratic protest movement (xviii, 20). The movement culture contains the educational tools that allow a community to organize itself democratically and to remain politically efficient. In *A Spoil of Office*, these institutions are respectively the Grange meetings, where Bradley encounters Ida for the first time, and the rural college, where orators receive their formal training. College students develop their skills by rehearsing such classics of Latin and American oratory as Spartacus' address to the Romans, Antony's eulogy of Caesar, or Webster's reply to Hayne. New thematics of public speaking are hammered out in the fraternity debating club, an extension of the oratory class, which accommodates pre-Populist controversies on free trade and the tariff.

The well-structured movement culture of the midwestern farmers guarantees that populist oratory, as awesome as it may be, will remain true to its democratic goals—thus, on the side of white magic. Speeches in this context are endowed with a power that borders on the supernatural: to Bradley, Ida Wilbur's address to the Grange has the impact of "something whiter and more penetrating than the sunlight" (14). The same violence overcomes Bradley when he gives his first school address: struck with the "terrible weakness" and "nausea" of stage fright, he first feels "like a man facing an icy river . . . into which he must plunge" (63); then, Bradley finds himself pervaded with "a mysterious power," comparable to "something divine" (65, 66). Garland assumes, perhaps too lightly, that the magical force of public speaking will ensure the democratic representation of the farmers in a corrupt American polity. Thus, he attributes to oratory a function that Northrop Frye and Fredric Jameson, in their discussions of literary genre, regard as typical of romance:

regenerating a fallen world through the creation of a community cleansed of conflict and injustice (Frye 186; Jameson, *Political* 103–50). Ida Wilbur is the embodiment of this utopian impulse, which broadens people's sympathies and creates more inclusive chains of solidarity. In her voice Bradley discerns the promise of an idyllic mode of life—"the great dream-world that [lies] beyond his horizon, the world of poets and singers in the far realm and luxury" (14).

Bradley's antagonist in this story of education is the lure of federal politics and its attendant corruptions. The novel makes this moral peril visible by depicting Washington as a sublime metropolis: when Bradley first catches sight of the city, it appears as an immense mass with blurry edges, "weighing myriads of tons" (269), clouded in an "insubstantial" halo of mist (269). To politically minded westerners like Bradley, the "vastness . . . complexity and noise" of the U.S. Congress are centers of fascination as powerful as are Chicago and New York to Dreiser's and Norris's ambitious protagonists. Yet, perhaps more easily than in these writers, Garland exposes the insubstantiality of the city, lurking behind its magnificent facade. Over time, Bradley becomes able to discern the comedy of greed hiding behind "the vast mass, and roar, and motion" (281) of the halls of Congress; he thereby breaks free from the taint of corruption. After he has left Washington, Ida tells him that, by failing to be reelected, he has escaped becoming a spoil of office.

In their struggle against corruption, the Populist speakers of *A Spoil of Office* seem, however, endowed with energy in excess of what is required for their immediate political needs. Because the deceitful charm of Garland's Washington is eventually unmasked, the city is not nearly as demonic as James's Boston; as such, it constitutes an imperfect match for the awe-inspiring Populist speeches. On the other hand, consciousness raising among gatherings of farmers does not in itself necessitate such momentous exertions as Bradley's and Wilbur's. I want to argue therefore that Bradley's and Ida's voices require an extra charge of power—a surrogate aura—because they are implicitly struggling against the social forces that constrain the Populist agenda from outside—industrialism and economic incorporation, particularly. Garland's paean to Populism presents indeed a vision of oratory that resembles mass politics without the industrial mass: the superhuman charisma that Sinclair will later attribute to Chicago socialists is here at work in the more convivial world of farming communities, where its intensity seems out of place. That the make-up of Garland's inspirational voices is thus overdetermined is discernible in the ambiguities of the utopian promise that Bradley perceives in Ida's speeches. Ida's sentimental allusion to the "great dream-world" beyond the farmers' limited horizon is bound to refer not only to the utopian future, but also to the more threatening shadow communities of the outside world—the open-ended space of the trusts and the urban-based market, which, in the 1890s, shaped the Populist farmers' perception of the American continent.

Through this fissuring of the orators' voices, Garland's text registers the fact that, as Bruce Palmer puts it, Populism occupied "a halfway position between two worlds"—between the Jeffersonian republic and the new world of factories and trusts (211–12). The Populist ideal of a producers' commonwealth, Palmer contends, tried to salvage the positive legacies of agrarianism by resorting to methods borrowed from the new economic order—by means of nationwide networks of solidarity that departed from the earlier "simple market society" (111). In an optimistic light, we might argue that Garland's depiction of oratory also fosters the hope that a democratic commonwealth might blend elements of the two modes of production: Garland's orators might be attempting to preserve the world of Jeffersonian farming by means of a superior unifying force whose origin lies in the mode of production that is superseding the agrarian republic. Still, the double affiliation of the charismatic voice—its anchorage both in the local realm of farming and in the shadow horizon of the continental market—is politically awkward: it implies that an orator like Bradley, ostensibly nurtured by the resources of the community, cannot entirely be an average man, speaking to his equals in their own idiom; he is indeed wielding a form of oratory that constructs a nostalgic, possibly deceitful simulacrum of the organic movement culture.

The Jungle

Nostalgia for a preindustrial community and its embodied voices is not a workable option for the protagonists of Upton Sinclair's *The Jungle* (1906): there is in the city of the Beef Trust no rooted community powerful enough to support such a political mode of representation. *The Jungle* depicts three types of social structures: the families of Old World immigrants, the economic machinery of capitalism, and the socialist utopia. Each of them is associated with specific cultural and economic practices: folk rituals for the Lithuanian community; a cycle of exploitation and death in industrial Chicago; and, for socialism, oratory and science. In the utopian logic of the novel, the inspirational speeches of socialist orators will vanquish capitalism and supersede the mechanisms of solidarity of the immigrant group. They will thereby initiate a broader chain of brotherhood, inspired by a tradition of thinkers, scientists, and artists. Sinclair's text does not, however, quite manage to impress on its readers the inevitability of the socialist victory: the world of the Chicago packing houses is sublime—both overwhelming and fascinating; as such, it cannot easily be swept away by political activists who boast oratorical gifts as uncanny as industry itself. Symptomatic of this political aporia is the fact that the community of socialism is never represented in the text, much less through realistic narration: the ending, in a sharp genre discontinuity, abruptly gives up documentary exposition for political prophecy.

The Jungle is highly dialogized: it accommodates a significant load of documentary information as well as strands of sentimentalism and naturalist gothic. The plot follows an allegorical logic: its *Bildungsroman* structure depicts through the story of Jurgis Rudkus the education of the American working class. Jurgis and his relatives are Lithuanian immigrants freshly arrived from Europe to the world of the Chicago meat-packing plants. Jurgis and his family try to transpose their Lithuanian customs to their new environment. The novel opens with Jurgis's and Ona's wedding, which is carried out according to the full decorum of Lithuanian peasantry. However, these rituals soon prove futile in the face of economic violence. The strong and healthy Jurgis is at first a prime subject for the recruiters of Packingtown. Yet, weakened by an injury, he is given ever less profitable jobs, so that his relatives have to seek employment in the slaughterhouses. From then on, the family members become allegorical scapegoats of urban poverty: they fail in their attempt to buy a house on the instalment plan; Ona, sexually abused by her boss, dies in labor, giving birth to an illegitimate stillborn child. Jurgis turns against his wife's seducer and is sent to jail. Blacklisted from the packing plants, he moves from steel mills to harvester factories, then drifts about the countryside. Back in town, he becomes a beggar, a strike-breaker, and a thug for machine politicians. By then, the protagonist is ripe for a conversion to socialism—an event that takes place when he seeks shelter in a meeting hall and is carried away by the socialist speaker's enthusiasm.

In allegorical terms, the economy of Sinclair's Packingtown functions as a sublime cannibalistic cycle: the packing houses are entropic biological machines that consume the population that keeps them running. The oceans of cattle that flow screaming to their death neatly parallel the streams of workers who, once hired in the stockyards on account of their vitality, face mutilation and physical exhaustion. In a passage that ensured Sinclair's *succès de scandale*, the novel reveals that occasionally, the machine accidentally grinds members of its work force into marketable sausage meat, in literal fulfillment of the text's cannibalistic allegory.[9]

Interwoven with the thematics of cannibalism is the suggestion that the economic degeneracy of the city must be made visible through tropes of threatening femininity. As in Norris's *The Pit*, the representation of production and exchange is carried out through maternal metaphorics that portray the city as a prosthetic scene of reproduction, antithetical to the agrarian cosmos. In the discussion of Norris, I relied on Catherine Gallagher's argument according to which nineteenth-century political economists make the female body, in its reproductive and nurturing functions, symbolically congruent with the whole economy or polity. Here too, I want to contend that Sinclair's text, obsessed as it is with pathological flows of life energies and with the splicing and grinding of bodies, creates a gendered discourse that can be read as the economics of a defiled woman's body. Sinclair's Chicago is a world in which women are sacrificed to profit, either through prostitution or—like Jurgis's wife Ona—to death in childbirth. In the logic of gendered economics, the ordeal of the martyred women becomes symbolical of the depravation of the economy—of its abject reliance on artifical mechanisms of (re)production. The moral perversion of this system of exploitation expresses itself in the discourse that Julia Kristeva calls abjection (9).

Because it feeds on tropes of excrements, the discourse of abjection blends easily into the documentary texture of naturalist city novels, whose sensationalistic aesthetic relies in part on an assumed affinity between realistic details and filth. In *The Jungle*, the description of Bubbly Creek—an arm of the Chicago River that absorbs the spillage of the meat-packing plants—illustrates how the whole abject economic traffic of the city can be signified allegorically by one single feature of the urban landscape:

> One long arm of [Bubbly Creek] is blind, and the filth stays there forever and a day. The grease and chemicals that are poured into it undergo all sorts of strange transformations, which are the cause of its name; it is constantly in motion, as if huge fish were feeding in it, or great leviathans disporting themselves in its depths. Bubbles of carbonic acid gas will rise to the surface and burst, and make rings two or three feet wide. Here and there, the grease and filth have caked solid, and the creek looks like a bed of lava; chickens walk about on it, feeding, and many times an unwary stranger has started to stroll across, and vanished temporarily. . . . Once, however, an

ingenious stranger came and started to gather this filth in scows, to make
lard out of; then the packers took cue, and got out an injunction to stop
him, and afterwards gathered it themselves. The banks of "Bubbly Creek"
are plastered thick with hairs, and this also the packers gather and clean.
    And there were things even stranger than this. (115)

In these lines, economic gain depends on the management of biological
waste. Like similar passages in London's *The People of the Abyss*, Sinclair's
"Bubbly Creek" vignette conflates the circulation of money with the
draining out of life: human and animal bodies are dissolved and recycled for money. This pattern of dubious regeneration informs many aspects of Sinclair's Chicago. In the meat industry itself, new bodies can
be recomposed out of refuse, as the plants concoct "devilled ham" and
other specialties out of the waste ends of animals, dyed and flavored in
order to conceal the nature of the meat and the presence of infectious
diseases (118). Similarly, the greenish waters of the Chicago streets,
which reek with the "ghastly odour . . . of all the dead things of the universe" (36), can be profitably recycled: holes in the ground, filled with
water coming from the roadbed, can be used to provide ice blocks in the
winter, even though they have been festering all year with the spillage
of nearby garbage dumps (37).

    On the basis of these examples, one may well wonder whether Sin-
clair's economics of abjection might not activate a form of literary pruriency that is incompatible with a socialist politics of demystification.
Indeed, the sensationalist descriptions of this perverted economic cycle
introduce into the text an ambivalence that threatens to blur the political direction of the novel. The "Bubbly Creek" passage, with its fanci-
ful mysteries-of-the-city rhetoric, suggests that even abjection, the most
negative of all sublime registers, can still inspire wonder for its debased
object. It is therefore impossible to rule out that the community of industrialism might not in itself become an object of desire—a focus of
emotional attachment that the reader would enjoy under the mode of
sensationalism. If Sinclair's novel fails to define a subject position that
allows its reader to take a clear stand toward an object condemned explicitly by the text, one can legitimately raise the question whether political fiction with a critical edge can be written within the medium of
sublime naturalism. Conversely, we may wonder what kind of ideal community—other than an overwhelming or abject one—can be represented on the basis of this form of discourse.

    The novel answers these question in part by implying that the injus-
tices of capitalism cannot possibly be redressed by a return to the kind

of communities that Jurgis knew in Lithuania. The machine of industrialism can in this perspective not be condemned as such, since the energies associated with it must partake in the creation of the commonwealth of workers. It is therefore not surprising to find in the novel passages such as the description of the steel plants, in which the sublime intensities of industry radiate an unadulterated sense of wonder: "Jurgis looked through the fingers of his hands, and saw pouring out of the cauldron a cascade of living, leaping fire, white with a whiteness not of the earth, scorching the eyeballs. Incandescent rainbows shone above it, blue, red, and golden lights played about it; but the stream itself was white, ineffable. Out of regions of wonder it streamed, the very river of life: and the soul leaped up at the sight of it, fled back upon it, swift and resistless, back into far-off lands, where beauty and terror dwell" (247). The vision of industry developed in these lines is spiritualistic; the fact that we learn a couple of pages later that Jurgis learned "to take all the miracles and terrors [of the steel plant] for granted" (249) hardly detracts from the fascination of a passage that constitutes one of the purest expressions of the animistic sublime in my corpus. In a form of alchemy that directly contradicts the image of industry as a machine of death, the furnaces of the steel plant—in the intensity of light, heat, and movement—confer the aura of life to a flow of incandescent iron. Of course, the steel industry is not comparable to the giant slaughterhouses: instead of turning live flesh and blood into filth, it shapes dead matter into tools and objects, thus fulfilling the Veblenian conception of socially useful work; most important, it is backed up by a long tradition of prestigious craftsmanship. By recapturing the aura of the industrial past within the ineffable realm of beauty and terror of modern factories, the steel plant epiphany provides a mediation by which the sublime affects of the gigantic industrial apparatus can be rechanneled for positive ends: these lines ensure therefore that the industrial commonwealth can escape the cycle of abjection. Accordingly, Jurgis will later learn from a socialist activist that the party's program involves "using the trusts, not destroying them" (381).

The hope that industrial Chicago might be regenerated out of its own resources informs Sinclair's depiction of socialist oratory: political speakers carry sublime energies—the source of their surrogate aura—that are in other passages of the text branded as abject. Jurgis's conversion to socialism takes place when the protagonist is a police suspect on the run, who has just discovered that two of his relatives have become prostitutes. In his first contact with socialist utopianism, the load of humiliation and violence accumulated up to that point is sublimated through the orator's voice, who talks in the accents of awe-inspiring forces:

> So all at once it occurred to Jurgis to look at the speaker.
>
> It was like coming suddenly upon some wild sight of Nature—a mountain forest lashed by a tempest, a ship tossed about upon a stormy sea. Jurgis had an unpleasant sensation, a sense of confusion, of disorder, of wild and meaningless uproar. The man was tall and gaunt, as haggard as his auditor himself; a thin black beard covered half of his face, and one could see only two black holes where the eyes were. . . . His voice was deep, like an organ; it was some time, however, before Jurgis thought of his voice—he was too much occupied with his eyes to think of what the man was saying. . . . and so Jurgis became suddenly aware of the voice, trembling, vibrant with emotion, with pain and longing, with a burden of things unutterable, not to be compassed by words. To hear it was to be suddenly arrested, to be gripped, transfixed. (358)

This spectacular epiphany plunges Jurgis into oceanic turmoil, holds him afloat by the tension of the speaker's hypnotic stare, and, in a gesture that resembles the movement of a revivalist meeting, pulls him up by the transfiguring power of the voice. Yet this oratorical feat is achieved by a speaker whose gift is affected by gothic dissonances: his figure displays an imbalance between biological strength—his gaunt physique makes him hardly stronger than a tramp—and the power of the sublime energies that flow through him. His voice has "strange intonations" that arouse in the listener "a sense of things not of earth, of mysteries never spoken before, of presences of awe and terror" (366). In the strains of the momentous speech, Jurgis discerns "powers . . . undreamed of," like "demon forces contending" (366). In these lines, the interweaving of the sublime of magnitude with animism and with the uncanny reveals that the texture of the political voice is consubstantial with the energies that animated the steel plants, as if the text equated breathing life into metal with raising the political awareness of the masses.

The surrogate aura that pervades the socialists' addresses is the manifestation of Chicago's shadow communities—here, industrial power and its "voiceless" constituencies (359). In Sinclair's political argument, this sublime excess of oratorical energies also makes visible the utopian communities of the future: the rhetorical energy projects a utopian glow around a political community whose ideals cannot be represented in narrative form within the documentary epistemology of the novel. The very term surrogate aura suggests, however, that Sinclair's appeal to supernatural accents remains a strategy of pseudo-totalization that might weaken the novelist's portrayal of socialism. In practice, the impact of the demonic powers aroused in Jurgis's epiphany remains unclear: the awakening of proletarian consciousness is followed by a narrative of proletarian struggle that boils down to the account in headline form of successive socialist victories at the polls. Thus, we are left with the sense that some obstacle prevents the energies invoked in the conversion scene from being consumed by the narrative developments, as if these forces exceeded the boundaries of the political program outlined in the text.

Faced with this sense of incompleteness, one might argue that a socialist novel published in 1906 still records the energies of a movement in full growth, and that it can securely shift the synthesis between utopia and reality into the future. At that point in history, Sinclair's hope in American socialism could seem warranted. James Weinstein shows that the years that preceded World War I marked the high point of the American Socialist Party.[10] The socialists, building on the legacy of mid-1890s Populism, enjoyed significant representation in town councils and in state assemblies; Eugene Debs, their presidential candidate, collected about one million votes at the presidential election of 1919. However, divergences over the rejection of the war effort and the Bolshevik revolution precipitated the decline of the party. In retrospect, we are, however, more acutely aware of the fact that it is precisely because the socialist utopia only has a tenuous organic connection with the Chicago scene that the charismatic powers of its militants have to be fleshed out with the demonic aura of the forces of industry. If judged by the standards of Lukácsian realism, Sinclair's utopian project acknowledges its political defeat when it tries to secure the passage from theory to practice by quasi-supernatural means: without a narrative synthesis of abstract principles and descriptive details, the text fails to embody the workings of a socialist community.

Though the political limitations outlined thus cannot be overcome in their own terms, it is important, I think, to venture an interpretation of *The Jungle* that circumscribes the utopian potential of Sinclair's strategies of pseudo-totalization. In this approach, the novel's glorification of political propagandizing and charismatic speeches weighs more than the creation of grass-roots networks of solidarity. Indeed, *The Jungle* offers the hope that a group can be held together by the culture of a new intelligentsia. In the absence of an organic movement culture, socialism is implanted into the novel in deus ex machina fashion; its appeal is identified with the charismatic personality of socialist orators, who act as messengers from a higher realm, distantly or partially related to the body of the narrative.

In the novel, the most prominent representatives of the new socialist elites are Tommy Hinds and Dr. Nicholas Schliemann—both of them important mentors for Jurgis. Hinds is the archetypal political activist: there are hints of sublime powers in the description of "the torrent of his eloquence," which can be "compared with nothing save Niagara" (380). Hinds's business life—he started out as a blacksmith's helper and has become a small hotel owner—serves as a model of solidarity between the proletariat and the middle class: as a socialist entrepreneur, Hinds applies exemplary labor rules to the management of his own staff. In the economy of the novel, Tommy Hinds's main function is of a genealogical nature: he has been "a reform member of the city council . . . a Greenbacker, a Labour Unionist, a Populist, a Bryanite" (380). The personal histories of Hinds and his associates "on the trail of the Octopus" (380) provide a political genealogy whose historical aura compensates for the impression that Sinclair's socialism is a movement decreed from above. Further on, the genealogical function of Hinds's narrative is complemented by the survey of socialistic theories provided by Nicholas Schliemann—a Veblen-like professor of philosophy whose dazzling conversation provides glimpses of the universal scope of the socialist movement. Through the medium of Schliemann's oratory, the novel puts together a canon of socialist thinking that includes the description of marriage as a form of prostitution, the belief that science will solve the problems of production in a noncompetitive fashion, the theory of conspicuous consumption, the indictment of capitalist waste, the condemnation of urbanization, Charlotte Perkins Gilman's theories of scientific homemaking, and Kropotkin's program of scientific agriculture. This utopian shopping list bathes in the prestige of an orator whose charismatic presence justifies the by now routine comparison to "a thunderstorm or an earthquake" (396).

Schliemann's lecture suggests that, when the narrative of *The Jungle* is suspended, the story of initiation is replaced by a course of reading. This suggests that Jurgis's education is incomplete, in the same way as Avis Everhard's was in London's *The Iron Heel:* it is remarkable that after an initiatory path that brings him face to face with many inspiring orators, Jurgis never develops a voice of his own; what he acquires instead is "the reading habit" (387). This deviation from the pattern that underlies the other novels of charismatic oratory can, I think, be interpreted in two ways. We have seen that, by ending his novel on the promise that "Chicago will be ours" (412), Sinclair is attempting to give voice to a community that, historically, is doomed to exist only in the abstract.

On the basis of the very last pages of the novel, I would however argue for a less pessimistic interpretation; if Jurgis is not empowered as a political speaker, the novel itself is: in the last paragraphs, the speech of a nameless orator merges into a series of political slogans that, in the fashion of a political tract, seem to emanate directly from the author and from the space of his text. So, the sublime ordeals of Jurgis are resolved in an allegory by means of which the novel gives itself a charismatic political voice; likewise, the form of community that is most vividly represented in the text is a community of politicized readers.

Teller's *The Cage* and Bullard's *Comrade Yetta*

Within the corpus of novels of oratory, it makes sense to read Jurgis Rudkus's conversion to socialism as an allegorical marriage. In this logic, the destruction of Jurgis and Ona's couple is compensated by the fact that the Lithuanian workman joins a collective dedicated to the redemption of America. In this, Sinclair concurs with Garland, Teller, and Bullard, who use the actual marriage of their protagonists as a symbol of unanimistic reconciliation. The socialist appropriation of romance has irked many readers of radical fiction: critics from Alfred Kazin to Peter Conn are wary of any departure from realism because they fear that it might induce a sell-out to the wish-fulfillment fantasies cultivated by capitalism.[11] I believe, however, that romance is not necessarily parasitical in this context. Michael Denning argues that 1890s dime novels develop allegories of the labor struggle through the conventions of popular fiction. Likewise, I wish to show that novels of oratory rewrite their narratives of emancipation through love plots of charismatic seduction. In this light, Teller and Bullard's heroines, as well as London's Avis Everhard, qualify as what we might call brides of socialism, deciding through their marriage choice the shape of the American future. Conversely, their suitors are romance figures carrying a dark form of charisma, whose ambiguous overtones allegorize the ideological lures to which the working classes may fall victim. Also, I think that weeding out the romance from these texts leads one to misread their political agendas, which are partly devoted to sexual and reproductive thematics—issues articulated essentially through romance and sublime tropes.

Arthur Bullard's *Comrade Yetta* (1913) and Charlotte Teller's *The Cage* (1907) were both written in response to traumatic political events. Bullard was a radical social worker who also coedited the Socialist daily *The Call*; he published his novel as a literary testimony to the 1909 "Uprising of the Twenty Thousand"—the massive strike of the New York garment workers (see Rideout 54). Teller's *The Cage*, Peter Conn writes, constitutes a socialist journalist's "reconstruction of the Haymarket riot and her reverential memorial to Haymarket's executed anarchists" (93).[12] In these romance narratives, politics is a matter of knowing where the socialist brides—respectively Yetta Rayefsky and Frederica Hartwell—will bestow their commitments and affections. Bullard's Yetta, David M. Fine reports, is modeled after Clara Lemlich, a teenage worker whose compelling address at a waist-makers' union meeting initiatied a general strike (95). In the novel, Yetta is Henry James's political nightmare come true: a Verena Tarrant figure rising from the Jewish ghetto to organize her fellow sweatshop workers. Yetta's exceptional oratorical skills attract the attention of several left-wing figures in New York—middle-class feminists, bohemian intellectuals, and socialists. Emotionally involved with several of her political mentors, she settles for Jewish socialist Isadore Braun—a marriage choice that commits her to Isadore's patriarchal values. Teller's Frederica, on the other hand, is the daughter of a pro-labor minister. Her sentimental ordeal consists in figuring out whether her charismatic fiancé Eugene Harden is a worthy union man or a rakish traitor to the socialist cause, involved in the Haymarket incidents. When all ambiguities are dispelled, the conclusion of Frederica's marriage signifies the dream of a union of workers and middle-class liberals.

The discourse of political charisma in these labor novels revolves around the paradoxes of representative mass leadership. Bullard and Teller's charismatic figures—Yetta and Eugene respectively—share their fellow-workers' conditions, but are in some respect marked off from their surroundings. Only thus can they project the aura of mystery necessary to mobilize the energies of urban crowds. Yetta radiates a mesmeric potential that, in romance fashion, matches her exceptional beauty. In accordance with Le Bon's concept of prestige, she is able to be "hypnotized by" and to become "one with" the crowds of her fellow workers (78). Her specific gift consists in amplifying the mesmeric power she picks up from her audience by mingling it with those aspects of her personality that single her out from the group. In the middle of a Carnegie Hall address, for instance, she lets "a look of communication with some distant spirit" (213) come over her face and switches from English to Hebrew; the whole crowd is "held spellbound by the swinging sonorous cadence" (213). Hebrew refers to the shadow community of a distant tradition whose energy can inspire New York strikers, Jewish or other. By anchoring Yetta's power in these religious sources, Bullard strikes a clever compromise between depicting a charismatic leader that blends within her own group or one that remains transcendent to it.

In *The Cage*, Eugene conflates so many markers of uncanniness that he seems overqualified for crowd leadership. A Hungarian aristocrat exiled to the United States for his socialist views, he is accused of seducing Frederica without telling her of a previous European marriage. More mysterious still, Eugene's alleged treachery is reflected in the figure of his evil *Doppelgänger*—his stepbrother Gustav Lange, who is guilty of all the crimes Eugene is suspected of commiting—abusing young women, betraying the union, and planting the Haymarket bomb. Thus characterized, Eugene stands at the intersection of two shadow communities— one based on class, the other on biology and desire. In social terms, Eugene enjoys a broader range of experience than does a stereotypical working-class figure. Both a worker and a foreign nobleman, he embodies a ubiquitous dime-novel type, which Michael Denning has dubbed the "natural aristocrat" (74). Denning shows that working-class heroes of popular fiction are often granted a secret aristocratic birth—a device that, if read allegorically, implies that valorous mechanics are not simply what they seem, but are also gentlemen in disguise—"Knights of Labor," for instance (74).

On the other hand, Eugene's ability to ignite the desire both of individuals and crowds makes him the herald of a vitalistic community—a set of people bound by libidinal, instinctual, or evolutionary ties. Like Freud or James, Teller assumes that hypnosis draws on libidinal mechanisms. In her novel, the union leader's bond to the workers feeds on the same energies as his love for Frederica. The seduction of oratory amounts therefore to a falling in love: "The power [Eugene] had held over the audience had been for [Frederica] the final draught of his personality, and it had intoxicated her. The magnetic vitality which had encompassed the several hundred listeners had embraced her and drawn her so close to him as she stood there that she could almost feel the touch of his hand on hers" (119). The "touch of Harden's hand upon hers," we learn a few pages later, is also the magical stimulus that stirs the "trembling pleasure" of "her body's song of love" (124). Teller articulates such stirrings of desire through the idiom of Darwinism: she regards the libidinal affects of the hypnotic bond as the outward manifestations of a hidden realm of animal instincts linking modern humans with their prehistoric kin. It is this world of evolutionary genealogies that Frederica glimpses in the seduction of Eugene's voice: her love for the enigmatic romance hero makes her discover that she is a "primeval woman, with instinct and passion as her motive forces" (220).

The Cage does not blindly proclaim the legitimacy of the vitalist energies carried by its mesmeric speaker: Teller ponders whether there might not be some black magic in Eugene's instinctual source of authority. In the political field, the dangers of excessive prestige are made visible in the figure of Gustav Lange, who possesses an ominous hypnotic power that "deafen[s], blind[s] . . . and frighten[s]" Frederica (60). Within the lovers' private relationship, Frederica utters misgivings about Eugene's animality when she points out that, "in spite of the conventional white cuffs and the carefully kept nails," Eugene has "savage hands" with "fine black hair on them" (28). Likewise, in a dream sequence, Frederica sees herself kissing Eugene's gloved hand, only to realize that her teeth are biting into the hand through the glove (307).

However, *The Cage* cannot denounce Eugene's patriarchally based charisma without undercutting the vitalist groundings of his leadership. Thus, the novel does not renounce its celebration of magnetic manhood—a choice that curtails Frederica's role in the political struggle. By way of compensation, Frederica gains empowerment in the private arena: Teller's use of the romance idiom produces a proto-psychoanalytical rhetoric that establishes the existence of a libidinal field of interaction and that, in so doing, promotes the legitimacy of female desire. The instinctual fascination of the vitalist community is a force that unleashes Frederica's "body's song of love," and keeps her "breathless and palpitating" (124). This romance discourse transcends the limitations of sentimental fiction because it articulates a critique of the institutions that regulate sexuality: Frederica learns "through her own consciousness of herself and of her body" the weight of "all the traditions of a thousand years, which have kept the woman away from freedom, have made spiritual restraint the spiritual law for the sex" (223). In the same logic, the novel advocates sex education. Less outspokenly, the narratives of illegitimacy and bigamy that revolve around Eugene read like allegories of free love: the melodramatic tangle by which Frederica finds herself married to an alleged bigamist allows the novel to evoke non-Victorian marital patterns without opprobrium. The novel suggests indeed that, when passion is genuine and mutual, biology is stronger than the cage of society's law: Frederica's "great desire," the "consciousness of her body" (223), leaves the heroine free to live by "the law of the spirit" (222).

Bullard is less anxious than Teller to cover up the patriarchal impact of vitalistic epiphanies. In *Comrade Yetta*, the revelation of the iron laws of instincts ushers in a trade-off: the movement culture of socialism, held together by charismatic organizers, gives way to "socialism for the babies" (445); the awakening of the heroine's sexuality entails the curbing of her ambition as a socialist orator. The novel makes this loss acceptable by hinting that, by embracing a sexually fulfilling marriage, Yetta Rayefsky escapes from the sterility of the overcivilized left. When Yetta marries Isadore, she is able to turn her back on lesbians, "unsexed" feminists (97), or shiftless aesthetes. The break with this environment comes to pass when "Nature's revenge" catches up with Yetta and her fiancé (419): the overworked Isadore is struck with typhoid fever. Their doctor, acting as the herald of vitalistic wisdom, berates the couple for turning their back on nature and advises them to have children.

Bullard himself does not present his paeans to socialist domesticity in this conservative light. By picturing his heroine "trembling at the threshold of the Great Mystery" of sex (427), Bullard, like Charlotte Teller, aims to create a new idiom for the representation of desire. Isadore voices this ambition when he lectures Yetta about the historical evolution that makes for an ever increasing spiritualization of love: "As we begin to get used to this startlingly new concept of love," he argues, "we'll develop the words to express it. It's too big a task for one generation" (473). The resulting celebration of the "mystic, unexpressible joy of sex" (473) is spiritual in that it testifies to the existence of a shadow community of ancestors linked by bonds of motherhood. To Yetta, sex means being included in the "unbroken line of mothers which stretche[s] back of her to that dim epoch when the new element of life first appeared on the shores of the primordial sea" (419). In this Bullard offers the vision of a vitalistic polity managed by scientifically educated men, but regulated by the values of the past. The unbroken nurturing chain of the "line of mothers" (419) reads like an allegorical equivalent of a preindustrial community, where conviviality is obtained at the cost of a tighter degree of social control. The empowerment afforded by this nostalgic polity may be gauged by the fact that Yetta—now Mrs. Isadore Braun—will from then on take pleasure in darning her husband's socks.

PART 4

Novels of
Artistic Education

Overcivilization and the Crisis of Writerly Manhood

Mesmeric orators like James's Verena Tarrant or Sinclair's socialist activists are, functionally speaking, performers—rhetoricians of the crowd's unconscious, aiming to capture the attention of an unruly audience. The continuity between hypnosis and art in naturalism manifests itself in the fact that both realms of experience are narrated through scenarios of regeneration. A striking allegorical illustration of this convergence appears in a passage of London's *The Valley of the Moon* where the protagonists Billy and Saxon witness an impressive instance of what Amy Kaplan calls the "spectacle of masculinity" ("Romancing" 665). The two characters become the fascinated observers of a powerful swimmer. The young man—a Viking-like muscle man, embodying the precepts of London's racialism—hails from a commune of athletically proficient artists. During his swimming routine, he rushes towards the huge breakers of the Pacific and, "when it seem[s] he must be crushed, . . . dive[s] into the face of the breaker and disappear[s]," plunging and re-emerging several times, eager "to win seaward against the sweep of the shoreward-hastening sea" (371). His gesture is a typical exploit of the oceanic sublime— a daring display transcending the immersion anxieties that haunt the inhabitants of the naturalist city. Specific to this scene is the fact that the swimmer's achievement defines a hierarchy of the mesmeric gaze, geared to a scale of artistic excellence. In the face of the athlete's exertions, Billy remains riveted, "tense with watching" (371), or "with blue eyes flashing" (372). Thus paralyzed with trance-like admiration, Billy and Saxon stand at the lowest rung in a pecking order of hypnotic dominance, under the sway of the superhuman swimmer. However, once they join the community and are enthroned as artists, they acquire the skill to arouse this mesmeric fascination themselves.

≈ଓ ୧≈

The cultural configuration that underlies Jack London's aspirations toward artistic mastery is revealed in more realistic terms in the opening chapter of *Martin Eden*. In this scene, the uneducated Martin, London's partly autobiographical protagonist, visits a middle-class interior—an environment whose trappings of feminized refinement he finds thoroughly unfamiliar. With his sailor's awkward, rolling gait, he negotiates reefs of uncanny bourgeois bric-a-brac, which include an oil painting of a stormy seascape. The canvas depicts a "pilot schooner" struggling through "heavy surf" and "storm-clouds," sailing around a threatening "outjutting rock" (33). "Irresistibly" drawn by the beauty of the painting, Martin is nevertheless surprised to discover that, seen from up close, the pattern disappears and is replaced by "a careless daub of paint" (33), as if the canvas were a "trick picture" (33). At this stage, Martin, "brought up on chromos and lithographs that were always definite and sharp, near or far," does not yet "know painting" (33). The novel describes, however, how he absorbs the unfamiliar cultural heritage and, in time, how he manages to "make it in [his] class" (42).

London's evocation of the power of art in this scene suggests that aesthetic practice, when carried through the rhetoric of sublimity, can function as a vector of personal and cultural regeneration. In this final section, I propose therefore to show that the naturalist representation of artistic work gives utterance to feelings of helplessness and mastery inspired by the sublime metropolis. The texts I use for this argument could be described as turn-of-the-century novels of artistic education— naturalist works that deal with cultural practice and artistic identity. The number of novels that, directly or figuratively, handle these issues is higher than one might expect of a genre stereotypically devoted to the investigation of urban poverty. The present corpus includes Norris's *Vandover and the Brute* (1914); Jack London's *Martin Eden* and *The Sea-Wolf* (1904); Dreiser's *The "Genius"* (1915); James Weldon Johnson's *The Au-*

tobiography of an Ex-Coloured Man; Willa Cather's *O Pioneers!;* Abraham Cahan's *The Rise of David Levinsky* (1917); and Ernest Poole's *The Harbor* (1917). These works reveal that the naturalist decades witnessed a pre-modernist reappraisal of the cultural and social status of writers. This process was articulated along several interrelated axes: the readings below take into account the writers' attempts to construct a masculine writerly identity, their narratives of class ascension, and their need to define their status toward two discourses that compete with literature—the social sciences and the mass market of popular culture.

Christopher Wilson provides a compelling description of the cultural and economic background of turn-of-the-century narratives of artistic education. He shows how far the professional persona of Progressive-Era novelists was shaped by the development of a mass market for popular literature and journalism. Wilson contends that naturalists tried to handle the tensions of their cultural environment by defining for themselves an identity based on literary professionalism—on the devotion to the "labor of words" (11). Against the dilettante ethos that characterized the literature of the Gilded Age, these writers made a point of earning their living in the cultural market. Their aim, Wilson argues, was to develop a literature of social didacticism spread through the new mass circulation media—through Progressive-Era magazines like *McClure's*, for instance (xiii).

The naturalist drive toward literary professionalism described by Wilson turns cultural empowerment into an act of masculine assertion. In London's *Martin Eden*, characteristically, the first major step in the protagonist's education consists in embarking on an affair with Ruth Morse, the daughter of his middle-class benefactors. Ruth is a sterotypical "lily-pale spirit" (52) who introduces the sailor to upper-class culture, and whom he later rejects because she fails to sympathize with his ethos of manly realism. By depicting a hero who stakes his integrity on the rejection of "bourgeois refinement and culture" (463), London joins the chorus of contemporary intellectuals who were, as Jackson Lears puts it, "seeking alternatives for modern softness" (113): they were resolved to stand up against what their contemporaries called overcivilization—the feminization of culture favored by the Victorian genteel tradition. Alan Trachtenberg argues that the turn-of-the-century reaction against overcivilization was the outcome of a historical context characterized by imperial expansion and by the growth of immigration in the cities (*Incorporation* 141). These social developments had stirred aspirations for heroism that could not be satisfied within the bounds of Victorian gentility, which favored the values of the domestic sphere. Instead, the early twentieth century ushered in a movement toward the exploration of the public world. Trachtenberg singles out as typical of the dissatisfaction with genteel constraints William James's belief that "great fields of heroism" can be found in "the daily lives of the laboring classes" (141). Investigating the urban proletariat for literary or journalistic purposes was therefore implicitly designated as a mark of masculine courage.

In their endorsement of the ethos of strenuous masculinity, naturalist writers were also responding to pressures that bore directly on the definition of their craft. Alfred Habegger and Michael Davitt Bell argue that, in their critical definitions of realism and naturalism, writers sought to counter the view that authors must be, as Bell puts it, "the bane of all fine manhood" (29). Bell shows notably that William Dean Howells emulated literary personalities who had managed to be "'men' and 'writers' at the same time" (29). Habegger contends that this drive toward a masculine reshaping of authorship involved a departure from what writers perceived to be effeminate sentimentalism or aestheticism in art: for decades, fiction had been dominated by sentimental women writers; the commitment to realism was therefore meant to wipe off the prejudice that male authors were "sissies" (Habegger 56)—"distinctly unmasculine figures" (65) who performed a woman's trade, and who remained dependent on the taste of their feminine audience.[1] The anxieties over the loss of intellectual manhood described by Bell and Habegger incited naturalist writers to lay down a course of education meant to reclaim their sense of masculinity. Jack London's *The Sea-Wolf*, I argue below, is a paradigmatic instance of these novels of overcivilization. Its protagonist, Humphrey Van Weyden, embodies the degeneracy incurred by men in a feminized culture. The young aesthete, lulled by the comforts of his upper-middle-class round of life, is totally helpless in the face of real-world disasters. When his San Francisco Bay ferry is struck by a ship emerging from impenetrable fogs, Humphrey fears he might have to share the fate of other passengers on the ship—the "tangled mass of women, with drawn, white faces and open mouths" (21), whose abject dying shrieks remind him of his own feminized self. Humphrey is saved from drowning by Wolf Larsen, the captain of a seal-schooner who submits "Sissy Van Weyden" to a grueling course of remasculinization destined to make him "stand on his own legs" (21). As in other novels of education, Humphrey's regeneration is depicted in a narrative that explores what David Leverenz calls "paradigms of American manhood" (73)—models of masculinity anchored in social and professional identities. I point out below that a successful artistic education consists in defining a work-gender profile that offers an acceptable compromise between aesthetic integrity, personal empowerment, and the pressure of the market.

While my interpretation of texts like *The Sea-Wolf* builds on Wilson's, Jackson Lears's, and Trachtenberg's descriptions of the revolt against overcivilization, I also wish to underline the obstacles that hampered the project of cultural remasculinization and made it stray from the writers' explicit agenda. Pure empowerment in the public sphere is, I think, not an option in novels of artistic education. The configuration described in these texts is rather a dialectic between the work market and the peripheral space of artistic life that Dreiser calls "Bohemia" (*"Genius"* 90). Likewise, the limits to literary empowerment are discernible in the fact that the connection established by naturalism between masculinity and writing remains paradoxical. Try as they may, naturalist texts fail to produce any consistent instance of the starkly dichotomized gender roles postulated by their program of male supremacy. This apparent inconsistency affects Norris's critical essays where, for instance, the novelist unwittingly indicates that the ties to the genteel tradition cannot easily be severed (13). There is indeed a note of strained self-confidence in Norris's claim that, "of all the arts, [literature] is the most virile" (*Criticism* 13). Though an exponent of Anglo-Saxon manhood, Norris does not seem to be able to shed his belief that the writing of fiction belongs to the sphere of women and genteel aesthetes. At best, he provides the oxymoronic reassurance that literature is not a "mademoiselle," but "a robust, red-armed *bonne femme*" (13). In Norris, the attempt to orient the craft of writing "away from the sexless aesthetes into a World of Working Men" (14) conjures up therefore an ambiguous vision of literature as a being "with an arm as strong as a man's and a heart as sensitive as a child's" (14). Accordingly, I mean to show that the difficulty in breaking with genteel roles, compounded with the contradictions of the naturalist gendered economy, incites writers like Norris, London, Dreiser, and Poole to entrust the responsibility of artistic empowerment to liminal or transgressive identities: I indicate that the authors' gender discourse makes room for trickster figures—androgynes and amazons, and that their class discourse favors protagonists who stand above or in between existing social categories.

Ironically, the naturalist appropriation of sublime discourse contributes as much to the miscarriage of the project of literary empowerment as it does to its initial elaboration: at each level—class, gender, and aesthetic discourse—the imagery of terror subverts what it promises to make possible. This logic of rhetorical backfiring is particularly visible in the problems raised by the novelists' commitment to a supposedly bolder form of realism. In chapter 2 I mentioned that, regardless of the theoretical complexities we may discern in the use of this label—its epistemological naiveté, its polysemy—the novelists analyzed here all pledged, directly or through their protagonists, their basic allegiance to some form of realist aesthetic. "Realism is imperative to my nature" (462), claims London's Martin Eden, as he tries to hammer out a compromise between "the school of clod"—fiction where humans appear as beasts—and "the school of God"—the effete symbolism of Maeterlinck or of genteel realism (284). Likewise, in Dreiser's The *"Genius,"* the protagonist Eugene Witla feels vindicated when an expert art dealer greets the young man's paintings by exclaiming "thank God for a realist" (223). Yet the radicalness of these characters' preferred realist aesthetic is explicitly tied to what are, in our perspective, the least realistic aspects of their discourse: their departure from genteel realism involves the recourse to tropes of sublime magnitude and abjection that allow them to make visible urban poverty or continental markets. By thus exploring the shadow world of urban realism—mysterious metaphysical realms and hidden psychological recesses in Dreiser, the netherworld of atavism in London and Norris—novelists foster the suspicion that their writing is a vehicle of degeneration. In the analysis of *Vandover and the Brute,* I indicate that Norris himself, who otherwise welcomed the romantic features of naturalism, denounces as a pathology of the text the distortions and transfigurations of his own grotesque idiom. A similar dialectic reversal affects naturalist gender discourse: in London's *The Sea-Wolf,* I propose to show that, when the rhetoric of sublimity is mobilized to depict a superlative form of artistic manhood, it conjures up grotesque figures branded as abjectly non-masculine—primitive, androgynous, or homosexual.[2]

Naturalist Gothic and the Regeneration of Artistic Identity

Strategies of artistic empowerment in naturalist novels are the more successful if they are carried out through the medium of gothic discourse. Naturalist authors use this subset of the rhetoric of sublimity in order to express the most defamiliarizing aspects of the urban scene; as such, the gothic idiom constitutes a decisive testing ground for writers eager to determine if their aesthetic practice and artistic personae measure up to the constraints of the metropolis. In the discussion of hypnotic persuasion, I have provided illustrations of scenarios of regeneration that function at the level of a whole social group. In those cases, oratory is represented through complementary romance idioms—through a dialogic pattern in which utopian wish-fulfillment counteracts the darker accents of the gothic. In the texts discussed in the present chapter—Norris's *Vandover and the Brute* (1914), Charlotte Perkins Gilman's "The Yellow Wallpaper," and London's *The Sea Wolf*—no such counterforce to gothic degeneration is forthcoming. The challenge these works have to meet consists in exploring whether gothic rhetoric, which of itself seems to signify degeneration, can reverse itself, as it were. In the context of novels of artistic education, the search for a dialectic reversal within the grotesque is a metafictional gesture: it amounts to evaluating

the potential of various literary discourses and the mode of social insertion that fits them.

Vandover and the Brute

Compared to other novels of artistic life, Norris's *Vandover and the Brute*
develops only a reluctant narrative of empowerment. In its discussion of
aesthetics, the text associates the departure from canonical standards of
beauty with sexual deviance and class declension; it ranks therefore as
one of the most spectacular narratives of degeneration and proletarianization in the turn-of-the-century corpus. Norris's tendency to submit
his protagonist to a tireless, though superficial, moral censure brings his
novel closer to the spirit of decadent literature than to the moral agnos-
ticism of naturalists like Dreiser and London.[1] This moralizing streak,
I wish to argue, confers a negative value to the gothic idiom through
which the protagonist's moral abjection is conveyed: *Vandover* is a text
that explicitly condemns the rhetorical tools on which it most relies.

Vandover and the Brute chronicles the moral and social decline of a young
San Francisco artist whose lack of sexual discipline (the novel focuses on
his visits to prostitutes, but there are also allusions to masturbation) leads
to a cascade of catastrophes: Vandover seduces a young woman who later
kills herself; he also squanders his father's real-estate fortune. Symptomatic of this degeneracy is Vandover's feeling that his personality is invaded by "the brute" (215); this grotesque creature manifests itself during fits
of lycanthropy and progressively despoils the painter of his artistic capacities. When he reaches the lowest depths of psychological and social abase-
ment, Vandover is reduced to taking a caretaker's job in the pay of his friend
Geary, the very person who betrays his trust in order to despoil him of
his inheritance. At that point, Vandover has "become the brute" (316); he
has reverted to an atavistic state that, the novel indicates, fits his situation
as a destitute proletarian.

Art in *Vandover* undergoes the impact of degeneration as deeply as the
protagonist's moral fiber. Through its reflections on Vandover's aesthetic
perversion, the novel develops a significant meta-cultural critique of the
fate of the various forms of aesthetic representation available in urban
culture—particularly, of the debasement of art through mechanical reproduction. We are told for instance that Vandover learned to draw by
painstakingly copying prints—pastoral kitsch and "Ideal heads" (14), for
instance—divided in checkerboard fashion. The vulgarity of this artistic training is mirrored in the fact that, as an adult, Vandover develops a

taste for bohemian bric-a-brac—Assyrian bas-reliefs, photogravures of the Mona Lisa and of works by Rembrandt and Vandyke. In the novel's logic, this taste for cultural artifacts is stigmatized as an indulgence in comfort and "pretty things" (221), antithetical to great art. Yet, when Vandover cannot afford the pretty things any longer, he resurrects the lost bric-a-brac by affixing to his walls labels that read "Mona Lisa Here," or "Window-seat Here" (280), thus substituting empty signs for what was decorative junk in the first place. The tendency of cheap art to mutate into even more uncannily vacuous versions of itself is illustrated at the end of the novel, when Vandover is reduced to the status of a commercial artist, obliged to paint small romantic landscapes on the door of iron safes; the aesthetic degeneration such an occupation involves is pointed out in one of the young man's raving fits, when he cries out: "When you paint on steel and iron, your colours don't dry out true; all the yellows turn green" (333).

The caricatural commodification of art and language depicted in the novel is brought about by a degenerative process whose paradigm is atavistic regression. The parallel between the degeneration of instincts, language, and aesthetics, is established in the scenes involving the presence of the Dummy, a mute character whom Vandover's friends take along as mascot during their drinking sprees. The Dummy, in his normal state, is able to write short sentences, but can only utter animal-like sounds; yet, when drunk, he manages to blurt out a few words that ring like "the sounds of a voice heard through a telephone when some imperfection of transmission prevents one from distinguishing the words" (298). Thus characterized, the Dummy is the mirror image of Vandover: the latter is an articulate artist plagued with lycanthropy, who, during his "dog act" (299)—as his friends uncharitably call his disorder—is reduced to uncontrollable barking sounds. We should, however, not infer from this that Norris is simply opposing the roar of the brute to civilized language: here as in *McTeague*, the author juggles with traditional concepts of savagery and culture. The comparison between the Dummy and Vandover reveals indeed that the hierarchy that organizes the different modes of expression in the novel is paradoxical: on the one hand, the text indicates that the loss of articulated speech represents the most severe form of degeneration—the descent to the level of the snarling dog, to the very bottom of the evolutionary ladder. This does not mean, however, that language as such constitutes a guarantee of civilization: when the text shows that it only takes alcohol to make the Dummy emulate the telephone, it voices the suspicion that the language and the technology of industrialism and commercialism have an uncanny link to savagery or pathology as well. The representation of art in *Vandover* is therefore conditioned by the fear that there can be degeneration—communicational entropy—in language itself.

Within Vandover's painting practice, artistic and instinctual degeneration emerges in the guise of the brute—an overdetermined figure that signifies both the young painter's moral transgressions and the debasement of urban life in general. The monster that appears in his sketches is symptomatic of a perversion of vital forces: "certain shapes and figures were born upon [Vandover's] canvas, but they were no longer the true children of his imagination . . . they were changelings, grotesque abortions" (229). Vandover himself interprets this evolution as a sign of his own sexual degeneracy: he had so far clung to the hope that artistic discipline could sublimate what he perceives to be his degenerate inclinations. Here, in a process that is both a stylistic abortion and a new birth, the repressed energies resurface on the canvas in the shape of the "deformed dwarves" or the "hideous spawn" of the brute, displacing "the true children of [Vandover's] mind" (229). Yet the degeneration of art instanced in Vandover's Brute is a citywide phenomenon. Thus, besides its obvious role as an allegory of individual degeneration or sexual repression, the brute is an embodiment of a dysfunctional gendered economics: in the brute's deformity are involved not only the protagonist's personal sins, but all the pollutions of "the great city's vice" (230). Besides the brute itself, the other "infinitely great monster" (230) that threatens the development of Vandover's art is indeed the urban sphere—the environment where "Life" deploys itself as a "mysterious force" manipulating "the infinite herd of humanity, . . . crushing out inexorably all those who [lag] behind" (230). In this light, the hideous changelings that emerge on Vandover's canvas are comparable to the misshapen population of the metropolis itself.

There might be a promise of artistic regeneration in the fact that the horrid sketches of the brute signify the proliferating urban crowd: if pursued along the brute's grotesque lines, Vandover's painting could mediate between his own abject personality and the decadent environment of the city. The narrative of *Vandover*, however, never envisages the possibility that proper art could arise from the "grotesque and meaningless shapes" (225) born on the painter's canvas: the brute is not allowed to play the part of the trickster figures that appear in Charlotte Perkins Gilman's or Jack London's stories of artistic education, for instance. Vandover's despair at seeing his painter's craft abort in the emergence of this aesthetic monster is the more poignant as the novel, in its decadent outlook, fails to define a space for artistic authenticity: it plays off pure aesthetic perversion against the most stilted form of academicism. Norris's description of Vandover's style, before it becomes affected by the brute, suggests indeed that the young man's painting combines a postromantic fondness for open landscapes with the allegorical didacticism of the late-nineteenth-century academic tradition, as it was practiced in France by William Bouguereau (1825–1905) and Ernest Meissonier (1815–91). The preparatory sketches of *The Last Enemy*, Vandover's "first masterpiece," are heavily influenced by the "melodrama of the old English 'Home Book of Art'" from which the young man used to copy his "Ideal Heads" (14). This future "salon picture" (64), which recapitulates in allegorical terms Vandover's own struggle with the brute, portrays "a British cavalry man and his horse, both dying of thirst and wounds . . . lost on a Sudanese desert" (64). In the painting, man and horse are gazing at a lion who is drawing near with "his lower jaw hanging" (64). By privileging such colonial and military subjects, Vandover's painting emulates the tendencies in European art that are most remote from the context of the American city.

From a socio-psychological angle, Vandover's aesthetic conservatism aligns the young painter with what David Leverenz calls the "patrician" paradigm of manhood (78). In a study of the American Renaissance, Leverenz points to the existence of a linkage between the work ethic, the choice of literary subjects, and the writer's sexual identity. The mid-nineteenth-century writer's notion of manhood, Leverenz argues, was patterned after artisan, patrician, and entrepreneurial ideologies. In this system, the patrician work-gender identity characterizes the ideology of the early-nineteenth-century patrician classes, which valued "property, patriarchy and citizenship" (80). The artisan model, on the other hand, defined manhood "in Jeffersonian terms, as autonomous self-sufficiency" (78). Both the artisan and the patrician paradigm assumed that a man must be "a model of industry and honesty" (78). As such, both were opposed to the ethos of the efficient but dishonest entrepreneurs, who hailed the advent of "a marketplace emphasizing competition, risk, and calculation, with all the instability attending the economic change to industrial capitalism" (85).

In Leverenz's logic, Vandover's commitment to patrician manhood betokens his hostility to the vulgarity of the entrepreneurial world. Norris's moralizing discourse stipulates indeed that art should be a support of character—it represents "what [is] best and strongest in Van-

dover," "the one good thing that yet survived" (214, 220). The threats
such a moralizing art form is expected to contain include all that, by those
standards, is non-masculine—dependence, that is, but also aggression.
Anthony Rotundo, concurring with Leverenz, remarks that before the
end of the nineteenth century, "selfishness" and "ambition" were viewed
as threats to masculine character (227). In *Vandover*, the character who
exhibits these unsavory traits is Geary, the man who profits from Vandover's degeneration. The novel, in this logic, revolves around the confrontation between Geary's ruthless businesslike mindset and Vandover's
would-be patrician—but actually decadent—lifestyle. Each of them embodies one facet of the debasement of urban life.

It is not clear, however, whether Norris's paean to patrician rectitude
and elegance is meant to be more than a narrative decoy. It is indeed
almost a narrative necessity for *Vandover* that the erosion of masculinity
and the proliferation of the gothic should be containable only to a limited extent. The novel thrives on the description of its character's loss
of independence, illustrated in the squandering of his inheritance, the
regression to animality, and the alienation of his art. Patrician manhood
can do little against the multiplication of these symptoms of degeneration, since the novel never implies that the protagonist could meet its
ideal expectations: the son of a slum landlord who was ironically nicknamed "the Old Gentleman" (7), Vandover is the very perversion of
gentility; he is branded as a social parasite and a seducer of young women.
His inadequacy for an aesthetic of moral rectitude is made plain in the
narrator's remark that "he [has] no idea of composition" (64): his melodramatic subjects tend to lose themselves in romantic "reaches of landscape, deserts, shores, and moors" (64). More damagingly, the text intimates that the pursuit of art is in itself conducive to degeneration. In the
account of Vandover's struggle against the "filthy inordinate ghoul" (215)
that lurks within himself, the narrator indicates that the good, disciplined
impulses of the young man have been shrinking "with the shrinking of
a sensuous artist-nature" (215).

What Norris gains by letting his protagonist thus paint himself into
a moral corner is the prerogative of deploying his own gothic discourse
under the cover of a moralizing tale. The degree of empowerment afforded by *Vandover* is therefore paradoxical: it is achieved by the author
at the expense of his own protagonist. The latter has very little to cling
to by the end of the narrative. The novelist, on the contrary, manages
to break with genteel literary decorum and fashion himself into a daring naturalist, probing into scandalous topics. The exploration of instinc-

tual pathology performed in the novel creates a field for the author to dish out the sensationalistic language that his own text brands as decadent. As in London's Darwinian gothic, Norris's paroxystic enumerations ("changelings, grotesque abortions, . . . deformed dwarfs, . . . hideous spawn"), his formulaic repetitions and hyperboles add up to a manneristic form of discourse that the writer seems to pursue for his own writerly pleasure.

Gilman's "The Yellow Wallpaper"

When Norris's Vandover reaches the end of his social descent, he can only afford lodgings in a small room that "at some long-forgotten, almost prehistoric period had been covered with a yellowish paper, stamped with a huge pattern of flowers that looked like the flora of a carboniferous strata, a pattern repeated to infinity as the eye turned" (318). This passage oddly evokes Charlotte Perkins Gilman's "The Yellow Wallpaper" (1892), which reports a character's obsession with what she takes to be the grotesque metamorphoses of a labyrinthine mural pattern. The convergence between Gilman and Norris is due to the fact that the two authors believe that Victorian home decoration fosters overcivilization. Norris's *Vandover* condemns bric-a-brac as a sign of unmanning degeneration, both in an aesthetic, and, more obscurely, in a biological sense. Gilman gives a feminist twist to this fear of the overcivilized domestic space. Her sociological writings suggest that, for women, overcivilization involves being confined among dusty gimcracks whose threatening bulk embodies the barriers placed by patriarchy against women's mobility (see *Home* 156–58; *Women* 257). In Gilman as in Norris, the combined struggle against bric-a-brac and the strictures of overcivilized selfhood is carried out within gothic discourse. More specifically, the two texts presuppose that their protagonists' fate depends on their ability to wrestle with monstrous shapes that grow on surfaces of inscription—wallpaper in Gilman, a painter's canvas in Norris. Unlike in *Vandover*, however, Gilman handles this thematics of writing and inscription with a positive bias: the protagonist of "The Yellow Wallpaper" discovers in the grotesque transfigurations of her walls a trickster figure that helps her shed her disenfranchised role.

"The Yellow Wallpaper" deviates from most naturalist texts by its confessional format, close to stream-of-consciousness narration; its treatment of madness carries a distinctly modernist ring, quite different from Norris's fin-de-siècle pruriency. The story, Gilman indicates in her autobiography, was written in response to her traumatic experience as a patient of Dr. S. Weir Mitchell's cure for neurasthenic women. Gilman came to regard Mitchell's method—a rest cure that precluded any activity—as a patriarchal trap meant to turn women back to domesticity (see Gilman, *Living* 89–95; Bederman 130–31).[2] The story occupies a privileged place in my argument about literary empowerment, precisely because its function as a vehicle of its author's personal disenfranchisement is well-documented. "The Yellow Wallpaper" contains the diaries of a woman suffering from nervous collapse, who, on the orders of her husband, must remain shut up in absolute inactivity in the nursery of a colonial mansion. The narrator, who must conceal her diaries, quickly becomes obsessed with the yellow wallpaper in her room, which boasts "sprawling flamboyant patterns committing every artistic sin" (4). She comes to distinguish "a strange, provoking, formless sort of figure" behind the horrid design. Ceaselessly crawling around the room, the narrator sets out to tear off strips of the "optic horror" (9) on the wall, so as to free the figure that has come to life behind the pattern. As this ghostly character takes on increasingly grotesque shapes—bulbous eyes, strangled heads, larvae—the narrator becomes progressively identified with her: the tearing off of the paper signifies their common liberation. When this task is completed, the narrator boasts to her husband and to her sister-in-law that she "has got out at last," that she has "pulled out most of the paper, so [they] can't put [her] back!" (20). The husband faints and falls to the ground, and his wife complains of having to creep over his reclining body in order to go on with her crawling.

Walter Benn Michaels, in a landmark interpretation of the story, has criticized the temptation to regard Gilman's text as inherently oppositional. Even as Michaels describes how Gilman's character writes "herself into existence" (5), he argues that this process of self-inscription does not fully enact a gesture of empowerment through feminine work. Michaels contends on the contrary that the thematics of writing and self-generation in the story conflates production and its alienating, feminizing opposite—consumption. The protagonist, as she inscribes her new self by tearing strips of wallpaper away, consumes "her body in order to produce her body" (12). Therefore, the construction of selves in this story is not an oppositional act that would draw its legitimacy from a Veblenian critique of patriarchal rituals of consumerism. Gilman's account of the act of "willed self-begetting" (6) does not so much demystify the construction of gendered subjects in the consumption economy as it "exemplifies" its mechanisms (27)—it illustrates it with no prior urge toward endorsement or opposition.

By arguing that Gilman's "Wallpaper" is a trickster's story, I mean however to indicate that the text loses too much by being submitted to an interpretation that flattens out the binarisms that it sets up. In Michaels's perspective, for instance, it becomes impossible to view the story as dealing with alienation—mental or social—or the transgression of norms. For Michaels, hysteria is indeed the very matrix on which personhood was articulated at the turn of the century (25); it is as such not primarily a condition of painful self-estrangement. Also typical of this reading choice is Michaels's decision to bracket off the story's handling of its own generic conventions: the various processes of inscription at work in the story—the metamorphoses of the wallpaper script, the writing of the protagonist's diaries, the smooch left by her body on the wall—are dealt with as if they belonged on the same plane of discourse. My point here is, on the contrary, that self-positioning and self-inscription in "Wallpaper" take the form of a struggle among differentiated levels of discourse and verisimilitude—realism, the gothic, social Darwinism. In this logic, the paradox of the story consists in the fact that self-construction is performed in a radically alienating medium—the "interminable grotesques" (9) on the wall.

The uncanny and elusive character of the wallpaper is made visible by tropes that evoke a form of geometrical irrationality or, conversely, a teratological biology: the pattern is a "kind of 'debased *Romanesque*' with *delirium tremens*" (9) that knows no "laws of radiation, or alternation, or repetition, or symmetry" (9), yet it also resembles "wallowing seaweeds" (9) and "waddling fungus growths" (19). Gilman's geometric and biological similes, like other naturalist varieties of tropes of sublimity, are tools that hint at a hidden world beyond realistic space. In graphic terms, the distorted wallpaper patterns produce their own quasi-supernatural form of referential illusion. It is in this way that they allow the narrator to discern in the two-dimensional surface of the nursery wall the distorted mirror-image of herself—the ghostly woman shaking the ugly design in order to get free. Thus, as in the description of the "deformed dwarves" on Vandover's canvas (*Vandover* 229), Gilman's gothic discourse yields a being that would have no place in a realistic configuration; it is as if the text itself, when submitted to degeneration and disfiguration, could act as a life-giving medium. There is an element of magic in the apparition of this animate shape among the inanimate traces on the wall: the nar-

rator alludes at one point to her fascination for the lifelike aspect of inanimate things; as a child, she mentions, she derived "more entertainment and terror out of blank wall and plain furniture than most children
could find in a toy-store" (6). The presence of the woman behind the
wall corroborates the fact that the story must accept such leaps into the
gothic as a valid medium of truth. While the description of the mansion
sounded at first like a parody of ghost stories, we now realize that the
colonial mansion, like Gilman's text, is "a haunted house" after all (1).
The husband's distrust of superstition, and his fear that "a nervous weakness like [his wife's] is sure to lead to all manner of excited fancies" (6),
are branded as a sign of repressive narrow-mindedness. Conversely, the
protagonist's ability to perceive a new-born self in the gothic script shows
that her empowerment amounts to the construction of a writerly identity: an avid reader of the signs on the wall, she leaves on its surface her
own "very funny mark" (15)—the "long, straight, even *smooch*" (15) inscribed by her wanderings around the room.

Besides the engendering power of writing, "Wallpaper" uses its biological tropes to make the birth of the woman behind the wallpaper
appear as a form of uncanny, vaguely sexual reproduction. The story
contains a complex network of ambiguous references to birth, sexuality, and children. On the one hand, a few elements in the text testify
to the narrator's concern for her own child, now in the care of a relative. Yet the narrative starts with an inchoate tale of a broken family
line, which conjures up an atmosphere of sterility and ambivalence
toward reproduction; the "ancestral halls" (1) where the narrator abides
are ghostly and have long been "untenanted" because there has been
"legal trouble . . . about the heirs and coheirs" (3). Suspicions about the
possibility or willingness to reproduce increase in the description of the
nursery. A room where the protagonist is both infantilized and regenerated, the nursery is an object of ambivalence: on the one hand, it is
a patriarchal space of confinement; the narrator views it therefore as a
site of aggression and barrenness, unfit for children. Yet, by virtue of
the dialectic of regeneration of the story, she is led to conclude that
she is "really getting quite fond of the big room" (5).

The narrator's acceptance of the yellow wallpaper amounts to embracing a form of self-engendering based on a mechanism of abjection. The
wallpaper, when it is described as "an interminable string of toadstools,
budding and sprouting in endless convolutions" (12), describes a primitive, nonsexual process of proliferation. Unlike in Norris's *Vandover*,
these gothic visions do not have to be exorcised: the protagonist wel-

comes the gothic distortions through which she sees herself transfigured into a host of "strangled heads and bulbous eyes" (19) or into fungus. It is in the absolute otherness of this animal and vegetal metamorphosis that her new self is reborn—a personality that is granted the privileged power and lack of inhibition proverbially attributed to insanity.

There are, admittedly, ambiguities in a mechanism of regeneration that takes the form of a birth into madness. Gilman's story is representative of the broader naturalist corpus in that it enacts a precarious transaction whose benefits do not entirely counteract the writer's overall sense of anxiety and loss. There are two types of such transactions in the present corpus—sacrificial gestures or games of rhetorical subversion. The sacrifice motif, I have pointed out, occurs in Dreiser's *Sister Carrie*, Robert Herrick's *The Web of Life*, or London's *The Iron Heel*, where the demise of one set of characters—Hurstwood, Alves, and the Chicago rioters, respectively—works to the empowerment of each novel's protagonist. In Gilman's story, the logic of sacrifice is implicit in the text's allusions to the protagonist's suicidal tendencies. The fascination that the "sprawling outlines" (4) of the wallpaper exert on the narrator is indeed characterized as mesmeric and potentially destructive: their "lame and uncertain curves" (4) seem to "commit suicide," as they "plunge off at outrageous angles [and] destroy themselves in unheard of contradictions" (4). Kenneth Burke's theory of symbolic action suggests that we should read such expressions of despair as elements of a strategy of exorcism— as a self-sacrifice involving the author and her character: "a symbolic suicide (on the page)," Burke writes, "is an *assertion*, the *building* of a role and not merely the disintegration of all roles" (39). Thus, in "Wallpaper," as in Edith Wharton's *The House of Mirth* or London's *Martin Eden*, the death of the autobiographical figure serves as an empowering gesture for the author. This reasoning strikingly applies to Charlotte Perkins Gilman, who survived depression and the rest cure, and made a point of testifying against it. The negative side of this literary strategy consists, however, in the fact that it performs a gamble with despair. The proliferation of narratives about suicidal artists at the turn of the century indicates that cultural regeneration remains a highwire act. In this sense, the fate of Gilman's character precludes an optimistic—or even a fully empowering—interpretation of the story.

That Gilman's regeneration strategy should also be performed through rhetorical subversion is in keeping with the narrative of writerly empowerment constructed in the text. The subversive language game in this case consists in reversing the pessimistic import of the biological and evolutionary language through which the protagonist's descent into madness is portrayed. This reshuffling of evolutionary tropes is comparable to the strategy by which Dreiser, in *Sister Carrie*, manipulates the meaning of his heroine's implied passivity; it betokens an attempt to twist the logic of the scientific laws that provide the ideological validation for the writer's social universe. Specifically, the gothic ramblings of "Wallpaper" twist around the patriarchal clichés of nineteenth-century science— women's propensity for hysteria, their ineradicable link to childhood, their unmanageable reproductive biology: Gilman's discourse of regression into the animal, even into the vegetable stage, rewrites in caricatural terms the evolutionary itinerary that, according to scientific wisdom, produces proper human beings, but here only leads to the genesis of an apparently disempowered, abject female.[3] Then, in a subversive gesture, the text intimates that the biological imagery that depicts this grotesque engenderment can be made to "shriek with derision" (19): the gothic language becomes the threatening voice of a character whose newly gained power is supported—and, to some extent, undercut—by tropes of disfigurement.

Jack London's Yukon Stories

Gilman's story reveals that the process of regeneration performed through gothic discourse involves a reshuffling of evolutionary tropes. It is along those lines that I propose to read Jack London's *The Sea-Wolf* and his stories of primitive life. Of course, London's fiction is too beholden to evolutionary doctrine to carry the sharp critique of science developed in Gilman's denunciation of medical sexism. In spite of their discontent about philosophical determinism and urban-industrial economics, London, Dreiser, or Norris do not envisage the possibility that the principles of the Darwinian world could be dislodged radically. Instead, they suggest that the Darwinian legacy can only be constantly renegotiated, through provisional bargainings, as it were. The trickster logic that informs this unstable redrawing of ideological boundaries can be analyzed in the light of Carroll Smith-Rosenberg's analysis of the Davy Crockett myth. Smith-Rosenberg contends that the value of the Davy Crockett figure for mid-nineteenth-century culture consists in the fact that the frontier man "epitomizes the liminal" (101): he straddles the limit of civilization and the wilderness, and therefore embodies the possibility of transgressing all social boundaries. It is by such a mechanism of local transgressions and reversal, I believe, that turn-of-the-century novels of education work out the threat of overcivilization. Ironically, the relevance of trickster narratives to naturalism resides in the fact that they embody a limited, compensatory form of subversion. Smith-Rosenberg, quoting Mary Douglas, writes that the trickster's humor "'produces *no real alternative*, only an exhilarating sense from freedom of form in general'" (Douglas, qtd. in Smith-Rosenberg 107).

Jack London's ability to submit naturalist science to trickster logic is visible in the fact that his stories of primitive life, though they flaunt their Darwinian affiliation, do not respect the conceptual boundaries of evolutionary discourse. In chapter 10, I pointed out that naturalist genealogies rework the neo-Darwinian controversies opposing Lamarckian to Weismannian theories—the beliefs, respectively, in the primacy of learning and in the predominance of biological atavism. In a gesture that blurs the evolutionary debate, London's stories of Arctic life draw on both of these two theories, but do not treat their claims as irreconcilable. This paradoxical configuration is illustrated in *White Fang* (1906) and *The Call of the Wild* (1903)—the twin narratives of a wolf who climbs the evolutionary ladder in order to become a dog, and of a dog who reclaims his atavistic roots. Lamarckian and Weismannian formulas are present in both texts, though in different degrees of dominance. White Fang's rise out of savagery toward civilization implies that education—the acquisition of cultural traits over atavism—is possible; his story is therefore predominantly Lamarckian. The surrender of Buck, the hero of *The Call of the Wild*, to his wolfish origins suggests on the contrary that atavism remains a potent force under the surface of civilization. Thus, in this novel, Weismannian discourse prevails over the claims of cultural education.

The coexistence within the same texts of these contrasted discourses is made possible by language games similar to those we have seen at work in Gilman's story. For instance, *White Fang* revolves around the Lamarckian slogan that instinct is "the accumulated experience of the generations" (247). Yet this Larmarckian view is too rational for London's purposes: *White Fang*, in spite of its paean to civilizing virtues, remains a novel that mythicizes the primitive; it is not the mechanical account of a process of Pavlovian training. The claims of ancestral instincts are therefore restated by means of tropes of sublimity. Thus, the incantatory repetition throughout the text of terms like "the Wild" (169, 170, 206), "Life" (243–45), or the "unknown" (234, 235, 247), projects the image of a mysterious atavistic realm immune to environmental change—an image of primitivism most spectacularly embodied in the landscape of "the savage, frozen-hearted Northland Wild" (169). London's constant tendency to renegotiate his concept of evolution indicates that his texts are the site of what the novelist perceptively calls "a battle of the instincts" (*White Fang* 247): the very notion of instinct is affected by deep ambiguities. *The Call of the Wild*, particularly, plays on the dual evolutionary status of its protagonist, a personalized dog who can be attributed a human and an animal perception of his own instinctual life. The instincts that take hold of Buck when he responds to the call of the forest are not the unproblematic animal impulses that regulated his behavior as a dog on the California estate where he originally resided; they are not anchored in the Lamarckian sedimentation of habits that, like an evolutionary capital accumulated over the history of the species, has turned wolves into peaceable dogs. Rather, these are instincts viewed from an ambivalent human perspective: they are atavistic impulses that belong to the "dominant primordial beast" (65)—the wolf inside the dog. Such ancestral memories do not point to the evolutionary future, as is the case in the Lamarckian view, but point back to the primitive past.

A primitive world based on such an unstable definition of instincts accommodates characters that can negotiate the dichotomies of evolutionary discourses. These figures are literally or figuratively half-breeds. Indeed, White Fang and his mother Kiche are cross-breeds of wolves and dogs; François, one of the sled-masters in *The Call of the Wild*, is a "French-Canadian half-breed" (53); like him, a fair number of men in the North Country are of ethnically mixed ancestry—part-Inuit, part-European, or simply linked to various European countries of lesser prestige in London's eyes, and thus racially tainted. London portrays Inuit Indians as a race poised between civilization and the animal realm. Buck, though a thoroughbred dog, is a metaphorical half-breed too, since he is receptive to the call of his wolf ancestors. Through this technique of characterization, London manages to inscribe the promise of regeneration in the very make-up of his protagonists: these figures are evolutionary tricksters; they are able to look either up or down the Darwinian scale, toward civilization or atavism. Liminality is particularly crucial to the make-up of the protagonist's mentors, who can share with their trainees their skills at transgressing limits. In *White Fang* and *The Call of the Wild*, it is these liminal adjuvants who make possible the protagonists' accession either to the ecstasy of the primitive or to the comforts of civilization: White Fang is educated first by his half-breed mother, then by the Inuit Indians, then by Weedon Scott, a city man who has learned the ways of the wild.

By thus turning the polarities of evolutionary discourse into objects of transactions, London makes sure that the romance of primitivism ceases to be equated with degeneration. In *The Call of the Wild*, for instance, Buck's decision to sound "the deeps of his nature" (77) as far as "the womb of Time" (77) triggers "a secret growth" (65)—thus, a movement upward—not a plummeting down. In a paradoxical formula that fuses Lamarckianism and Weismannism, the dog is submitted to an education into the primitive. The reward of this education is a form of existential ecstasy, the "forgetfulness of living . . . the sheer surging of life, the tidal wave of being" (77) experienced by the dog "sounding the old wolf-cry" (77)—or by "the artist, caught up and out of himself in a sheet of flame" (77). Here, the rediscovery of the ancestral impulses constitutes a utopian transcendence of the Weismannian conception of biological determinism: London's text manages to transform the neo-Darwinian vision of endless extra- and intra-species struggle from a degenerative nightmare into sublime wonder.

The Sea-Wolf

A course of education at the hands of liminal adjuvants constitutes the narrative backbone of *The Sea-Wolf* (1904), London's most important novel of overcivilization and regeneration. *The Sea Wolf*, in its account of Humphrey Van Weyden's rise toward manhood, places its protagonist in the midst of complex narrative transactions about the meaning of primitive life and civilization. The two liminal mentors who preside over these ideological bargainings are Wolf Larsen, the captain of the *Ghost* and Maud Brewster, a woman poet rescued aboard in the middle of the *Ghost*'s journey. Wolf and Maud have complementary functions. The former is a naturalist superman, whose impressive physique is portrayed through heaps of sublime rhetoric; his intimacy with primitive forces will help bring Humphrey closer to his own instinctual life. Wolf eventually proves an awkward role model, however, as the form of masculinity he embodies appears uncomfortably charged with sadomasochistic and homoerotic affects. Maud Brewster's role consists therefore in breaking the hold Wolf exerts on the young man. In this, she performs a trickster's function equivalent to Wolf's, albeit higher up on the evolutionary scale: a self-reliant professional woman, she shows Humphrey how to carve out for himself a position in society that does not lead him to forsake his newly won primitive manhood.

As an evolutionary trickster, Wolf offers Humphrey a way of relating to the world characterized both by ecstasy and control: he embodies the superhuman existential joy that he himself describes as "the bribe for living, the champagne of the blood, the effervescence of the ferment" (68). The naturalist superman's liminal subject position involves the capacity to take pleasure in the spectacle of the chaotic social world while not letting oneself be engulfed in it. In the first chapters of the novel, this psychological profile is defined as a form of fascinated spectatorship. It is illustrated in a scene where Humphrey, awake on the deck at night, discovers "the unending glory of what [he] never dreamed the world possessed" (67). At that point, the young man lets himself be hypnotized by "the spectral ripple of foam thrust aside by the *Ghost*'s forefoot" (67), which marks the trace of the ship as it ploughs into the water. The spectacle, Humphrey says, "lured me away and out of myself till I was no longer Hump the cabin-boy, nor Van Weyden, the man who had dreamed away thirty-five years among books" (67). The promise of ecstatic empowerment articulated here is precarious, however, because it articulates the fantasy of a preoedipal union with the sea; as such, the hypnotic pull of the water uncomfortably recalls the image of the sinking San Francisco ferry where Humphrey nearly perished. Wolf's appearance on deck in the midst of Humphrey's dream of aggrandizement is in this respect quite timely. The captain tears the young man away from a mesmerizing oceanic vision, and reminds Humphrey of the necessity to keep such ecstasies under strong paternal control.

With its dialectic of maternal and paternal affects, the narrative of Humphrey's education fits the (pre)oedipal models of the sublime elaborated by Thomas Weiskel or Bryan Jay Wolf. Weiskel's preoedipal paradigm locates the primary source of sublime affects in the "original ambivalence" (105) experienced by the subject toward maternal entities that appear as fascinating and overwhelming—romantic landscapes, or, in *The Sea-Wolf*, the "crooning song" (67) of the sea's "spectral ripple of foam" (67). It is to help the subject break away from preoedipal fascination, Weiskel contends, that the sublime activates an oedipal scenario of identification with the father. Thus, under the surface of one single overwhelming moment of terror, Weiskel discerns two levels of affects: the preoedipal longing for engulfment and, secondarily, "superego anxiety" (105)—the fear of the castrating father, which affords a shelter against the more powerful maternal bond. The father-oriented part of the sublime dialectic, Bryan Wolf suggests, pits the son (less convincingly the daughter) in "oedipal rivalry" (201) against the sublime father; the child, in this scenario, is affected with feelings of "secondariness" (201) toward a parent whose authority may, however, be subverted.

The Sea-Wolf diverges from the (pre)oedipal script of sublimity in that it does not represent the father figure as a stable anchorage of authority: Wolf is an object both of identification and desire, as perilous as the maternal sea that threatened to annihilate Humphrey in the opening chapter. It is indeed a feature of London's failed sublime that the crisis brought about by preoedipal fears of oceanic engulfment should not be put to rest by Humphrey's identification with Larsen, but, on the contrary, chronically rekindled. At first, the novel promotes paternal authority as an antidote to overcivilization. The captain steering the steamboat that hits Humphrey's ferry is a "trim and quiet" (20) paternal ruler, who marches "hand in hand" with destiny and runs "a calm and speculative eye" over the victims of the collision (20). In an uncanny association, this Olympian character, never to appear again in the text, announces the arrival of Wolf, whose ship emerges out of the fog, as if by magic. Like the captain of the steamboat, Larsen is a creature of preternatural calm whose glance means "life and death" to Van Weyden (23). Thus, at the end of the shipwreck scene, the dread of the feminine seems to have been counteracted by a masculine take-over. Wolf can, however, not consistently fulfill his function as a paternal mentor. He is all too eager to denigrate the ideal he himself embodies: delight in the power of nature, he argues, is no more than "the drunkenness of life, the stirring and crawling of the yeast, the babbling of the life that is insane with consciousnssess that it is alive" (68). Behind this self-subversive remark lies the more fundamental fact that Wolf's persona, because of its sublime magnitude, exceeds the limits of one role—of the oedipal object of identification, say. It would indeed be impossible for Humphrey to model himself after a primordial superman that mixes such diverging features as the primitive brutality of a McTeague and the cultural acumen of a reader of "Shakespeare, Tennyson, Poe . . . De Quincey, Tyndall" and "Darwin" (50).

His impossibly protean outline makes Wolf a naturalist brute, portrayed by means of gothic tropes of abjection. Humphrey's awkward attempts to characterize the captain yield a portrait based on the paradoxical tropes of weakness and strength used by London in *The People of the Abyss*. An atavistic figure, the captain is associated "with things primitive, with wild animals, and the creatures we imagine our tree-dwelling prototypes to have been" (29); the root of his masculinity is "a strength savage, ferocious, alive in itself, the essence of life" (29); yet, by the same token, he embodies the more threatening and incongruous energy "which writhes in the body of a snake when the head is cut off, and the snake, as a snake, is dead" (29). On the one hand, there are connotations of remarkable power in the sight of an animal so full of the motion of life that it maintains its spastic activity even when cut in two. The image is, however, also one of castration and of abject degeneration: it is as if London were trying to represent in this repulsive reptilian shape a masculine power so blind that its striving for absolute activity makes it unconscious of its own death or of its own futility.

What Humphrey detects in the abject aspects of Wolf's primitive energy is the threat that the captain's and his crewmen's masculinity might tip over into a form of homoeroticism that he fears is neither manly nor even human. Humphrey remarks about the sailors of the *Ghost* that "their masculinity, which in itself is of the brute, has been overdeveloped. . . . They are a company of celibates, grinding harshly against one another and growing daily more calloused for the grinding. It seems to me impossible sometimes that they ever had a mother. It would appear that they are a half-brute, half-human species, a race apart, wherein there is no such thing as sex; that they are hatched out by the sun like turtle eggs, or receive life in some similar and sordid fashion" (107). This description of a self-generated breed of males, entirely independent from women and sexual reproduction, contributes to the novel's surprisingly developed discourse of homosexuality and androgyny. The crew of the *Ghost*, like Norris's wheat speculators, are characterized by a pattern of homosocial relations of the type defined by Eve Kosofsky Sedgwick in *Between Men:* the seamen are involved in an oedipal triangle in which the male-male ties are mediated by the presence of a metaphorical maternal figure. In Norris, this maternal third term was the engulfing vortex of the Board of Trade; in London, it is the mesmerizing flow of the sea: manhood, on the *Ghost* is measured by the ability to weather storms or to hunt seals. Since the sea represents a partner of a nonhuman, symbolic order, affective relations—very often aggressive ones—are established between men only.

On the ship itself, homoerotic intensities are fostered by the system of charismatic hierarchy to which the aggressive males are submitted. In this logic, Larsen's homoerotic attraction is constructed by means of the same theatrical configuration as the one Sedgwick describes in Melville's *Billy Budd:* the ship serves as a showcase for subjects and objects of homosexual desire, thus setting up a homosexual spectacle of masculinity

(*Epistemology* 92). For instance, in the most erotically charged moment of the relationship between Humphrey and Wolf, the captain strikes bodybuilder's poses in front of the young man; the latter becomes "fascinated by the perfect lines of . . . Larsen's figure" (116) and he suitably reflects that this paragon of the "man-type, the masculine" has a body "as fair as the fairest woman's" (116) as well as eyes "large and handsome, wide apart as the true artist's are wide" (33). Thus, Wolf might easily fit in the gamut of nineteenth-century icons of homosocial desire recorded in Sedgwick's studies of homosexual discourse: he comes close to the Nietzschean admirer of Grecian manhood, for instance (Sedgwick, *Epistemology* 136).

In this psychological configuration, Humphrey's first trial of manhood exorcises not only cultural feminization but also the homosexuality embodied in Wolf's unstable sexual definition. The confrontation pits Humphrey against the ship's English cook, Thomas Mugridge. In charge of all the women's tasks performed on the ship—cooking, cleaning up—Thomas is abjection incarnate; he is servile, cowardly, and cruel—a petty tyrant with feminine traits, who manages to be repulsive even in his Cockney intonations, in his fawning "greasy smile" (27), and in the smells of filthy cooking that emanate from his person. Formerly the lowliest creature in the hierarchy of the ship, he relishes the fact that he has been granted authority over Humphrey, the cabin boy. The struggle between Humphrey and Thomas is a farcical analogue of the sadomasochistic cat-and-mouse game that opposes Humphrey to Wolf. Since Humphrey has toughened up since his arrival on board, the fight is fated to be the mutual slaughter of "a pair of beasts" (77): Humphrey feels his lips lifting and "snarling like a dog's" (77). In practice, it takes the form of a symbolic masturbation contest in which the opponents obsessively whet dirks and kitchen knives in front of each other, carefully listening to other sailors—all of them experts at stabbing—eager to share technical advice. The cook concedes defeat to Humphrey, who will from now on run the galley himself, carry a dirk in a sheath on his side, and browbeat Mugridge whenever he feels like it.

Comic as it is, the narrative of Humphrey's victory over Thomas signals that survival on the ship is secured by adopting a ruthless entrepreneurial work-gender profile. There is no end to the cycles of regeneration on the *Ghost*, as the men must ceaselessly exorcize fears of feminization that are stirred by the very organization of their competitive homosocial universe. As Humphrey himself remarks, the *Ghost* is at bottom an "industrial organization" manned by employees at the mercy of a cruel boss—a world where life is "a cipher in the arithmetic of commerce" (61). As such, the seal schooner fulfills Leverenz's definition of the entrepreneurial mentality, which privileges strife and produces personalities obsessed with the threat of humiliation at the hand of other aggressive males. *The Sea-Wolf* contains characters who match Leverenz's description of the protagonists of Herman Melville's *Moby-Dick:* in either case, the sailors are "craving to be humiliated and thus to be fused with manly power" (283).

The novel defines two strategies through which Humphrey can respond to the entrepreneurial violence of Wolf's world. One of them is fulfilled within the novel: it consists in escaping from the arena of male-male aggression by entering a heterosexual union with Maud Brewster. The other is only adumbrated through the depiction of Wolf's transgender features: it involves the acceptance of an androgynous personality that can withstand both preoedipal dissolution and oedipal competition.

Maud's alternative to the violence of Wolf's homosocial polity is a psycho-economic ethos based on artisan self-reliance. The young woman is a likely advocate of this set of values because, contrary to what Humphrey initially thought, she is no "delicate, ethereal creature" of romance (165), but rather a naturalist amazon. Her immunity to overcivilization is established when, questioned by Wolf about her economic status, she proudly replies that she earns eighteen-hundred dollars a year through "piece-work" (154)—that is, by writing poems. As such, Maud embodies what Leverenz calls the artisan work-gender identity—the psychological profile that abides by principles of autonomy, industry, and honesty (Leverenz 78). In this light, Maud's dedication to an artisan work-gender profile carries the positive connotations of the early-nineteenth-century work ethic: her life as a self-employed poet stands in complete contrast to the infighting of Wolf's seal-hunting venture.

The artisan values introduced into the novel by Maud inform Humphrey's second cycle of trials of manhood—his lessons in survival on a desert Alaskan island. At the end of the novel, Humphrey and Maud escape from Wolf's dominion and end up on a rocky stretch inhabited by bands of seals—a place the two lovers quizzically name Endeavor Island. These scenes, drawing on the atavistic discourse of naturalism, present the reconstruction of married life in quasi-prehistoric conditions. Humphrey and Maud, like Robinson Crusoe, or, more accurately, like characters in the Flintstones cartoons, are pictured performing household tasks in the primeval realm of an island that resounds with the cries of rutting seals. This celebration of strenuous labor is meant to display both the strengthening of Maud's physical courage and to provide illustrations of Humphrey's newly acquired artisan masculinity: the young man, having rebuilt a ship out of the debris of the *Ghost*, exclaims: "All my handiwork was strong [though] none of it beautiful; but I knew that it would work, and I felt myself a man of power as I looked at it" (268). Maud, for her part, is revealed in all her amazon glamor; at the end of the characters' stay on the seal rookery, Humphrey proudly exclaims that Maud is his "mate-woman, fighting with [him] and for [him] as the mate of a cave-man would have fought, all the primitive in her aroused, forgetful of her culture, hard under the softening civilization of the only life she had ever known" (256). These lines indicate that the work of remasculinization is complete, for either character.

The second strategy of adaptation to entrepreneurial violence defined by *The Sea-Wolf* involves, I have indicated, the adoption of a transgender status; it corresponds to a work-gender paradigm not provided for in Leverenz's classification, which I wish to call corporate androgyny. By using this label, I seek to do justice to the fact that the psychological and economic discourse of naturalism does not define manhood or the hardships of real life on the basis of oedipal, male-male conflicts alone: the gendered economics of London, Dreiser, or Norris create a situation where male characters have to measure themselves against entities that are modeled as feminine—the urban market, the corporation. In this context, corporate androgynes are protagonists—predominantly males—whose claim to power is not only backed by the prerogatives of patriarchy but is paradoxically enhanced by the addition of feminine features.[4] They derive their heightened economic power from an ability to bracket off their sense of individuation and to merge with the feminine entitities of the urban economy that would otherwise threaten their sense of selfhood. Naturalist characters that fit this definition—Wolf in London's *The Sea-Wolf* or Eugene Witla in Dreiser's *The "Genius"*—are liminal tricksters in two respects: they transgress the boundaries of gender and economic identities.

The aspects of Wolf's androgyny that I described in the beginning of this section were generated by the logic of the spectacle of masculinity—the game of self-display to which the captain lends himself with relish. In order to bring to light what links his androgyny to the corporate economy, we need, however, to take into account another component of Wolf's persona—his role as a Darwinian shaman, in touch with the primordial cosmos of evolutionary forces. Wolf's role as an evolutionary trickster is made visible in the moments when he appears terrified and fascinated by the idea that his energy might turn into "strength and movement in fin and scale and the guts of fishes" (68). These regressive fantasies contribute to his androgyne persona insofar as Wolf acts as a seducer of men—a "Male Circe" (188)—able to make himself and his underlings regress to a nonhuman status. The reversal to an animal state is an aspect of the trickster's ability to dissolve all boundaries—sexual, natural, or social. Smith-Rosenberg shows that, in the Davy Crockett myth, the regeneration of masculinity is created out of "the violation of categories and the fusion with chaos" (197). Here too, the primitive imagery implies that a protean personality like Wolf's increases its power even as it seems to lose itself through alienating—thus also feminizing—metamorphoses.

In the make-up of Wolf's trickster persona, we may discern that androgyny is associated with a mode of social integration that is both interstitial and transcendent: androgyne supermen are able to assume incompatible work-gender identities. Wolf, for example, is defined by two contradictory economic logics: entrepreneurial manhood and the feminized economics of overcivilization. While his seal schooner is an organization of virile entrepreneurs, seal hunting itself, Mark Seltzer remarks, links Wolf with the feminized urban economy because, as London writes, it consists of a "wanton slaughter, and all for woman's sake" (*Sea-Wolf* 125; qtd. in Seltzer, *Bodies* 171). The dog-eat-dog squabbling of the entrepreneurial work-gender identity is, however, something that Wolf can, through his superman persona, both fulfill and transcend. As a fighter, the captain is at least the equal of his crewmen; as a social Darwinian philosopher he is able to probe into the mysteries of the struggle in nature, and can therefore lift himself above the scuffle. On the other hand, the androgyne component of the superman's profile promises to neutralize his dependence on the feminized urban economy by making him interchangeable with the city women who embody the metropolitan markets.

The capacity of androgyne tricksters such as Wolf to slip through the constraints of appointed social roles can be understood within the economic logic of what cultural historians such as Alan Trachtenberg and Martin J. Sklar have called the age of incorporation. Sklar points out that the 1890s debate over the trust was vitally affected by the passing of the Sherman Act, which tranferred the status of the legal person to "intangible" bodies—that is, the corporations (49). In practice, Sklar explains, this legislation partly freed corporate stockholders from the legal accountability to which they would have been submitted had their money remained invested in the full-fledged ownership of a company. Walter Benn Michaels argues that the creation of such intangible persons in the economic field led Populist pamphleteers and novelists to express the fear that corporations might be too large and insatiable for any form of limiting embodiment: rather, they must be disembodied entities—in fact, immaterial souls (185–88).

The corporate economy and the profile of androgyne tricksters thus share a common logic of disembodiment—capital is transferred and reinvested as gender roles are donned and shed. The link between economic and sexually transgressive shifts is overdetermined: the gendering of the economy that prevails in naturalist novels brings about a situation where the androgynes' gender mobility emblematizes their ambition to transgress class boundaries. In these works, the men who mimic the economic practices of the corporate economy should be tied neither to the roles of the nineteenth-century work ethic nor to traditional masculine identities.

Wolf's eventual downfall reveals, however, that, contrary to Humphrey's revitalized manhood, regeneration through male androgyny cannot substantially be constructed in *The Sea-Wolf*. The full-fledgded development of the male corporate androgyne self would involve a radically positive appraisal of primitivism that even London's fiction cannot endorse: though Wolf's regressive fantasies of disindividuation offer the promise of neutralizing the fears of engulfment that plague Humphrey, they still bear the stigmata of degeneration. The androgyne trickster partakes in the same form of abjection as his subhuman underlings who seem to have received life "in some . . . sordid fashion" as if they had been "hatched out by the sun like turtle eggs" (107). In this context, Wolf, as a transgender type, performs the ambiguous function of illustrating the degeneration that affects men—especially artists—in the overcivilized context of the corporate economy, and of sketching out in a utopian mode a form of accommodation with the new economic scene. Denied the full enjoyment of this androgyne transformation, the captain of the *Ghost* is, however, cast out from the narrative.

On the Threshold of the Metropolis: The Construction of Naturalist Bohemia

Gilman's "The Yellow Wallpaper" and London's *The Sea-Wolf* provide allegorical narratives of artistic education set in surroundings remote from the naturalist artist's round of life. In the present chapter, on the contrary, I discuss works that portray the actual mode of social integration available to cultural producers in the early twentieth century. The contradictions of artistic practice in naturalism are brought to light in a scene of Dreiser's *The Titan*, where financier Frank Cowperwood, after a performance of Puccini's *La Bohème*, exclaims that the "makeshift studio world" represented in the opera "may have no connection with the genuine professional artist, but it is very representative of life" (408). Cowperwood's formula implies, on the one hand, that writing or painting are social functions, performed in the commonplace environment of professional activity, not in a romantic "makeshift studio" (408). On the other hand, artistic labor carries a project of cosmic scope: in Cowperwood's vitalist idiom, it manifests the presence of "life" in the social world (408). From a Lukácsian perspective, we could, however, argue that American naturalists dissociate the professional routines of art from the totalizing function implicit in Cowperwood's description: they do not enjoy indeed a direct, organic access to the vital historical struggles of their time. Obsessed by the limits placed on individual agency by urban-industrialism, they, as Lukács writes of Zola and Flaubert, "stand aloof as observers and critics of capitalist society" (119). While I agree with Lukács's diagnosis of the fragmentation of the writers' experience, I believe, however, that the naturalist rhetoric of sublimity constructs for protagonists and narrators a subject position that is more complex than mere aloofness. The involvement of naturalists in turn-of-the-century affairs was, as Christopher Wilson's discussion of "popular naturalism" (xii) indicates, substantial, though not up to Lukács's utopian standards. The naturalists' ambiguous form of social integration, compounding commitment and distancing, is, I have argued, expressed in the novelists' predilection for trickster protagonists: Carrie Meeber or Wolf Larsen are very active *flâneurs* who bypass established hierarchies by ingenuity or self-transformations.[1]

The unstable negotiation by which naturalist artists define their place in the urban-industrial metropolis is enacted in a literary space that, following Dreiser's cue, I wish to call naturalist bohemia. Indeed, the novels in the present chapter portray creative activity taking place in a marginal area of society, be it the literal environment of urban artists or other liminal spaces from which artists express themselves in naturalist novels. The term bohemia designates in this perspective the universe of protagonists in Dreiser, Willa Cather, James Weldon Johnson, Abraham Cahan, and Ernest Poole, for whom being an artist means shuttling between established social identities: the trickster heroes of these texts are professionals, farmers, entertainers, or political activists, yet are also committed to an artistic activity that, they hope, gives them the freedom to negotiate or discard these roles if they become too constraining. Conversely, the liminality of bohemia is characterized in some of these novels—Cather's, Johnson's, Cahan's—as a condition enforced on the creative protagonist by gender or ethnic inequalities, or by the logic of capitalism.

The *"Genius"*

Theodore Dreiser's *The "Genius"* (1915), one of the novelist's least critically successful works, is the text that, from my perspective, provides the paradigmatic representation of naturalist bohemia. It traces the evolution of Eugene Witla, a painter who seeks to be both an artist and a successful executive.[2] To Eugene, aesthetic regeneration means acquiring the survival skills necessary to navigate the capitalist market. Eugene leaves his native Illinois small town for Chicago and New York. First a magazine illustrator, he enjoys a meteoric ascension as a painter, until his reputation sags. Eugene's marriage to Angela Blue, a morally conservative midwesterner, is jeopardized by the several affairs he has before and during his marriage, mostly with women he meets in artistic circles. Due to his failure both in art and in his emotional life, Eugene suffers from a nervous breakdown. He obtains from a railroad executive the opportunity to do a manual-labor cure in a carpenter shop of the company. As an "amateur laborer" among proletarians, the painter recovers his mental balance.[3] Still too fragile for artistic creation, Eugene decides to satisfy his financial ambition in the field of advertising and publishing. Eugene realizes, however, that he cannot withstand the infighting within the company hierarchy. His regeneration is, in the amoral logic of the text, triggered by the timely demise of his wife, who dies in childbirth. Eugene, now a proud father, enjoys a new spell of creativity.

The "Genius" might qualify as a novel of overcivilization were it not that, unlike Jack London or Frank Norris, Dreiser does not view the crisis of masculinity as an instinctual dysfunction. Eugene's sexual and cultural malaise is not due to his artistic sensibility but to the pressure of small-town values. Art, in this perspective, is a vehicle of existential emancipation, fueled by the desire to "get out of the ranks of the commonplace" (49). There is an anti-proletarian dimension in this program: Amy Kaplan indicates that the novelist valued the prestige of the artist's status as a goal in itself, and that his "conception of authorship meant distinguishing himself from wage laborers" (133). By these materialistic standards, all successful forms of art are worthy of praise, because all "artists [are] different from the rank and file of mankind" (66).

Dreiser deals with what he perceives to be the forces of conformity by means of a strategy of rhetorical devitalization: he depicts them in such sentimental terms that they cease to represent a threat. The anchoring places of tradition in the novel are Eugene's family in Illinois, Angela's homestead in Wisconsin, and the carpenter shop where Eugene recovers from depression. These locales are literally embalmed in yeoman and artisan kitsch: they are peopled with nostalgic stereotypes of American life. For instance, Angela's father, Jotham Blue, is elevated to the dignity of icon of midwestern manhood. In accents reminiscent of Norris's *The Octopus*, he appears as a "farmer in the big sense of the word—a cultivator of the soil," who lives in "the new paradise of the world" (116). His children display the yeoman virtues of "character [and] strength" (117).[4] Artisan virtues are also the hallmark of the railroad laborers with whom Eugene spends his work cure. These "heavy clods of souls" (307) work in a "little carpenter shop" (310) in a pastoral nook along the Hudson. Dreiser remarks that "there was a veritable song of labor" arising from the workplace (301). By thus clothing the activity of railroad laborers in the sentimental garb of craft work, Dreiser denies the existence of proletarianization. To Eugene, wage labor and the dependence on the market are permanent threats that cannot be ignored outright, but that can still be presented in sanitized form.

In his evaluation of the philosophical role of the artisan ethos, Eugene acts as a proper spokesman of Dreiser's discourse of urban sublimity. Eugene perceives artisan virtues as a set of principles that he "heartily respect[s] in others" but may not bear "any fixed or important place to him" (113). The young artist's decision to live beyond good and evil is based on the insight that society and nature are sublime fields that outspan all systems of value:

> He was always thinking in his private conscience that life was somehow bigger and subtler and darker than any given theory or order of living. It might well be worth while for a man or woman to be honest and moral within a given condition or quality of society, but it did not matter at all in the ultimate substance and composition of the universe. Any form or order of society which hoped to endure must have individuals like [Angela's mother] Mrs. Blue who would conform to the highest standards and theories of that society, and when found they were admirable, but they meant nothing in the shifting, subtle forces of natures. (113)

The fragmented, destabilized moral systems depicted here are homologous to family farms inserted in a fleeting nationwide market or to small companies, like Eugene's father's sewing-machine concession, at the mercy of the vagaries of a business landscape dominated by trusts. This passage indicates that Eugene, as a bohemian amoralist, may hope to thrive in the "shifting, subtle forces" (113) that have set the fragments of the old pastoral and artisan world adrift.

By attributing to his protagonist a subject position that incorporates and circumvents all other values, Dreiser constructs a utopian blueprint of what I call the corporate identity. Corporations play an important mediating function in Eugene's project of empowerment: they are the medium through which the philosophically inclined artist can implement his or her fantasies of social ascension. If, during his depression, Eugene seeks help from a railroad company, it is because he believes that only corporations are broad-based and powerful enough to respond to an artist's neurasthenia. The "'Engineer of the Maintenance of Way'" (300)

Eugene meets in the head office of the railroad is "a pale, dark man" who acts as "captain of thirteen thousand men" (300). In these lines, Dreiser portrays corporations through a rhetoric of empire: Daniel C. Summerfield, head of the advertising agency where Eugene later works as an art director, is presented as a "remarkable individual" who uses "Napoleonic" methods for the management of men (390, 393). Empires, like the naturalist corporate self, throw an overarching structure over a set of discrete parts. Thus, Eugene comes to conclude that "life might possibly be ordered to the best advantage" under a system akin to the railroad hierarchy, in which "all were striving to do the work of intelligence" (313). In this way, to borrow Fredric Jameson's terminology, Dreiser's corporations serve as "representational shorthand" for the subtle currents that govern life (*Postmodernism* 38).

The *"Genius"* places the protagonist's vision of the imperial corporation on the same footing as his utopian representation of the world of art. What links these two realms is, according to Dreiser, the role they attribute to insatiable desire, as well as the fact that they offer a field of expression for androgynous identities. The *"Genius,"* like most narratives of artistic education, depicts art as inherently linked to sexuality. For Dreiser, the gendering of art seems to take place at first strictly along heterosexual lines. On the one hand, Eugene's sensibility was fashioned by William Bouguereau's "warm-tinted" (50) nudes, which, the narrator suggests, testify to the artist's "astonishingly virile" (222) gaze. The same kind of masculine toughness, Rachel Bowlby indicates, is the hallmark of realistic representation in the novel (Bowlby 123). Yet the author attempts to place himself beyond the view that valuable art should be a man's prerogative. He suggests indeed that the aesthetic libido is fueled by the intensity of desire and the refusal of conventions, not by the gender of the subject. Thus, he opens the artistic realm to women who are not tied to the domestic sphere. Dreiser's bohemia is therefore presented as the abode of the New Woman, of "women of distinction" who have achieved "completeness and sufficiency" by combining masculine intellectual pursuits and feminine sensibility (132). The most prominent of these are Miriam Finch, a sculptor, and Christina Channing, a singer; both of them are "self-directed, self-controlled personalities" with "ideas of [their] own" (132). These artistically oriented New Women exhibit the contradictions of liminal characters, at pains to reconcile their intellectual goals with their love life. Miriam Finch is "a student of life . . . with keen appreciative intelligence." Yet she still longs "intensely for . . . the charm of face and form to compel the impetuous passion of a lover" (132). Likewise, the beautiful Christina has sacrificed her marital prospects for her career as a singer. Sympathizing with her plight, Eugene remarks that there should be "a new sex for artists—like they have for worker bees" (148).

The third-sex definition of artistic androgyny applies, of course, fully to Eugene himself: the young painter is the more able to find acceptance in bohemia as he is endowed with a mixture of masculine and feminine features that constitute the distinguishing mark of his artistic sensibility. Like Jack London's Wolf Larsen, the painter's androgyne make-up is particularly evident in his ability to play both sides of the spectacle of masculinity—as the subject and the object of the desiring gaze: Eugene is able to seduce both women and men. Christina, when taking Eugene out in artistic gatherings, flatters herself that he is "like his pictures . . . and as good to look at" (141); Hiram C. Colfax, the publisher who hires the young painter as artistic director, acts partly because "he liked Eugene's looks" (440). What these people appreciate in the young painter are not the muscular achievements praised in Jack London's heroes, but subtle, feminine qualities: Eugene is "somewhat like a lighted lamp casting a soft velvety glow" (133); he has a "sensitive, high-strung nature" (218).

The artist's androgyne personality proves useful to the corporate world insofar as it is associated with seduction and intuition. These qualities are intimately linked to saleability, since both commodities and persons need to stir desire in others in order to be exchanged. In this, *The "Genius"* develops a metaphysics suited to the advertising world: the author remarks that Eugene, as an artist and a businessman, lives in a universe where "life is apparently striving, constantly, to perfect illusions and to create spells" (472). Far from demystifying these illusions, Dreiser suggests that spells should function as creative fictions. The result is a social scene where psychological magnetism regulates personal relations among artists, in the same way as it helps characters negotiate the instability of the capitalist market. In its artistic and erotic form, this system of mesmeric intuition allows Eugene to recognize his kindred spirits: on their first encounter, Miriam Finch appears to the young painter as "intensely magnetic and gratifying" (132). In its commercial function, intuitive seduction is embodied in the figure of Daniel Summerfield, who, as a young canvasser, was "so smiling, so bland, so insistent, so magnetic, that business came to him rapidly" (391). The homology between artistic and commercial intuition is best illustrated in Eugene himself; as an artist, the young man is praised for being "quick to get impressions, especially of talent" (140). This aesthetic gift is, however, no different from the technique of the professional talent scout: it is the kind of gaze that Daniel Summerfield casts on the same Eugene, when the latter applies for a position as an art director.

However, Dreiser's theory of intuition undercuts the standards of verisimilitude of his novel. The upshot of the author's psychology is the creation of an androgynous hero who visits astrologers, adheres briefly to Christian Science, and trusts the popular superstitions about encountering "cross-eyed women" (389). In a text whose epistemological premises remain tied to realistic positivism, the introduction of parascience appears as a rather desperate strategy of containment. It covers up indeed the fact that the alliance of art and business within corporate selfhood may merely be Eugene's life-saving illusion: Eugene has to be endowed with gifts of intuitive perception the more magical as they might be suspected of lacking any substance whatsoever.

The weakness of Dreiser's conception of corporate selfhood lies in a flawed understanding of how corporate hierarchies work. Many of the adventures that befall Eugene are due to the fact that the business world falls short of being the real-world embodiment of the cosmic totality of phenomena. What lurks behind the facade of the "splendid vision of empire" (404) of the corporate realm is instead the backbiting of the entrepreneurial mentality. At the Summerfield corporation, the young painter's efforts are checked by a hierarchy ruled by fear, slavish subjection to the master, and selfish dishonesty: Eugene's colleagues "seemed little mannikins to him—little second, third, and fourth editions or copies" of their boss (415). Against this stultifying competition, Eugene opposes a dashing lifestyle that undermines his professional trustworthiness. His superiors come to the conclusion that "like all artists, [Eugene] is flighty" (419). Colfax, a perceptive corporate executive, dismisses Eugene by telling him: "You're a genius, I fancy . . . but like all geniuses you are afflicted with tendencies that are erratic" (644). After this, Eugene returns to his artistic vocation. Though advertised as a spiritual regeneration, this development marks in fact the failure of his utopia of self-aggrandizement.

Willa Cather's *The Song of the Lark* and *O Pioneers!*

Dreiser's *The "Genius,"* the autobiographical work of a German-American writer, focuses on a character who stands at the threshold of the city's power centers in several respects—as a midwesterner, as an American bearing a non-Anglo-Saxon patronym, and as an androgynous subject.[5] I have argued that a liminal status is the hallmark of all *flâneurs* of the urban sublime, who keep exploring a world that is never completely their own. *The "Genius,"* a stereotypical novel of bohemia, reveals through its gender and ethnic problematic that this subject position has a broader field of relevance than artistic life in the city. There are, in pre–World War I fiction, texts that investigate how artistic expression can develop from the margins of patriarchy or in between lines of ethnic segregation. Among those, Willa Cather's *O Pioneers!* (1913) and *The Song of the Lark* (1915), James Weldon Johnson's *The Autobiography of an Ex-Coloured Man* (1912), as well as Abraham Cahan's *The Rise of David Levinsky* (1917), express different levels of optimism about the possibility of creating disenfranchised subjects from an off-center position. While Cather celebrates an empowering feminine sublime, Johnson creates a protagonist mired in ambiguities. Cahan, in his realist novel, criticizes liminality as a trap laid by the structures of capitalism.

Alexandra Bergson and Thea Kronborg, the Swedish-American heroines of, respectively, *O Pioneers!* and *The Song of the Lark*, share the uncommon ability to flourish in environments where, according to Willa Cather, only liminal characters can thrive: the Iowa frontier for Alexandra, Colorado and the New York bohemia in Thea's case. In spite of the apparent dissimilarity of each novel's narrative concerns—a midwestern farmer's life and an opera singer's education—it is illuminating to discuss them in parallel. I believe indeed that *O Pioneers!* transposes the narrative features of artistic biographies to a frontier context. Conversely, the sharper characterization and more compelling narrative structure of *O Pioneers!* brings into relief a dialectic of feminine empowerment that *The Song of the Lark* articulates less convincingly.

In the two novels, the mark of the artist's education is the struggle against moral conformity and philistinism. The narrative of *O Pioneers!* resembles a story of bohemia because it shows the imaginative Alexandra waging the artist's struggle against creatures of habit—her own kinsmen, that is. After her father's death, Alexandra is left in charge of a farm covering supposedly unprofitable acreages. She believes that visionary intuition is necessary to make the "wild land" of the high country thrive (*Pioneers* 20). Accordingly, she adopts new farming methods that help her raise the farm out of debt and turn it into a prosperous matriarchal utopia. In this endeavor, Alexandra acts as an artist in the management of real life, working from the domestic sphere. That Cather deliberately inverts the narrative pattern of artistic education is visible in the fact that the novel's only professional artist—Carl Linstrum, Alexandra's future husband—only has a peripheral function in the story. Carl sees himself as a frustrated painter, reduced to working as an engraver. Aware of Alexandra's superiority, he exclaims, "I've been away engraving other men's pictures, and you've stayed at home and made your own" (116). The community Alexandra creates remains, however, marginalized: it is destabilized by Alexandra's brothers, who resent acting on a woman's instructions; also, it is weakened by Alexandra's own self-centeredness, which prevents her from interpreting the motives of the members of her clan: she fails to notice the secret love affair that develops between her brother Emil and a married woman, Bohemian neighbor Marie Tovesky. Marie and Emil are eventually killed by the young Bohemian's husband, an event that shatters Alexandra's world.

In *The Song of the Lark*, Thea Kronborg, a Lutheran pastor's daughter, feels like a cultural outcast in Moonstone, Colorado, her native small town. An extraordinarily gifted pianist and singer, she is supported by some of her family members—particularly by her mother. Townspeople, however, rate her below other local prodigies whose artistic inclinations respect the artistic pieties of church life. By contrast, Thea cultivates the esteem of those few characters who understand her gift—the local doctor Howard Archie, freethinking railroad man Ray Kennedy, or Spanish Johnny, a Mexican drifter with a keen sense of music. Once she moves to Chicago, to the East Coast, and later to Germany, the tension between genuine artists and dull professionals still informs Thea's itinerary within musical bohemia. Her most effective mentors at that point are a Hungarian piano teacher, and Fred Ottenburg, the son of a beer magnate turned patron of the arts. The novel ends with the image of Thea musically triumphant as a Wagnerite soprano, yet alienated from most of the social world and genuinely understood only by a scattered group of admirers. We learn in the epilogue that she eventually marries Fred.

What sets Thea and Alexandra apart from most of their contemporaries is a gift of genealogical intuition that, Cather suggests, lies at the root of the pioneer spirit: the two heroines are trickster figures able to communicate with the sublime past of the West. In *O Pioneers!* Alexandra's sublime epiphanies occur when the young woman senses within a landscape seemingly "unfriendly to man" (20) the presence of the "Genius of the Divide, the great free spirit that breathes across" the land (65). Alexandra is the first person "since [the] land emerged from the waters of the geologic ages" (65) to turn "a human face" inspired by "love and yearning" (65) toward the midwestern wilderness (65). Under her gaze, the Iowa highlands are no longer "an enigma"—they radiate the "power of growth and fertility" (76).

Likewise, Thea Kronborg's musical talent is rooted in the American landscape in that it is embodied in a heroine moved by the Western "feeling of empire" (485): Thea shares with her friend Ray Kennedy the impulse to roam about the West and to visit the sites where the "wagon-trails of the Forty-Niners" are still visible (340). These imperialistic undertones, similar in some respects to Jack London's Anglo-Saxonism, are given a bohemian twist in *The Song of the Lark:* the novelist indicates that Thea must empathize not only with the European conquerors of the West but also with the "Ancient People" (*Song* 544)—the ancestral cliff-dwellers who inhabited the Arizona desert. Exhausted after her second stay in Chicago, Thea, on Fred Ottenburg's suggestion, spends a few weeks in Panther Canyon, a cliff-dwellers' abode. The experience forever clarifies the stakes of her singer's gift. Letting her "intuitions" (550) merge with the bodily experience of the Indian women who once trod "the rocky trail," Thea feels in the flesh "the hardness of the human struggle" (550). The regeneration she enjoys there follows the pattern of the genealogical sublime: "The Cliff Dwellers," Thea feels, have "lengthened her past" (555). Forever pledging her hostility to the "self-satisfied people" who spurn "any serious effort" and remain "at the mercy of blind chance," she feels endowed with "older and higher obligations" (555)—the duty to devote herself to a musical endeavor of cosmic significance.

The Song of the Lark suggests that the broadening of genealogical and existential perspective Thea enjoys in the cliff-dwellers' pueblos is the proper foundation for a singing gift tuned to the requirements of the modern metropolis. Up to that point the narrative had defined musical inspiration in contradistinction to urban life: when Thea attends her first symphonic concert in Chicago—a performance of Dvořák's "Symphony of the New World" and excerpts from Wagner's tetralogy—she not only becomes "conscious of the city" (469) for the first time but also realizes that the chaotic urban crowd will try to make her "let go of" (470) her precious musical insight. However, her stay in the canyon provides the psychological dialectic that allows her to reconcile artistic intuition with the social environment of the city. The deserted Indian dwellings embedded in the rock walls form indeed "a dead city" (546) whose houses are set "in a row, like the buildings in a city block" (546). They stand therefore as a deeply hidden genealogical double of Thea's urban universe: in contrast with the befuddling environment of Chicago or New

York, they form a "cleft in the heart of the world" (567) where things are "simple and definite" (554) as "they had been in childhood" (554). In this sense, the canyon epiphany makes Thea "united and strong" (554) by embedding within her personality a realm of sublime genealogical depths. The heroine will from then on be able retreat to these emotional recesses in order to find "the things that [are] really hers" (554).

Alexandra's dialogue with the "Genius of the Divide" (65), as well as Thea's communion with the experience of cliff-dweller women, constitute instances of what Patricia Yaeger calls the "'feminine sublime'" (205). Yaeger argues that women poets like Elizabeth Bishop develop a preoedipal variety of the sublime that differs from the angst-ridden scenarios of masculine romanticism; in the moment of "'feminine'" sublimity, the subject glimpses a powerful maternal figure that "does not threaten to obliterate" the self (207) and promises instead to fulfill "a pre-oedipal longing for otherness and ecstasy" (209). In this process, the sublime object does not need therefore to be exorcized, repressed, or fetishized.

In Yaeger's formulation, the "feminine" sublime amounts to "domesticating" the Romantic experience of terror and wonder (Yaeger 209). This term should be understood in its etymological meaning since, in Yaeger's reading of Bishop, the upshot of the confrontation with the sublime is the creation of what Jean-François Lyotard calls a *"domus"*— a family-based group defined against a background of cosmic forces (*Inhuman* 191). The reconstitution of this extended domestic sphere is literally achieved in *O Pioneers!* where a matriarchal farm community is wrested from Alexandra's struggle with the land. Under Alexandra's aegis, this group gathers the different branches of the Bergson family, the farm hands, as well as characters ostracized by more conservative townspeople. There is a direct continuity between the cross-ethnic and philosophically unorthodox character of Alexandra's extended clan and the eccentric nature of Alexandra's visionary power. In her function as a matriarch, the young woman follows the repressed traditions of immigrants who, in the Old World, had been "tree-worshipers before the missionaries came" (152). Typically, Alexandra's main adjuvant is Crazy Ivar, a pagan hermit who lives on a half-sunken "wild homestead" (38), interacts more comfortably with animals than people, and listens to the "strange voices" (39) of the country. In *The Song of the Lark*, the bohemian community attracted by the performer's charisma is more distended than Alexandra's group since it relies on the elective affinities of music rather than on a domestic settlement. As in Alexandra's story, Thea's constituency includes an eclectic set of adjuvants—from Anglos like Dr. Archie to Mexicans like Spanish Johnny. The utopian possibilities offered by this group are illustrated in the festive moment when Thea returns home from Chicago and displays her newly acquired singing skills to her Mexican friends—people Thea regards as the members of "a really musical people" (495). The scene perfectly delineates the liminal integration available to the heroine: singing among the Mexican chorus of Spanish Town, she is the pivot of an eccentric community, relegated to the outskirts of Moonstone. As she performs the Mexican songs, a few of her Moonstone friends listen, entranced, to the "yellow butterfly" of her voice soaring from a distance in the summer night (498).

Against these glimpses of artistic and interpersonal victories, Cather's novels suggest that bohemian liminality carries an inescapable burden of alienation. Predictably, the boundaries constraining the heroines' empowerment through the feminine sublime are due in part to the discriminations forced by social conventions on cultural outcasts. Alexandra feels like a superman figure whose "fate [is] to be always surrounded by little men" (*Pioneers* 181) and whose imaginative efforts are not regarded as "real work" (170). Yet Cather also traces the origin of her protagonists' discontent to the very nature of their visionary inspiration. In *O Pioneers!* this pessimistic appraisal of the trickster's power is noticeable in the fact that Alexandra's landscape epiphanies are worded in a pastoral idiom that has, in Cather's time, been thoroughly refashioned by Norris's and Dreiser's city novels. The vitalist imagery in which Cather's landscapes are portrayed carries the dark ambivalence of the urban sublime: as in Norris and Dreiser, Cather's vitalism relies on a guessing game with uncanny life currents. In the case of Marie Tovesky's fated affair with Emil Bergson, for instance, Alexandra fails to discern where the forces of life run. Unaware of the two lovers' feelings, she reproaches Marie for jeopardizing through her lack of discretion the integrity of the farm community. Carl is, in this case, the more perceptive observer. Emil and Marie's love, he tells Alexandra, brought about "an acceleration of life"; it "was something one felt in the air, as you feel spring coming" (305). This form of pastoralism differs radically from the Whitmanian glorification of natural landscapes overflowing with vitality. The universe that it defines is one where channels of fertility have to be guessed at. It is therefore as unreliable as a speculative market. Accordingly, the characters that inhabit it are liminal in a negative sense: convinced that "the land belongs to the future" (Cather 307) and that

pioneers "should have imagination, should be able to enjoy the idea of
things more than the things themselves" (48), they remain, however, on
the threshold of durable empowerment.

The Song of the Lark, is, I believe, less straightforward than *O Pioneers!*
in its final assessment of its protagonist's achievement: the novel tends
to pass off as a full-fledged idealistic revelation what is in fact an insight
of an uncannily disquieting nature. Fred Ottenburg, Thea's musically lit-
erate suitor, explains that the young woman's superiority as a singer is
based on her ability to "simplif[y] a character down to the musical idea
it's built on" (649) so as to make her audiences able to hear "the idea,
the basic idea pulsing behind every bar she sings" (649). The practical
emotional impact of Thea's singing is, however, not in tune with this ideal
of essential clarity. When Dr. Archie, after Thea's long stay in Germany, attends one of her Wagner performances, his response is indeed "admiration" but also "estrangement" (640). Initially, the Elsa von Brabant
figure on the stage stirs in him "something like buck-fever" (638)—the
paralyzing fear that assails hunters confronted with an elk for the first
time, making them unable to shoot. Recovering from this sublime dread,
Archie resigns himself to the thought that a new being has "devoured"
the "little friend" (64) he knew in Moonstone "as the Wolf ate little Red
Riding Hood" (640): Thea seems now "much farther away than she had
seemed all those years when she was in Germany" (640). This negative
impression is born out when Archie meets the diva later at her hotel. At
first, the doctor finds Thea distant, suspicious, and prematurely aged; he
soon realizes that she is tied to a work schedule that cuts her off from
the world. We might argue that it is legitimate for Thea, the empowered soprano, to appear as a forbidding force of nature: her Cliff-Dwellers' canyon epiphany taught her not only to connect to her "earliest
sources of gladness" (545) but also to take inspiration from a "geological world" (56) whose "silent, immense operations" (560) could "get on
very well without people, red or white" (560). Still, by the end of the
novel, we feel that Thea's alienation carries a more bitter ring than what
her uncanny gift requires. This sense of unease is fueled by the fact that,
once the singer leaves for Germany, she is described mostly through the
consciousness of friends who know her only from a distance, and she
becomes an ever-receding presence in the narrative. In the epilogue,
through the Moonstone point of view of Thea's adoring aunt Tillie, we
get to understand that the soprano's legacy consists in her capacity to stir
ambitious fantasies in people mired in the mediocrities of everyday life.
Thea's trickster function boils down therefore to the power of implant-

ing in others the liminal status that keeps her partly disenfranchised: through her art, she reveals the existence of a fascinating threshold her audiences cannot cross.

The Autobiography of an Ex-Coloured Man

Relegation to a liminal status is the very condition of the narrator of James Weldon Johnson's *The Autobiography of an Ex-Coloured Man* (1912). Johnson's text is a novel of artistic education chronicling the itinerary of a light-skinned colored man who, in his early childhood, believed he was white. The son of a black sewing woman and of a prominent white southerner, the narrator belongs to the black middle classes. This group, he complains, enjoys a precarious, unrecognized status in turn-of-the-century America. Many of its members, shunned by the white establishment, live in absolute social invisibility; they are, in white people's minds, conflated with a black underclass for which the narrator expresses nothing but contempt; some middle-class blacks, like himself, straddle the color line. The narrator, nameless to the end, exacerbates his own interstitial condition by earning his living as a musician who performs a mixture of classical and rag-time music to audiences of white dilettantes and "coloured Bohemians" (105); his ultimate ambition as an artist is to make African-American music known to white audiences by making "it classic" (142), that is, by adapting it to European norms. Eventually, after witnessing a lynching that leaves him scared and shamed, he chooses to pass for white and to make a living in real estate. It is from this standpoint as a white man that he tells his autobiography.

By entrusting the novel's narration to a character that falls so radically in between ethnic and class lines, Johnson creates a text that switches with bewildering ease between different generic frameworks of reading. Overall, *Autobiography* is a story of the color line in the fashion of Charles W. Chesnutt's tales: its story of education allegorizes the situation of a whole community. *Autobiography* can also be read—though, I think, less compellingly—as the psycho-existential story of a single individual whose "choices . . . define him," even though "each is the wrong choice" (Rosenblatt 183). However, either reading option—allegorical or "novelistic," to take up Michael Denning's terms (74)—smoothes over the disruptive picaresque features of the text. The "novelistic" interpretation seems untenable in view of the fact that the novel covers a range of African-American experience that far outreaches the scope of a single character. The story includes, among other things, sentimental memories of a childhood in the South and in New England, an incursion into the universe of Pullman Porters, descriptions of urban poverty in Atlanta, the narrator's apprenticeship as a Jacksonville cigar maker, a sublime panorama of his approach to New York, his initiation into the gambling clubs of Harlem, travels to Europe, and so on. Conversely, even if Johnson's peripatetic protagonist fits the narrative requirements of a panoramic social allegory, the melodramatic climaxes that motivate his move from one locale to the next introduce breaches of verisimilitude so conspicuous that they verge on metafictional irony. Above all, Johnson's *Autobiography* surprises its readers by what we might call its dialogic fractures—by the fact that, under the surface of one protagonist's continuous narration, it accommodates apparently incompatible voices. The narrator's confessions switch from his self-portrait as an overcivilized pianist, whose own playing brings tears "rolling down [his] cheeks" (27), to fiery vindications of Negro empowerment through education, and to the narrative of his success as a white businessman, in Horatio Alger style.

Bernard W. Bell attempts to pin down the political orientation of the *Autobiography* by analyzing its unstable narrative voice in terms of ironical distance. Bell argues that, even as the narrator flaunts his adhesion to white culture, the "implied author" of *Autobiography* manifests his "sympathy for the rising black middle class" (89) and he "subtly divorces himself from his narrator's decision" to repress his "black American identity" (89). Though Bernard Bell thereby compellingly describes the overall political drift of Johnson's novel, he takes, I think, too much for granted the author's reliance on clear-cut ironies. I believe instead that *Autobiography* resorts to mechanisms of ventriloquism comparable to those that Michael Bell discerns in *Sister Carrie*. Dreiser's writing, Michael Bell argues, works by "an effacement of ironic distance" (161), which leads the novelist "toward an affective stylistic identification with the sensibilities of his characters" (162). In *Autobiography*, this polymorphous handling of the voice underlies, for instance, the narrator's depiction of his own educational efforts. Once the young protagonist learns he is a Negro, he manifests his "pride that [he is] coloured" (46) by enshrining Frederick Douglass "in the place of honour" (46) of his pantheon of black leaders. When appropriated by Johnson's narrator, Douglass's call for the education of blacks becomes, however, a blind, selfish race for excellence that leaves the character so intent on impressing white society that he loses the ability to make a contribution to African-American culture. In this psychological evolution, it is difficult to determine at what point we are encouraged to distance ourselves from the character's thirst for achievements. There might be some benevolent self-irony in the protagonist's reminiscence that, as a young piano student, he resented being given "the handicapping title of 'infant prodigy'" (26). Yet his ensuing claim that he "never played the piano like a child" (26) is backed up by an exposé on musical technique too specialized and informative to be viewed ironically. Likewise, the narrator's declaration that he has devised "what [is], so far as [he] knew, an original system" (132) for the study of French might, in the novel's context, be foregrounded as ridiculous bragging, were it not that the character goes on for one whole page to lay out the specifics of what is indeed sound educational methodology.

It is easy to imagine how a voice with multiple allegiances may be appropriate to a protagonist who is, as Johnson writes, constantly in "transition from one world into another" (20). By eschewing a stable narrative perspective, Johnson introduces indeed into his protagonist's idiom the logic of what W. E. B. Du Bois calls the "double-consciousness" of African Americans—the biracial affiliation that Johnson himself calls the "dual personality" (21). The narrator of *Autobiography* explains that the black American "is forced to take his outlook on all things, not from the view-point of a citizen, or a man, or even a human being, but from the view-point of a *coloured* man" (21). There ensues a "dual personality" that, he argues, forces blacks to disclose "one phase" of themselves "only in the freemasonry of [their] own race," while they are obliged to approach whites "under cover of broad grins and minstrel antics" (21–22). Johnson's achievement in *Autobiography* consists therefore in enacting these grins and antics within the narrator's voice itself. He describes a liminal protagonist who, like a trickster playing a "capital joke" (199) on the readers can, in the same voice, weep over the purity of sentimental matrimony, empathize with the mishaps of Harlem gambling addicts, and, overhearing white men discussing the Negro question, feel "compelled to accord [some] . . . admiration to the Southern white man for the manner in which he defends not only his virtues, but his vices" (165).

In spite of the overall impression of rootlessness induced by the protean make-up of Johnson's picaresque hero, *Autobiography* defines, I think, a space that serves as its center of narrative gravity. Through most of his adventures, the hero seems indeed to find his bearings among a homosocial fraternity of young men, which remains liminal toward other institutions. Johnson's novel, like Dreiser's *The "Genius,"* differentiates between its locales by granting them various degrees of generic verisi-

militude—from sentimentality to realism or uncanny romance. In this
system, family life and courtship are portrayed in the most abstract terms:
the narrator's childhood reminiscences are cloaked in sentimental tears,
while his several fiancées as well as his wife and children remain distant
shadows. The cigar-making episode, on the other hand, is sharply realistic, but, like Dreiser's account of the carpenter shop in *The "Genius,"*
it stands apart from the rest of the narrative. Most substantial, by comparison, is the constellation of men who help the protagonist in his wanderings, by offering him accommodation or, as in the case of a white New
York millionaire, by hiring him as a travel companion. These characters
pop up magically when help is needed. As such, they play the part of
fairy-tale adjuvants or, in the context of naturalism, of those figures revealed through what I have called genealogical epiphanies—providential kinsmen encountered in the trajectory of a romance narrative.

The homosocial fraternity is most vividly brought to life in Johnson's
portrayal of African-American bohemians in Harlem. These scenes unfold against the background of a metropolis depicted as a sublime "en-
chanted spot" (89) whose "stimulating influences"—"the crowds, the
lights . . . the gaiety" (90)—exert an addictive attraction on its inhabitants. The narrator's initiation into the Harlem bohemia proceeds according to the logic of the mysteries of the city. The gambling den is composed of mysterious hallways and parlors that lead the protagonist from
one fascinating game to the other. The cultural "Club" (97) is located
under a Chinese restaurant; behind its "gloomy facade," the narrator
discovers "a veritable house of mirth" where artists, intellectuals, and
sportsmen congregate (97). In this environment, the narrator learns,
respectively, gambling and rag-time; in the former case, education takes
the form of masculine ritualized challenges; in the latter, it consists of a
quick apprenticeship at the end of which the protagonist earns the title
of "professor" (115). The gambling place and the "Club" (97) make up
the utopian center of the novel; with regard to the city, they are interstitial places, with a highly positive connotation—centers of culture and
entertainment standing, from the narrator's point of view, at a welcome
remove from black urban poverty. The narrator's departure from New
York (typically, on account of a melodramatic imbroglio) has therefore
the effect of a slow narrative fade-out: as he moves to other, less envi-
able borderline identities, the text recedes into clichés and ventriloquist
parody, a process that culminates with the narrator's forsaking his music—his last tie to the community of black bohemians.

The Rise of David Levinsky

In Cather and Johnson, liminality, even when it is forced on the protagonist by sexism or racism, is rewarded with the glamor of tricksterdom. In Abraham Cahan's *The Rise of David Levinsky* (1917), on the contrary, the temptation to stay in between work identities is branded as a cultural maladjustment induced by urban capitalism. *Levinsky*, a confessional novel narrated by the main protagonist, is a narrative of liminal identity, though it is only indirectly a story of artistic life: its protagonist contemplates a career in the field of learning, opts for the garment business instead, is relegated to the sidelines of the dominant Anglo community, and ends up slumming on the confines of bohemia. The text ranges through a broad sweep of European and Jewish-American locales. It begins with the protagonist's childhood in the Russian town of Antomir. The young man, an orthodox Jew raised in poverty, is from the very first an eager Talmudic scholar. After his mother is killed by Russian anti-Semites, he emigrates to the "magic shores" (67) of America, where, for the sake of the job market of the Manhattan East Side, he has to give up his orthodox customs. David starts off as a push-cart peddler, then moves to the fast-developing garment industry. First hired as a machine operator in a sweatshop, he resents his new status as "a workman, a laborer, one of the masses"—that is, as a "degraded wretch" (152). To him, even a penniless peddler belongs "to the world of business, to the same class as the rich, the refined" (152). This Dreiserian distaste for proletarian work leads David to set up his own business, which, after initial mishaps, becomes a thriving company. The secrets of David's success are his ability to trick his acquaintances into his own capitalist schemes and, on the other hand, the systematic use of non-union labor—practices for which he finds an ideological vindication in the writings of Darwin and Spencer. Culturally, David is at first ashamed of his own greenhorn manners, which he unlearns by strenuously mimicking the manners of Jews more Americanized than himself. Also, throughout his life, he regrets his inability to pursue his studies, if not as a Talmudic scholar, as least at the College of the City of New York—an institution he calls "my Temple" (146). Divided between his achievements in business and his intellectual ambitions, Levinsky remains to the end of his life a frustrated character. His alienation is, in typical realist fashion, made visible by the fact that he never marries, but keeps shifting from one impossible courtship to another.

By using a confessional format for this novel of business life, Cahan risks the challenge of borrowing the voice of a character with whose values he, as a socialist, radically disagrees. Though there are moments when the author seems to give his narrator free rein—David's historical panegyric of the garment industry on the East Side is a compelling tribute to entrepreneurial zeal—the text as a whole makes clear that David's voice defends the principles that bring about his own maladjustment. It is, I think, important to keep this structure of ironical distancing in mind when interpreting Cahan's discussion of the relation between religion and business—a major issue in the novel. *The Rise of David Levinsky* attempts to explain how a man raised in the religious traditions of the Old World is led to embrace American capitalism. Faith and business are, on the surface, antithetical practices, linked, respectively, to the Old World organic community and to the secularized New World. Yet I believe that, in the novel, the relation of the Old World and the New is not a matter of simple contrast. David Fine argues that Cahan's exiled protagonists are "unable and unwilling to extricate themselves from the grip of the past," and that their yearnings for what has been lost constitute "positive forces . . . in their lives" (121). I would nuance this by arguing that Cahan does not portray Old World values along sentimental lines. Religious education, in *Levinsky*, is granted an extended and respectful discussion. Yet these passages also describe a world where piety and the fervor of learning are promoted by sadistic disciplinarians nicknamed, for instance, "the Pincher" (18) or "the Cossack" (20), and where even earnest scholars are not immune to mutual jealousy. Deeper down, Cahan's novel implies that religion fosters a disenfranchising form of otherworldliness: it is, in other words, a vehicle of alienation. The very mechanics of worship, Cahan indicates, create divided selves. David explains that reading the Talmud favors a "sense of duality" (35): with their minds "absorbed in the meaning of the words" and their hearts listening to the singsong of the text, Talmudic scholars "live in two distinct worlds at once" (35)—neither of them being the world in which the protagonist could find ideological tools to help him resist the pressure of urban capitalism.

Cahan's ambivalent portrayal of religion establishes an unexpected continuity between Talmudic scholars, suspended in between two worlds by their religious trance, and the plight of David in his New York exile. The connection between religious alienation and its secular equivalent in the city is made visible in the description of David's Atlantic crossing—a scene where Cahan relies on the discourse of oceanic sublimity.

In the "awesome whisper of the waves" (85), David discerns "an uncanny force" (85) that he associates with the "divine inspiration" (86) that created the Book of Psalms. Further down, this vision of divinity in nature merges with the protagonist's wonder at the "gorgeousness of the spectacle" (87) of New York harbor, where even ferries appear as "multitudinously windowed palaces" (87). David's "ecstasy" (87), however, soon gives way to misgivings as he faces the "icy inhospitality" (89) of immigration officials. One might argue that, in the progression of this passage, Cahan contrasts sacred values with a form of meretricious glamor that can easily be unmasked. I believe, however, that this anticlimax calls into question any form of submission to grandiose power. Both religion and business construct a harmful liminal position: in the former case, the subject is forever kept glimpsing into the "mystery" (38) of the "Master of the World" (39); in the latter, the protagonist's mind is set on an ever-receding horizon of financial aggrandizement.

Because the novel is focalized from David's point of view, there is little room for Cahan to display characters who struggle against the alienation of capitalism. Potential role models—socialist activists, for instance—occupy a peripheral position in the narrative. One of them is Matilda Minsker, the Russian-educated young woman who, in Antomir, had a brief affair with David and partly financed his voyage to America. After twenty years, David meets her again in New York; she is now an activist, married to an ideologue of the party. In her eyes, David has become a soulless capitalist who shows up at union meetings sporting a mink overcoat. Typically, Cahan's novel, because of its demystificatory logic, does not substantially define a mediating bohemian space where David and Matilda could interact more positively. The liminality of bohemia is, in the novel, the very condition of the market, and therefore not the prerogative of art. Still, we do get a glimpse of a Jewish bohemia in those scenes where David is, against all odds, courting the daughter of Hebrew poet Abraham Tevkin. The aging poet had been famous in Russia for the impassioned love lyrics he wrote for his wife. In the United States, Tevkin finds himself the head of a family in which each member "worship[s] at the shrine of some 'ism'" (474)—Zionism, socialism, or the modernism of little magazines. There could be regenerating energy in this depiction of young people committed to new causes. Yet the picture is blighted by the fact that, like David, the great Tevkin has betrayed his vocation: forsaking poetry, he has become a speculator obsessed with the development of New York real estate.

The Harbor

In contrast with the realist disenchantment of Cahan's *Levinsky*, I want to conclude the present discussion of stories of education with Ernest Poole's *The Harbor* (1915), a novel that, at the end of the naturalist period, churns out the rhetoric of urban sublimity in its full romantic glamor. In Poole's story of education, the narrator is brought at one point to wonder if he might "not try becoming one of the workers" (176). This blatant expression of *flâneur* politics appears in a work that, Peter Conn indicates, is "designedly pro-socialist" (117) and was widely read in its own time. After a long critical eclipse, Conn suggests that *The Harbor* still ranks as "the best"—though also as the last—of the socialist novels of the early twentieth century (110). From my perspective, *The Harbor* stands also as one of the works that signify the end of the first wave of naturalism. The text displays indeed most of the features of the rhetoric of terror—oceanic imagery, gendered economics, stories of hypnosis and regeneration, the problematic of liminality—which it mixes with proto-modernist elements such as explicit psychoanalytical allegories.

The Harbor is a story of education, narrated in the first person by a protagonist named Bill, whose existence is defined by his liminal relation to the New York harbor. This locale allegorizes the development of American industrialism. "I have seen three harbors," the narrator muses retrospectively, "my father's harbor which is now dead, Dillon's harbor of big companies which is very much alive, and Joe Kramer's harbor which is struggling to be born" (373). The three ages thus defined correspond respectively to the period of post–Civil War entrepreneurs, to Progressive-Era trust-sponsored scientific management, and, finally, to the advent of the socialist masses. Initially, Bill is a timid bourgeois youngster, partly educated in the Paris bohemia. On his return from Europe, with the help of several mentors, he discovers the harbor of the trusts. Two sublime epiphanies are needed to make him commit himself to the politics of the harbor, and to make him become, first a pro-capitalist publicist, then a socialist writer. The pro-capitalist mentors are Eleanore Dillon, Bill's future wife, and her father, an advocate of what James Weinstein calls corporate liberalism.[6] Bill outgrows his father-in-law's capitalist outlook at the instigation of Joe Kramer, his radical high-school friend. Joe introduces Bill to the harbor of the crowds who fight against capitalist oppression. Bill realizes then that "the spirit of the crowd" (315) can coalesce from its initial chaotic state and produce organized action. He records this experience in an autobiographical manuscript. Though the strike fails and the workers mobilize for the oncoming imperialistic war, the text closes on a vague promise of hope and vitalistic unity.

Poole's representation of the harbor follows the tradition of the naturalist sublime in that it defines class boundaries and work identities in gender terms. Accordingly, Bill's exploration of the docks is structured by the preoedipal and oedipal scenarios I have analyzed in London's *The Sea-Wolf* or Norris's *The Pit*. The domestic sphere, in this logic, is the abode of benign maternal influence. Industry, on the contrary, is the men's world, a universe "immeasurably stronger than [Bill]—in fact, like [his] father" (20). Bill realizes, however, that this masculine space is activated by feminine energies—abject ones, that is: on a spree with a youth gang, he discovers prostitution. The memory of the "hideous, disgusting" whores, the narrator writes, "loomed over my whole childhood" (15). From then on, Bill cannot see "or even [think] of the harbor" without feeling "the taste of foul, greasy water in [his] mouth and in [his] soul" (19).

In order to dispel his ambivalent perception of the harbor, Bill needs father figures who are equal to the crushing power of industrialism. Bill's own father is unfit for that function: his utopia of entrepreneurial capitalism has been defeated by "the smoke and soot of an age of steam and iron"—the age of the trusts (108). Dillon and his daughter Eleanore are, on the contrary, highly charismatic figures. Dillon—"the first really big man [Bill had] ever come close to" (149)—is "a giant" from whom emanates "some queer magnetic force" (152). Eleanor, motherless at a young age, is a daddy's-girl amazon who deftly steers her personal motorboat through the New York docks. It is during an outing on Eleanore's boat that Bill experiences his pro-corporate epiphany: in a revelation patterned after Coleridge's "The Rime of the Ancient Mariner," he becomes able to discern beauty in the dirt and disorder of the docks. Gazing at two "foul sluggish columns of smoke" (139) rising on the Jersey shore, he lets himself be entranced by the smoke's "wonderful purple" (140). These "monster snakes" take on the guise of "the rush and the vigor of life" (140–41).[7] Both Coleridge's and Poole's epiphanies enact a scenario of reconciliation with natural forces and sexuality. For Bill, the epiphany represents simultaneously the transcendence of industrial abjection and his sexual coming of age—his falling in love with Eleanore. Also, the conversion scene describes a dialectic of regeneration that will later focus on the labor crowds.

Bill's newly won perception of the magic of industrial life expresses itself at first in "glory stories" (162)—press articles that celebrate the capacity of capitalists to determine "how it is that everything has become so frightfully snarled" (144). Dillon and Eleanore help the young writer by offering him the ability to "see [the] harbor or city or state as a whole" (184)—whether from Eleanore's boat or from Dillon's high rise. This building, a transparently phallic symbol, is "a garish tower of lights that [seems] to be keeping a vigilant watch over all the dark waters" (138). From up there, the engineer enjoys over the harbor's "smoke and dirt and disorder" (138) what Michel de Certeau calls a "god's eye view" (*Invention* 171, my translation)[8] and what, in Michel Foucault's terminology, qualifies as a perspective of panoptic surveillance.[9]

In practice, the engineer's agenda blends the social-reform zeal of the Progressive Era with the money-mindedness of the corporate world. "For every abuse that [Bill] could discover," Eleanore contends, "her father was working out some cure" (142). Simultaneously, Dillon and Eleanore make no secret that, as far as the harbor's rationalization goes, "Wall Street" is "the brains of it all" (154): "In all you'll see while exploring the wharves," Dillon says with pride, "you'll find some string that leads back there" (154). These passages speak in the accents of Norris's pro-corporate sublime. Seen from Eleanore's boat at daybreak, the "homes of the Big Companies" (154), towering over the sublime city, offer a breathtaking spectacle, as "sunshine" is "reflected from thousands of dazzling window eyes" and the corporate city produces "a deep humming" (154). It is unanimistic visions of this type, in which big companies serve as symbols of the unity of all life, that Bill tries to capture in his "glory stories" (162). His series consists of interviews of important businessmen whose glory lies in their ability to bring together the fragments of industrial America, and to turn social chaos into a well-ordered worldwide flow of commodities. The novel makes visible the power of these "invisible gods" (221) in sublime insights of global interconnection, worded in Whitmanian catalogs: "the men of the mines, the factories and the mills, the promoters of vast irrigations on prairies" (212) are, in this logic, reconciled under the benevolent aegis of imperialistic capitalism.

Peter Conn argues that Poole's astonishing ability to emulate Norris's pro-corporate rhetoric weakens his socialist agenda (117). Conn's objection is compelling provided we place *The Harbor* within the framework of a politics of realist demystification. I believe, however, that Poole's novel, unlike, for instance, Cahan's *Levinsky*, is an instance of the naturalist sublime precisely because it does not condemn its character's capacity to empathize with the city's fascinating spectacles. In this perspective, Bill's political commitment is less a matter of argument than of emotional shock tactics. To tear him away from the glamor of corporate rule, the forces of socialism need to evince a spectacle more powerful than what capitalism delivers. The object of this second major epiphany is the crowd as a factor of historical change. The mentors who help the narrator bridge the gap that separates him from the nameless masses are Joe Kramer and Jim Marsh, Kramer's unionist friend. Kramer, a perennial radical, is the most pronouncedly allegorical character of *The Harbor*: Eleanore remarks to her husband that Joe "has a real place in the deep unconscious part of you" (248). This proletarian mentor has the magical ability to appear whenever and wherever a radical voice must be heard.

Just as Dillon and Eleanore take Bill on a trip up the tower, Joe takes the young man on an initiatory descent to the engine room of an ocean liner. The ship has an explicit class system that spreads on a vertical spectrum—from the sunny upper decks, where "dainty women" (250) sport their furs, to the furnaces buried "within ten feet of the keel of the ship." The men Bill meets below are the abject refuse of capitalism. Their quarters are a "foul" place, "encrusted with dirt" (246). Bill notices that "the smells of [the men's] bodies [fill] the place" (246); the stokers' breakfast—a "greasy, watery soup" (247)—is reminiscent of the oily water of the docks and, as such, concentrates all the abject features of the harbor. Bill, at first, sees only despair in these men. To Joe Kramer, however, there is a dialectic of hope working through the process of proletarianization; ships, he claims, now employ hands with "factory views" (248): they are eager to go on strike.

Bill's ambivalence toward the "surging multitudes of men" (304) is eventually resolved when the young writer realizes that the crowd is capable of self-organization. Throughout, Bill views the mass through the categories of order and disorder that are central to the elder Dillon's corporate liberalism. Since the multitude possesses no managerial hierarchy, the only feature that can redeem it in the eyes of the young artist is a quasi-magical quality of self-structuring that he calls "the spirit of the mass" (246). This phenomenon becomes visible during the first strike meeting where, "in some mysterious fashion a crude order" appears (314):

> Gradually I began to feel what was happening in this hall. That the first "strike feeling" . . . was condensing as in a storm cloud . . . attracting swiftly to itself all these floating forces. Here was the first awakening of that mass thought and passion which swelling later into full life was to give me such

flashes of insight into the deep buried resources of the common herd of
mankind, their resources and their power of vision when they are joined
and fused in a mass. Here in a few hours the great spirit of the crowd was
born. (315)

This oceanic depiction of the fusional group, with its allusion to coalesc-
ing vortices and magical illuminations, constitutes the apex of the discourse of sublimity of *The Harbor*. It seals Bill's conversion to socialism.

The end of the novel expresses a note of hope for the future, while
acknowledging defeat in the present. The narrative records the slow
dismantling of the strike. The narrator, though, enjoying the freedom
of his liminal status, lives these events through the ebb and flow of the
"'strike feeling'" (315). Its disappearance is experienced as the eclipse of
a mystical insight. But, Bill adds, "back we would go into the crowd, and
there in a twinkling, we would be changed. Once more we were members of the whole and took on its huge personality. . . . And this to me
was a miracle, the one great miracle of the strike" (321). Though the
endless "miracle" of this regeneration remains fragile, Bill chooses to
trust to it until the end of the strike.

By accepting the immersion into the disordered crowd, Bill commits
himself to a paradoxical form of mass politics that reads like a socialistic
rewriting of Le Bon's theory of the feminine crowd. Like the French
sociologist, Poole views the "common herd of mankind" (315) as a sublime body whose power is immanent but also chaotic. In Poole's socialistic crowd psychology, the power of prestige, which Le Bon attributed
to leaders, is restored to the mass itself. Poole's vision of self-organization posits the existence of a charismatic principle in the mass, which
manifests itself as a magical crystallization of force, perceptible during
political epiphanies. Peter Conn's dissatisfaction with this mystical pseudo-totalization is understandable (113): by characterizing the revolutionary mass in those terms, Poole endorses the dialectic of distance and
regeneration that forms the basic structure of the fascinated gaze of
naturalism. This subject position belongs to outsiders, unable to grasp
the inner dynamic and structures of a movement. Bill's gaze remains
indeed peripheral to proletarian commitment: as an artist, he admires
the sailors' chanties, but condemns their lyrics as too crude. Logically,
it is not Bill himself, but an Italian unionist who writes the "Revolutionary Songs of the Sea"—the politicized versions of the chanties that inspire the striking sailors. Instead, Bill submits his autobiographical manuscript to mainstream publishing houses, which turn him down on account
of his radicalism; eventually, he manages to release his narrative of the

strike in the little magazines of New York bohemia. His drifting away from militancy is expressed in the vitalist finale, which, as Peter Conn points out (117), replaces the specifics of militancy with a blurry invocation to life.

It would, however, be simplistic to take Bill's eventual movement away from politics as the sole measure of the political impact of *The Harbor*, or as the decisive proof of the limitations of naturalist liminal artists. Doing so would, for instance, render incomprehensible the novel's enthusiastic reception among pre–World War I socialists. I argued in the discussion of James Weldon Johnson that the liminal heroes of naturalism need not exclusively be viewed along novelistic lines—that is, as fictional persons paralyzed by what Conn calls the divided mind of pre–World War I culture. I believe indeed that the main attraction of Poole's *The Harbor*, Johnson's *Autobiography*, and Cahan's *Levinsky* resides in the fact that their narrators are to some extent picaresque devices that make visible the whole gamut of ideological commitments available to their politicized readers. In this logic, *The Harbor* fulfills its agenda by its expository function alone, leaving readers free to focus on one specific ideological narrative and disregard the others.

Of course, the reduction of the naturalist fictional artist to the role of picaresque mediator is in itself a sign of marginalization, since it precludes a synthesis of consciousness—here reduced to a mere expository mechanism—with the urban world. Willa Cather's *O Pioneers!* and Dreiser's *The "Genius,"* whose protagonists do not act as mere picaresque puppets, reveal that naturalist bohemia is the site of artists whose perimeter of action is shrinking, even though their creative ambitions are unchanged. In the beginning of this chapter, I defined naturalist bohemians as figures endowed with a perspective that is both totalizing and interstitial; characters like Dreiser's Witla confront the sublime city from the vantage point of a forced or chosen alienation, and manage to infiltrate it by slipping through the grid of its social classifications. The novels discussed here reveal that, in this, naturalist bohemians want too much: their utopian aspirations, instead of moving toward fulfillment, signal a break-up of artistic perception. Characters in Dreiser, Cather, Johnson, Cahan, and Poole stand indeed both at the threshold of the city and at the inception point of American modernism. The decade following World War I brings about an eclipse of naturalism and of the urban sublime in that it suggests that writing can satisfy itself with exploring fragments of experience—artistic practice and consciousness, typically—through a highly tightened-up idiom. The stylistic terseness of writers like Hemingway, the dislocation of their speech into apparently self-contained fragments, stands as the dialectic counterpart of the sprawling romantic cadences of the naturalist idiom. Hemingway's discontinuous prose, for instance, represses any upsurge of the romantic idiom of earlier sociologically oriented literature. This aesthetic asceticism is predicated on the belief that literature can do without the world—or at least, without the world in the sense of a social scene broad enough to stand as a metaphor of a totality of human activities.

Conclusion

The plight of the protagonist of Ernest Poole's *The Harbor*, constantly trying to revive his feelings of solidarity with a proletarian crowd that he finds otherwise disquieting, is paradigmatic of the urban sublime in literary naturalism. This narrative idiom, I have argued, consists of a set of romance tropes and textual strategies allowing characters to manage their relationship to an urban environment that is overwhelming in its physical mass, yet never entirely self-present. As a sociologizing discourse, the sublime is meant to enable writers to establish a configuration of the gaze that negotiates the illegibility of the city's economic, ethnic, and gender relations. In its most ambitious moments, the rhetorical momentum of the sublime, even as it proclaims the lack of intelligibility of the metropolis, attempts to turn its unknown realms from a menace into a source of power. The texts, however, seldom fulfill these aspirations: in practice, the urban sublime makes the threatening and mysterious city available to spellbound *flâneurs*—characters like Poole's narrator, Howells's Basil March, Dreiser's Carrie, or London's Avis Everhard. The turn-of-the-century predilection for characters that act as observers on the verge of the city remains ideologically ambiguous, however: though this subject position betokens powerlessness, it is endorsed by writers and social scientists engaged in a frantic political reassessment of their environment. The sublime, because it posits the existence of mysterious depths in the social world, makes it possible for writers to back up their sociologizing discourse with the power of unseen, unde-

cipherable authorities. The political strategies elaborated in this way
range from Frank Norris's advocacy of the trust, through Upton Sinclair's
and Charlotte Teller's commitment to socialism, to the celebration of
Anglo-Saxon masculinity in Norris and Jack London.

From a literary-historical perspective, the analysis of the urban sublime has led to a reshaping of the literary landscape at the turn of the
century. Against the view that naturalism is a later development of realism, I have argued that the two genres are mutually imbricated, yet carry distinct epistemologies and discourses. One aspect of this argument
is the recognition that the realist genre persists alongside naturalism
throughout the turn-of-the-century period. Simultaneously, I have contended that the specificity of naturalism as a genre resides in its handling
of romance: the subsets of the rhetoric of sublimity mentioned above are
all to large extents beholden to the nineteenth-century romance tradition and to the gothic. This emphasis on naturalist romance has resulted in a shift of canonical emphasis. When I started working on this
project, I expected Frank Norris and particularly Theodore Dreiser to
be the central figures of my corpus. Yet I discovered that the logic of
sublimity finds some of its most striking statements in Jack London's
surprisingly diverse fiction. It is through London's work, particularly, that
I have attempted to establish the structural links that connect Norris's
and Dreiser's sublime economic vision to other aspects of naturalist urban sociology, such as the psychological and political discourse of hypnosis and the genealogical theories of Darwinian primitivism. What
emerges from these readings is the picture of a broad flowering of romantic realism at the end of the century. The literary corpus thus defined constitutes what might be called the moment of sociological vitalism in American literature: it includes texts that use the social Darwinian
rhetoric of instincts and atavism in order to map the metropolis. This
form of literature, I suggest, dies out by the end of World War I, after
which fiction moves away from the panoramic representation of social
conditions.

In this light, evaluating the ideological work performed by turn-of-
the-century city novels entails specifying the status of romance within a
literary project stereotypically regarded as socially mimetic. In this matter, I have followed Fredric Jameson's contention that we should assess
texts if not by their capacity to reproduce the real, at least by their apti-
tude to provide what Jameson himself calls "cognitive mapping" (*Postmodernism* 52)—insights into the processes by which texts construct the
social sphere. The present book indicates that cognitive mapping in

naturalism is performed primarily through the dialogic interplay of documentary discourse and sublime rhetoric. Traditionally, Marxist criticism, particularly in its Lukácsian form, has uttered the suspicion that the romance is the accursed portion of the naturalist text—that it constitutes the textual site where the novel gives in to alienating fantasy. I have contended on the contrary that the impact of naturalist romance on the representation of the city consists in initiating a reflection on the possibility of a totalizing grasp of the urban experience. In this logic, the function of the rhetoric of sublimity consists in expressing metaphorically the dimension of the urban scene that a realist gaze cannot comprehend—what is radically other, irreparably fragmented, or excessive in terms of magnitude. The naturalist urban sublime expresses, in this logic, the anguished awareness that the city's environment might preclude a unified perception of its own social world and that, by the same token, even preindustrial ideals of organic solidarity may be exposed as figments. In this context, vitalism, which constitutes the mainstay of the sublime rhetoric of naturalism, appears as a pseudo-totalizing idiom: its metaphorical tropes—the vocabulary of Life and instincts—attempt to name a totality of experience that resists any literal form of encoding. The rhetorical impact of the naturalist sublime is therefore irremediably two-sided: it expresses the need to retotalize the illegible city, yet, even as it does so, it makes plain the resilience of fragmentation.

In order to reach the above description of what is at stake in naturalism, I have adopted a writing perspective that alternates between two discussions of the sublime in postmodern culture—Fredric Jameson's and Jean-François Lyotard's. From Jameson and the Marxist tradition he embodies, I have derived the insight that there is no absolute theoretical grounding for the gesture that proclaims the inevitability of sublime fragmentation and alienation in contemporary culture—or, retrospectively, in the naturalist city. In this optimistic perspective, the presence of romance fantasies and nonpositivistic discourses within naturalism acts as a call for epistemological postponement: on the one hand, it acknowledges the limits of the writers' sociological investigations; on the other, it leaves open the possibility that the remainder of unmapped social space might, to observers endowed with more comprehensive reading paradigms, be reduced to the clarity of what Lyotard calls a *domus*—the economy of a familiar world (*Inhuman* 191). From Lyotard's point-of-view, however, the hesitation of the naturalist text between incompatible social epistemologies should be taken at face value—as the acknowledgment of the increasing unmappability and self-alienation of what Lyotard himself calls the postmodern "megalopolis" (*Inhuman* 191). In this respect, the romance discourse of the naturalist sublime fulfills, through its early-twentieth-century vitalist idiom, a function that Lyotard ascribes to postmodern art—the elaboration of an aesthetic that makes perceptible the dissonant "feeling that there is something unpresentable" in the social world (*Postmodern* 16). In the case of urban space, specifically, the sublime warns us against seeking a forced reconciliation between the apparent certainties of local space and the overall unmappability of the megalopolis; though in itself "conceivable," this synthesis is "unpresentable" in that it could only manifest itself through discourses engaged in an unsolvable *differend* (*Postmodern* 15).

The cultural legacy of the naturalist sublime can, I think, be traced in the fact that its dialogization of urban space trickled down through the whole twentieth-century corpus of American city novels. To round off this essay, I wish therefore to indicate how this pattern of dialogization informs mid-1980s cyberpunk science fiction, a genre I have referred to in the course of my theoretical argument. Cyberpunk resembles naturalism in that it constitutes a flowering of urban fiction with the explicitly didactic purpose of mapping a new stage of urban development—in this case, the spread of computer-managed information in the 1980s. As it appears in William Gibson's *Neuromancer* (1984), the informational metropolis of cyberpunk is sublime in the "unthinkable complexity" of its "clusters and constellations of data" (51), in its discontinuities, and its grotesque details. Like the naturalist city, the cyberpunk environment exists on several planes at once; real space, the cyberspace grid of information storage and exchange, orbital space, and so on. There is therefore a coexistence within the novels of several literary discourses, obeying various modes of verisimilitude—literary and technological. The cyborg characters who negotiate this heterogeneous environment—part human, part circuitry—are high-tech descendants of the naturalist liminal tricksters. The sublime paradox of this universe is that, though it is in principle unified by a process of informational encoding, it is fissured by discontinuities that the novels investigate with painstaking realism.

From the perspective of Marxist criticism, cyberpunk conjures up a hair-raising vision of the reification of work, and above all, of language. The memory banks of cyberspace constitute a dystopian embodiment of the "alienated power" (31) that Fredric Jameson calls "dead human labor stored up in our machinery" (*Postmodernism* 31). In their moments of realist demystification, cyberpunk novels denounce this alienation—a gesture praised by Jameson (38). In the twenty-first-century world of

Bruce Sterling's *Heavy Weather* (1994), for instance, it is possible to fit the power of a "twentieth-century phone company" (154) in small appliances. Yet the narrator warns that "there [isn't] a single being left in the world who fully underst[ands] what [is] going on in these little boxes" (154). Keeping track of those "million lines of code" is "far beyond the direct comprehension of any human brain" (154).

However, like naturalism, cyberpunk cannot solve the postmodern breakdown of social legibility through realist/Marxist channels: it cannot specify how the informational world could be regenerated into a self-present, directly intelligible community of human producers. Instead, these novels manifest their characters' irreducible sense of sociological bafflement through a nonrealistic metaphorical idiom. In *Heavy Weather*, this resurgence of romance is noticeable in the author's descriptions of "bellowing . . . screeching and humming" (102) twisters—vortices comparable to Norris's speculation maelstrom, whose incomprehensible dynamics Sterling's punk scientists scrupulously document. Likewise, in William Gibson's *Count Zero* (1986) and *Mona Lisa Overdrive* (1988), cyberspace appears as a sublime field whose totality and shape can only be discussed in an animistic idiom reminiscent of Dreiser's economics: the cyberspace matrix is haunted by Voodoo gods—in fact, Artificial Intelligences—who communicate with privileged individuals. In the face of this mixture of technological realism and romance, what matters, I think, is neither to follow the techno-psychedelic stance of cybercritics who take for granted that technology carries a demiurgic power,[1] nor to assume that we find ourselves in a historical situation where reified relations can summarily be unmasked. Gibson's texts indicate rather that it is worthwhile to keep the mechanics of dialogization going: in this perspective, the discourse of sublime romance serves as mediating idiom between what can be made familiar and what remains beyond the horizon of intelligibility of the city.

Notes

Preface

1. Among naturalist writers, Theodore Dreiser has been a prime target for accusations of literary ineptitude. Julian Markels, in "Dreiser and the Plotting of the Inarticulate Experience," points out that by the early sixties, the critical tendency to catalog Dreiser's limitations had "settled into a rather dry routine" (431). F. O. Matthiessen, in *Theodore Dreiser*, feels obliged, in spite of his sympathetic readings of Dreiser's texts, to emphasize the fact that, unlike Hawthorne, the novelist was "only half-educated" (59). A recent disparaging evaluation of Frank Norris appears in Michael Bell's book on American realism, where the critic contends that, instead of developing a language "of scientific description and explanation," the novelist favored the "abstract, melodramatic cliché" (123).

2. Jean François Lyotard, in his discussion of Kant's philosophy of history, emphasizes the narrow connection that links the emotions of sublimity and big historical upheavals (*Reader* 393–411). Lyotard, following Kant, argues that in the absence of the metaphysical certainties of a dialectic paradigm of history, human progress can only be inferred from the sublime "enthusiasm" (401) caused by momentous political crises, which serve as "'signs of history'" (393).

Chapter 1: From Natural to Urban Sublime

1. For studies that use either Burke or Kant as theoretical foundation for the aesthetic of sublimity, see Thomas Weiskel, Neil Hertz ("Notion"), Patricia Yaeger, Fredric Jameson's *Postmodernism*, and Jean François Lyotard's *Leçons*.

2. Peter De Bolla argues that Burke's view of the sublime as a healing process had a direct ideological reward: De Bolla links the development of the aesthetic of the

sublime in mid-eighteenth-century England to anxieties about the growth of the English national debt.

3. Kant's theory of the sublime does not revolve around terror, but rather around the impact of the notion of infinity on the limited perceptions of the human mind. Sublimity is "what is purely and simply great," hence also "what is excessive for the imagination" (186, 200).

4. This aspect of the romantic sublime has elicited psychoanalytical readings that detect in the dialectic delineated by Burke and Kant a mechanism of gendered construction and empowerment of the self (see Weiskel, Hertz, Yaeger, and Wolf).

5. See Elizabeth McKinsey's *Niagara Falls*.

6. The typical object of the "rhetoric of the technological sublime" in Leo Marx's study is the railroad.

7. The legitimacy of this skepticism is borne out by the fact that the ultimate development of urban and technological sublimity is the feeling of awe inspired by the threat of nuclear annihilation—what Rob Wilson and Frances Ferguson have called the nuclear sublime. Contrary to those who describe all forms of the sublime as a power strategy, McKinsey's argument about Niagara Falls suggests that the natural sublime, even if reduced to a "necessary fiction," constitutes a relation to nature that can still serve as an oppositional force to industrialism (272).

8. Joseph Tabbi, in *Postmodern Sublime* (209–27), analyzes the relation of cyberpunk to the tradition of the sublime. He argues—with, I think, undue harshness—that cyberpunk is a debased form of the aesthetic of technological terror and wonder. Tabbi credits Jameson with laying down the critical theory of cyberpunk sublimity at a time (1984) when this science fiction movement barely had any public existence.

9. Theodore Dreiser, *Sister Carrie* (Pennsylvania 177). The Norton Critical Edition of Dreiser's *Sister Carrie* reproduces the text originally published by Doubleday in 1900. I have used this version as basic reference for the interpretation of Dreiser's work. However, I have found it useful to resort occasionally to the University of Pennsylvania edition of the novel, which reproduces an earlier version of the text. Parenthetical references to the Pennsylvania manuscript include the word "Pennsylvania."

10. A major point in the critical reappraisal of naturalism has consisted in departing from the view that naturalist authors shared the Jeffersonian distrust of urban life, and that their works establish an acute contrast between city and country. On the contrary, the turn-of-the-century novels that depict new economic realities in the accents of nature romanticism blur this dichotomy to such extents that they deprive themselves of the possibility to characterize either the metropolis or nature as phenomena in their own right. From our perspective, it would be tempting to conclude that naturalism defined itself in sheer opposition to pastoral or small-town ideology. However, in order to avoid any reductive dualism, it makes sense to assume, as Raymond Williams and William Cronon do, that, to borrow Cronon's words, "the city-country story" should be told "as a unified narrative" (Cronon xvi; see Williams 3–7). Cronon criticizes the pastoralist credo that makes the nightmarish city appear as antithetical to beneficial nature. Provocatively, Cronon even claims that the commodities of the urban market "are among our most basic connections to the natural world" (xvii).

Chapter 2: Critical Reassessments of American Realism and Naturalism

1. Michael Bell ranks June Howard, Amy Kaplan, and Walter Benn Michaels as neo-historicist critics of turn-of-the-century fiction (23), a list to which might be added Mark Seltzer, who nevertheless rejects this affiliation.

2. Berthoff dedicates his study of realism to "liberalism and democracy, the good old causes, in whose ambiguous service the work surveyed in this volume was mostly written" (3).

3. The deconstructive zeal of the new historicist interpretations of naturalism should, I think, not obliterate the fact that Parrington's and Kazin's readings develop a powerful and consistent narrative of the realist's struggle against sexual censorship and social injustice. In a critique of Walter Benn Michaels's *The Gold Standard and the Logic of Naturalism*, Fredric Jameson makes the interesting remark that exposing the falsehood of previous radical interpretations of Dreiser still begs the question why "readers made [these radical misreadings] in the first place, and continue to do so" (*Postmodernism* 209).

4. Despite his rejection of the neo-historicist label, Seltzer shares with Michaels some of the methodological features stigmatized by Fredric Jameson in his critique of neo-historicism (*Postmodernism* 181). By focusing on what Foucault calls "systems of micro-power" and on the ceaseless reproduction of inegalitarian relationships, Seltzer and Michaels depict historical development as an inert given, whose issues, though constantly negotiated at a local level, seem unrelated to any diachronic development (Foucault qtd. in Seltzer, *Bodies* 88).

5. Among contemporary genre criticism, Jameson distinguishes a "semantic" and a "syntactic" approach, focusing respectively on the thematic and structural features of genres (*Political* 107).

6. When referring to Bakhtin's theory of dialogism, I have in some instances used the terminology that appears in *Esthétique et Théorie du Roman*, the French translation of the Russian critic's essays on fiction. These terms—"plurilinguism," "pluristylistic," "plurilingual," "plurivocal"—[*plurilinguisme, pluristylistique, plurilingual, plurivocal* (*Esthétique* 95, 87)]—are self-explanatory to readers of English and allow of more flexible derivations than Caryl Emerson's and Michael Holquist's sometimes unwieldy "heteroglossia" and "heteroglot" (*Dialogic* 263, 272).

7. Jameson's model is inspired from V. N. Voloshinov's and Mikhail Bakhtin's theories of language, as they are formulated in Voloshinov's *Marxism and the Philosophy of Language*.

8. Bakhtin does not advocate radical discursive heterogeneity, however: he views the text of the novel as an organic structure. To him, the "heterogeneous stylistic units" of the novel make up a "harmonious literary system" endowed with stylistic and generic characteristics of a different order than those of its component (*Dialogic* 262); each unit receives its literary meaning from its inclusion in the whole.

9. On the face of it, one might believe that recent studies have focused on a rather limited set of writers—Howells, Dreiser, Wharton, Gilman, Norris, London, Sinclair. By comparison, a pre-1980s analysis like Charles Child Walcutt's *American Literary Naturalism: A Divided Stream*, seems more comprehensive, as it includes Fredric, Garland, Crane, London, Norris, Churchill, Dreiser, Anderson, Farrell,

Steinbeck, Hemingway, and Dos Passos. Yet the impression that 1980s critics interpret the boundaries of the canon in narrow terms is, I think, due less to an actual difference in the number of authors covered than to the fact that they are not discussed within a cohesive literary-historical narrative.

10. The periodization of naturalism in French literature is probably only marginally easier to establish. With the publication of Zola's first novels and manifestoes, the movement seems well demarcated in time; it is, however, anything but homogeneous: a writer like Guy de Maupassant, who was officially affiliated with Zola's literary school, wrote texts that are much closer to mid-century realism than to naturalism. In his periodization of the genres, Georg Lukács ranks Flaubert among the naturalists, though his work precedes Zola's by about fifteen years ("Narrate" 119).

11. Chase argues that "since the earliest days the American novel, in its most original and characteristic form, has . . . defined itself by incorporating an element of romance" (viii).

12. Kaplan's technique for interpreting textual heterogeneity draws on Fredric Jameson's "Reification and Utopia" as well as on his "Magical Narratives" (*Political* 103–50).

13. Frank Norris, in "Zola as a Romantic Writer," argues that Zola's naturalism is not, as most readers think, "an inner circle of realism," but rather "a form of romanticism after all" (*Criticism* 71).

Chapter 3: The Limits of Urban Realism

1. William Cronon analyzes this "cityward journey" in the works of Hamlin Garland and Robert Herrick (9).

2. The impact of anti-urban ideology on intellectuals and writers is discussed in Morton and Lucia White's *The Intellectual vs. the City*. John McDermott indicates how Americans who had moved to the city evaluated this new environment by the standards of pastoral ideology (1–20); this argument is further developed by Kirk Jeffrey.

3. Alfred Habegger, in *Gender, Fantasy, and Realism in American Literature*, argues that "American realism descended from popular women's fiction" by way of Henry James and William Dean Howells, two novelists who served as middle-men between the feminine world of domestic-oriented sentimental fiction and realism proper (56, 65).

4. The foundations of Lukács's Hegelian approach of the novel were laid down in *The Theory of the Novel*; the Marxist transposition of this argument was performed in Lukács's later works, such as *Studies in European Realism* and "Writer and Critic."

5. In "Narrate or Describe," Lukács argues that texts that meet the standards of organic realism are identifiable notably by the fact that they privilege dialogue and action in dramatic form—what Lukács himself calls "narration"—over "description." The distinction between "narration" and "description" is perfectly congruent with the categories of "scene" and "summary" elaborated in the Anglo-Saxon theory of the novel, from Henry James to Percy Lubbock's *The Craft of Fiction*. Lukács's distinctive contribution to this problematic is his willingness to anchor these terms in his Hegelian philosophy of history.

6. It would be easy to demonstrate that Balzac's fiction, Lukács's favorite example for organic realism, does not fulfill the Hungarian critic's requirements: Balzac's

realist prose is highly heterogeneous and contains many grotesque, romantic, even gothic passages.

7. Ronald E. Martin, in *American Literature and the Universe of Force*, uses this term to designate the rhetoric of social evolutionary energies that pervades naturalist texts.

Chapter 4: Sublime Horizons, Vitalist Mysteries

1. Among Dreiser's novels, only *The Trilogy of Desire* (*The Financier*, *The Titan*, and *The Stoic*) focuses on characters born and raised in the city.

2. See June Howard's *Form and History* and Mark Seltzer's *Bodies and Machines* for interpretations of naturalist narration as a medium of surveillance.

3. Peter De Bolla indicates that the impact of Longinus on eighteenth-century aesthetics was primarily due to the fact that his text could be "accommodated within the growing body of works on oratory and prescriptive rhetoric" (36).

4. Like Kenneth Burke, speech act theorists J. L. Austin and John R. Searle regard reference—realistic description—as a speech act (Austin 130–34; Searle 72–96).

5. *Carrie*, 1–2. Dreiser borrows his conception of the "Unknowable" from positivistic philosophers like Herbert Spencer and Edward L. Youmans, who argue that the realms beyond scientific perception can both be "sensed" and represented metaphorically: according to Spencer, the Unknowable is an "uncomprehendable [*sic*] reality" of which "scientific laws [are] but proximate representations" (qtd. in Bannister 43). Youmans contends that, if we cannot objectify the Incomprehensible, "we are, by the laws of thought, equally prevented from ridding ourselves of the *consciousness* of this power" (qtd. in Bannister 62).

6. The cultural manifestations of the paternal scenario of sublimity are discussed in Bryan Jay Wolf's interpretation of Thomas Cole's landscapes. The emotional issues of the preoedipal stage, which lie at the basis of the maternal scenario of the sublime, are described in Nancy Chodorow's *Mothering* (99–110) and in Karen Horney.

7. Howard argues that naturalist novels use oceanic metaphors in order to convey the action of the forces of determinism. The sublime impact of such seascapes has been underlined by Immanuel Kant in his *Critique of Judgment* (203).

8. Alan Trachtenberg and Michael Denning have emphasized how deeply the mysteries of the city have shaped the perception of urbanization in late-nineteenth-century America (see *Incorporation* 103; *Mechanic* 85–117).

9. The role of the gothic as a discourse that brings about the breakdown of totality is discussed in Vijay Mishra's *The Gothic Sublime*. Mishra writes that the gothic is "the voice from the crypt that questions the power" of "totalizing grand" narratives like the Kantian construction of ego and reason (38).

Chapter 5: *Domus* versus Megalopolis

1. The fact that object of study and methodology mutually contaminate each other, as it were, corroborates Jameson's remark that "postmodernism theory" is "necessarily imperfect or impure" (*Postmodernism* xi)—that it is obliged to rely on the very concepts that it means to deconstruct. I have argued elsewhere that this caveat is par-

ticularly relevant to theoretical discussions of the sublime: these arguments—includ-ing Jameson's supposedly critical analysis of the postmodern sublime—borrow their structure and imagery from the rhetoric of terror itself (Den Tandt, "Invoking" 806, 813–14). Jameson's efforts to make visible the nontextual foundations of history as well as his descriptions of the workings of cognitive maps are indeed systematically conveyed through formulas that qualify as sublimity speech acts.

2. Lyotard outlines several historical steps that have led to the delegitimation of totalizing (for him, Hegelian) thinking, chief among which is the Nazi holocaust (see "Discussions; or, Phrasing 'after Auschwitz'" in *Reader* 360–66).

3. In this respect, postmodern theory relates to totalizing systems (Hegelian Marx-ism, typically) much in the same way as William Wordsworth's sublime poetry does toward the mystical insights of William Blake: Thomas Weiskel indicates that Blake's poetry of "the visionary" (7) places the subject on equal footing with absolutes, while Wordsworth's aesthetic of sublimity views the same objects as overwhelming and unknowable entities (16). Like Wordsworth, Lyotard and Jameson reject the possi-bility of a theoretical intuition of essences (Lyotard, *Reader* 324ff., 369; Jameson, *Unconscious* 35). In their postmodern version of the sublime, what is glimpsed through the emotions of terror and fascination is a shadow image of these metaphysical groundings, which are no longer accessible to human speculation.

4. The contention that totalizing dialects are defined by their anchoring in a spe-cific area of experience is formulated along different lines in Slavoj Žižek's discus-sion of the Lacanian theory of the "nodal point" (Žižek 87). Žižek argues that in ideological discourse, "the multitude of 'floating signifiers,' of proto-ideological el-ements, is structured through the intervention of a certain 'nodal point' (the Laca-nian *point de capiton*) which 'quilts' them, stops their sliding and fixes their mean-ing" (87). In Žižek's Lacanian argument, the nodal points of all separate ideologies ultimately point back to the ultimate nodal point of discourse, the phallus.

5. Compared to Lukács's imperative to achieve an immanent synthesis of the real, Benjamin's theory of the aura positions itself closer to the open-endedness of the sub-lime. Benjamin's utopia of a culture revolving around ceremonial contemplation is indeed not based on immanent self-presence. Because Benjamin grants so much im-portance to absence and distance, his texts enjoy a particular affinity with the urban scene that they analyze.

6. Terry Eagleton objects to postmodern theorists (Jameson, in this case), saying that many people in contemporary societies go through their round of life without fully—if at all—experiencing the destabilizing pressure of the alleged postmodern dislocation. Thus, he argues that those who decree the death of the bourgeois-hu-manist subject and the correlative advent of a "dispersed, decentred network of li-bidinal attachments" ("Capitalism" 39) ignore the persisting power of older psycho-logical or economic configurations. This critique of the discourse of detotalization is reiterated in Eagleton's *Ideology*.

Chapter 6: The Discovery of the Urban Market

1. A large segment of the critical literature devoted to *Sister Carrie* revolves in-deed around the different ways in which the ideological import of the novel's disso-

nant voices can be resolved—or left dangling. Alan Trachtenberg, in "Who Narrates? Dreiser's Presence in *Sister Carrie*," reviews previous critical attempts to interpret the fragmented voices of the novel. Trachtenberg's own reading aims to demonstrate that, in spite of the apparent contradictions of Dreiser's narration, the narrator does serve as a controlling narrative agency in the text.

2. Donald Pizer points out that Ames, while discussing Balzac with Carrie, criticizes the French novelist's obsession with money. Pizer later adds that Carrie is "deeply responsive" to Ames's advice (*Novels* 64). There is, I think, no sign that the heroine follows up on the financial aspect of these instructions.

3. Cynthia Griffin Wolff provides a discussion of the parallels between Wharton's sociological vision and Thorstein Veblen's theory of conspicuous consumption (xxi).

4. Veblen argues that industrial activity—in his view, the basis of an equitable polity—must handle nonhuman things (*Theory* 26). His celebration of the "instinct of workmanship" is predicated on the rejection of epistemological "anthropomorphism" and "animism," that is "the naive imputation of a workmanlike propensity in the observed facts" of nature (*Instinct* 53).

5. Walter Benn Michaels and Rachel Bowlby have analyzed the role of money as object and vehicle of Carrie's inexhaustible desire, as well as the fascination exerted by commodities in Dreiser's fiction (Michaels 31–58; Bowlby 52–65).

6. Donald Pizer points out the autobiographical dimension of Carrie and Ames by arguing that these characters "blend into an honorific self-portrait of Dreiser as both a soulful artist, driven by a quest for beauty, and a practical, successful man of affairs who is also a speculative thinker" (66). Pizer's argument is implicitly based on the gendered dichotomy between intuition and reason, thus corroborating the view that these two protagonists blend into an androgynous personality.

7. Dreiser's own bewilderment and wonder are amply documented in *Newspaper Days* and in the autobiographical segments of *The "Genius."*

Chapter 7: Sublime (Re)production

1. For discussions of these aspects of the pastoral tradition, see Henry Nash Smith and Leo Marx.

2. For the movement culture of Populism, see Lawrence Goodwyn's *The Populist Moment*. Richard Chase himself bases his view of Populism on Richard Hofstadter's *The Age of Reform*, a study that describes populist politics schematically, and therefore makes it more difficult to distinguish between the farmers' insurgency and the ideology of the California novelist. Norris's supposed sympathy for the plight of the farmers is difficult to reconcile with his pro-corporate stance, which has been described by Walter Benn Michaels.

3. Peter Conn emphasizes the political importance of Parry's novel. Conn argues also that the anti-trust connotation of the term "Octopus" is indeed largely due to Norris's influence (83–92).

4. Horney's discussion of the whirlpool trope is based on Schiller's poem "The Diver." Seltzer discusses the same kind of maternal imagery in Norris's *Octopus*, where the coiling hair of a milkmaid "seemed almost to have a life of its own, almost Medusa-like" (Norris qtd. in Seltzer 33). Seltzer argues that these tropes endow the

young woman with connotations of "unmanning fecundity" (33). A contemporary instance of vortex imagery appears in Bruce Sterling's cyberpunk novel *Heavy Weather*, where the twisters provoked by global warming are depicted in sublime accents reminiscent both of Poe and Norris. As in Norris, Sterling's vortices, with their "grinding and rattling and keening noise" (102), are metaphors of social chaos.

5. Penley's conception of the bachelor machine is borrowed from Michel Carrouges's whimsical essay *Les machines célibataires*. Carrouges himself borrows the term from Marcel Duchamp's early-twentieth-century *Large Glass, The Bride Stripped Bare by Her Bachelors, Even*. An influential theoretical elaboration of Carrouges's concept of "bachelor machine" appears in Gilles Deleuze and Felix Guattari's *L'anti-Oedipe*, where the bachelor machine ranks among the possible libidinal devices that structure the processes of the unconscious (see Deleuze and Guattari 24–26).

6. Julia Kristeva, in *Pouvoirs de l'horreur*, points out the role of the tropes of abjection in signifying and averting the fear of the archaic mother: excremental imagery is, in this logic, the only channel through which the power of the mother is allowed to express itself (90–94).

Chapter 8: Pastoralism Reconstructed

1. Judith Butler argues that gender and sexual norms are produced through performativity and reiteration (see Butler 2, 12). Her argument, meant to deconstruct essentialist conceptions of gender, provides a useful framework for the analysis of practices where gender roles are explicitly enacted.

2. London's views of domesticity and the urban market stand out in sharp contrast with Charlotte Perkins Gilman's discussion of the same issues in *Women and Economics* (1898) and *The Home* (1904). Unlike London's celebration of "lawless and terrible" desire (*Valley* 144), Gilman's *The Home* assumes that what "is really sacred can bear examination," and that "mystery and shadow belong to jugglers, not to the truth" (4). Gilman's direct target is the "blind idolatry" (5) that surrounds "domestic mythology" (36); her larger project consists in helping women accede to what might be called a civic individualism—"a wider, keener civic consciousness," as the author puts it (11). Compared to this project of empowerment in the public sphere, the home economy so cherished by London's characters represents an evolutionary throwback—a social configuration partly outgrown by human development. Some of the most resilient obstacles to Gilman's program are the ritualistic aspects of home life—in particular the components of domestic culture that mingle consumerism and sexuality. Thus, Gilman campaigns against waist-binding—a form of mutilation for the sake of seduction—and against the "tyranny of bric-a-brac"—that fetishistic "magpie instinct," which, she argues, many women use as a debased substitute for real art (257). In a passage reminiscent of *The Valley of the Moon*, Gilman singles out as most representative of the perversion of domestic art the practice of trimming lace with fur; this unfortunate habit "combines the acme of all highly wrought refinement of texture" with "dressed hide with the hair still on," thus with "the symbol of savage luxury and grandeur, of raw barbaric wealth" (*Home* 156). In Gilman's logic, the vaguely obscene primitivism of domestic art must wither away once women are freed from their confinement.

Chapter 9: The "Common Lot" of 1890s and 1900s Realism

1. Characteristically, in *Twenty Years at Hull-House,* Addams indicates that her social project originated in an apocalyptic conversion experience: on a tour of the London East End, Addams watched from the top of an omnibus a huge crowd of "the submerged tenth" struggling for rotten food sold at auction (61–62). There, Addams went through a quasi-mystical experience, which resulted in a call for a therapeutic dialogue across social groups. Admittedly, in Jane Addams's overall biographical development, the sudden discovery of men with teeth tearing into uncooked cabbages, or of "myriads of hands . . . clutching forward for food which was already unfit to eat" (62) represents only one among several determinants that drove the author to social action; the influence of Lincoln, or Addams's own missionary ideals had already laid the spiritual foundations by which this vision of poverty could acquire its moral meaning. Within the context of *Twenty Years at Hull-House,* however, the cataclysmic East End epiphany provides a symbolic rationale for the author's social commitment.

2. In *The Incorporation of America,* Alan Trachtenberg argues that the White City should be seen as a cultural expression of the newly achieved hegemony of corporate classes, thus marking the political defeat of the ideals of solidarity represented by the labor movement or Populism.

Chapter 10: Naturalist Gothic

1. Tzvetan Todorov argues in *Introduction à la Littérature Fantastique* that the fantastic is not a unified style, but rather an effect created by the text's strategic management of generic discontinuities (28–29). Gothic fiction channels the reader's response in such a way that he or she hesitates to attribute a fixed epistemological value to the unsettling events that overcome the characters of the narrative. In Todorov's typology, fantastic phenomena are supposed to be perceived either as uncanny or as supernatural. At the end of the story, the epistemological hesitation disappears and the fantastic effect cancels itself out as the narrative settles for one specific genre. In the uncanny, every unfamiliar occurrence is explained rationally, whereas the supernatural affirms the presence of non-positivistic forms of causalities.

2. On this point, I follow Gallagher's interpretation, which underlines the economic significance of the grotesque representations of women in the urban scene. Seltzer, on the other hand, reads the gothic slum mothers within a problematic of surveillance and policing: in this logic, the bodies of foulsome working-class women are paradigmatic "visual displays," required for the construction of the structure of the gaze fostered by "statistics and surveillance" (*Bodies* 100).

3. Contemporary instances of this equation between the maternal and the social body are discussed in Janice Doane and Devon Hodges's "Undoing Feminism: From the Preoedipal to Postfeminism in Anne Rice's *Vampire Chronicles.*" Doane and Hodges discern in vampire stories of the 1970s and 1980s a privileged connection between the gothic, maternal metaphorics and the representation of the urban economy that is quite similar to naturalist gendered economics. Moreover, Doane and Hodges argue that the specter of the monstrous feminine also haunts contemporary

discussions of mass culture—Jameson's and Ariel Dorfman's, notably. Doane and Hodges suggest that, contrary to what these critics claim, the use of maternal metaphorics in theoretical discussions generally implies a complicity with the affects carried by the gothic tropes.

4. Jack London borrows the term "blonde beast" from Nietzsche's *Genealogy of Morals*, where it designates an avatar of the Superman or the Free Spirit. The occurrences of this phrase in Nietzsche are, however, much scarcer than in Jack London. In the American novelist's racial sociology, the blonde beast embodies an Anglo-Saxon utopia of instinctual health.

5. Critics of naturalism who insist on the realistic affilation of the genre have criticized atavistic characterization as a sensationalistic offshoot of Darwinian science, or as the outcome of excessive realist shock tactics. Vernon Louis Parrington warns that, by studying the "inner drives of low-grade characters[,] the naturalist is in danger of creating grotesques" (325); ultimately, he or she "may turn man into an animal" (325). Likewise, Warner Berthoff faults Jack London's primitivism for bringing naturalism to the level of the gothic (246).

6. Donald Pizer has emphasized the importance of this dialectic of everydayness and romance in *McTeague*. He argues that, for Norris, "the romance of the extraordinary is not limited to the distant in time and place"; on the contrary, "beneath the surface of our placid, everyday lives there is turbulence" (15).

7. It is characteristic of the repetitive character of Norris's sublime idiom that this sequence of tropes should appear practically verbatim for the description of a cityscape in the author's *Vandover and the Brute*.

8. The status of Social Darwinism marks a dividing line in the critical readings of naturalism, recent or older. Against the canonical definitions of the genre—in Parrington, Kazin, Berthoff, Walcutt—where the writers' professions of deterministic scientism are taken quite literally, 1980s critics such as Howard, Michaels, and Bowlby have regarded naturalist Darwinism as an allegory of another historical narrative—proletarianization, for instance—or as a field of discourse where power relations are enacted. Other interpretations of the 1980s—Harold Kaplan's *Power and Order*, Ronald E. Martin's *American Literature and the Universe of Force*, and Bannister's *Social Darwinism*—still view naturalist fiction from the perspective of science; these "scientist" readings are methodologically close to intellectual history, and they usually rely on a larger corpus than naturalist fiction proper.

9. See Robert Bannister's *Social Darwinism: Science and Myth in Anglo-American Social Thought*; this study attempts to nuance the stereotypes of evolutionary sociology elaborated, for instance, in Richard Hofstadter's *Social Darwinism in American Thought*. Bannister argues that no current in American thought ever claimed the social Darwinian label as its own: the term was only used derogatorily by critics of evolutionary sociology. Bannister shows, however, that evolutionary thinking, in its various misappropriations, did define the field of social debate in the 1890s. However, Bannister's analytical caution sometimes verges on political exoneration, as in the case of his euphemistic account of William Graham Sumner's theories.

10. These naturalist stories of atavism rewrite in scientific terms the broader Victorian fascination for demonic *Doppelgänger*, illustrated for instance in Robert Louis Stevenson's or Oscar Wilde's urban gothic fiction.

11. Gail Bederman, in *Manliness and Civilization*, points out the importance of this mechanism of overdetermination when she argues that "race and gender cannot be

studied as if they were discrete categories" (239). Anthony Rotundo, in *American Manhood*, analyzes another axis of overdetermination when he discusses nineteenth- and twentieth-century masculinity as a function of the "culture of the workplace" (194).

Chapter 11: The Politics of Hypnotic Persuasion

1. I choose to read *The Iron Heel* as a naturalist work, in spite of its science fiction affiliation because, like most pre-1960s science fiction texts, it abides by some of the key precepts of realistic verisimilitude. Darko Suvin suggests indeed that science fiction follows a literary epistemology cognate to realism, though not entirely identifiable with it (26). Science fiction emulates realism in its refusal to adopt the logic of fairy tales or myths (27). In this perspective, it is possible to argue that *The Iron Heel* shares the concerns of the naturalist muckraking novel: it voices the concerns about insurrectional crowds that characterize the urban sociology of naturalism.

2. This Faustian rhetoric, though unexpected in an essay by Zola, is representative of positivist triumphalism. Zola shares these romantic strains with, for instance, Herbert Spencer, whose doctrine of the Unknowable carries mystical overtones. Also, Gaston Bachelard underlines how close Zola remains to pre-scientific romance (*Psychanalyse* 156). Zola's *Le Docteur Pascal*, the volume meant to serve as the scientific summary of *Les Rougon-Macquart*, contains the anecdote of an alcoholic who dies in a painless process of spontaneous combustion (*Docteur* 299).

3. The respective claims of objective observation and social activism are never clearly defined in Zola. The French novelist, who transposes the principles of Claude Bernard's experimental method into literature, does not consider detached observation a sufficient basis for experimental science: observation must be followed by experimentation, manipulation. Yet the larger claims to neutrality are never abandoned, as Zola, quoting Bernard, asserts that the experimental method is not dependent on "any philosophical system" ("Experimental" 164). The ethos of objectivity is restated later, as Zola appropriates Claude Bernard's formula, which states that "the experimenter is the examining magistrate of nature" (168): "we novelists," Zola writes, "are the examining magistrates of men and their passions" (168).

4. Nietzsche's concept of "revaluation of values" is set forth in *Twilight of the Idols*. Revaluation rules out impartiality: Nietzsche contends that war—not detachment—constitutes the best tool in the serious task of the inversion of values (31). His hostility to the professed neutrality of scientism, which he regards as an avatar of idealism, is expressed notably in *Beyond Good and Evil*, where he condemns "those hotch-potch philosophers who call themselves 'philosophers of reality' or 'positivists'" (131). In *The Genealogy of Morals*, science is ranked alongside the ascetic ideal among the factors that induce "biological impoverishment" (290). In *Twilight*, literary naturalism is also listed among the items that are Nietzsche's "impossibles" (78). He accuses Zola of taking "delight in stinking" (*Twilight* 78).

5. In spite of its ambivalence toward the urban poor and its commitment to the superman mystique, *The Iron Heel* has long remained a classic for the culture of socialist movements in Europe. From Leon Trotsky's praise of the novel, it appears that socialist readers were struck by London's prophetic anticipation of fascism. Trotsky, in a letter of 1937 addressed to Joan London, remarks that the novel provides a blueprint of the economy and the political psychology of fascism (25). Lon-

don's foresight, Trotsky argues, is enough to silence the arguments of those who accused the novel of self-deflating pessimism: the negative vision of the revolution-ary inclinations of the proletariat—developed notably in the "People of the Abyss" chapter—has been perfectly vindicated by the development of postwar fascism.

6. The patriarchal bias of Freud's theory of hypnosis is noticeable in the fact that the psychoanalyst rules out the prospect that a maternal figure of authority could be introjected into the superego. In this, Freud deviates from Ferenczi's parental theory of hypnosis, which influenced his own paradigm of group formation. Ferenczi, Freud explains, distinguishes between "two sorts of hypnotism . . . : one coaxing and soothing, which he considers is modeled on the mother, and another theatening, which is derived from the father" (*Group* 59). This is, however, the only passage in which Ferenczi's concept of maternal hypnosis is mentioned in the text; this hypoth-esis is neither explored nor refuted. Instead, Freud attempts to buttress his account of the paternal foundations of the group mind by digging up archaic roots for the phenomenon of paternal hypnotic authority.

7. Douglas regards the process of feminization that she discerns in nineteenth-cen-tury culture as a factor of intellectual trivialization. Unlike Jane Tompkins, who at-tempts to redeem domestic fiction against the masculine bias of the literary canon, Douglas interprets Melville's proto-modernism as a revitalizing rebellion against the taste of the feminized public (349–96). In this respect, Douglas's position is not dis-similar from James's.

8. The relevance of Derrida's "Speech and Phenomena" to oratory is easier to bring out if we translate the original French title as "Voice and Phenomena" (*La voix et le phénomène*). In this work, Derrida deconstructs Husserl's claim that the voice of con-sciouness in the living present can be a site of absolute presence and immediacy.

9. Christopher Wilson reveals that the success of the novel was due to the fact that middle-class audiences reacted to the sensationalistic exposure of health hazards in the meat industry, but safely ignored Sinclair's socialistic indictment of capitalism (113).

10. Weinstein, in *The Decline of Socialism in America*, argues that the social and elec-toral power of American socialism peaked around 1912 (93).

11. Alfred Kazin patronizingly describes socialist writers as "the most romantic novelists of their time" (84). Similarly, Peter Conn evaluates Teller, Bullard, and Ernest Poole's achievement by their capacity to stick to analytical realism (96–100). Conn follows on this point the tradition of readers who, for instance, attribute the millenarian overtones of *The Jungle* to Sinclair's lack of "narrative ingenuity" or to the failure of his political vision (Gottesman xxvi). Against this restrictive view of socialist discourse, Jameson points out that even Marxism includes "'a romance par-adigm,'" pointing to the reconciliation of alienated mankind (*Political* 103).

12. For critical discussions of Bullard's and Teller's novels, see Peter Conn (98–104, 96–98) and Walter Rideout (54–58, 63). Conn analyzes Tellers's *The Cage*.

Chapter 12: Overcivilization and the Crisis of Writerly Manhood

1. The cultural dominance of women's literature and domestic fiction in the mid-nineteenth century has been pointed out by Jane Tompkins. Tompkins argues that

this feminine tradition was later obscured by modernist writers and critics, who refashioned the canon by foregrounding the male tradition of the American Renaissance. By arguing that realist writers refashioned the conventions of sentimental family novels along masculine lines, Habegger's discussion of American realism acknowledges the importance of the tradition of domestic fiction.

2. The paradoxical presence of transgender characters—New Woman figures, male androgynes—within naturalist scenarios of masculine empowerment is attested even in texts distantly related to artistic education. For a more detailed discussion of this issue, see Den Tandt, "Amazons" (639–60).

Chapter 13: Naturalist Gothic and the Regeneration of Artistic Identity

1. Warren French, in his introduction to *Vandover*, argues that Norris's novel, rather than a naturalist work, should be regarded as a significant text of the small corpus of American decadent fiction (xi–xiv). This interesting argument suggests that the distinction between decadentism and naturalism should be redefined: neo-historicist readings of naturalism have indeed focused on semiotic practices that were so far considered typical of the fin-de-siècle (the link between consumerism and sexuality, for instance).

2. Gail Bederman relativizes the import of Gilman's critique of women's confinement in the domestic sphere by showing that Gilman's feminist argument is tied to a racial agenda. Bederman points out that Gilman viewed her own access to the public sphere in terms of racial duty; she believed "she must choose between woman's sphere and racial advance" (133). Relegation to the domestic sphere was, in this perspective, synonymous with regression not only to childhood, but to savagery.

3. For a discussion of the connection established by nineteenth-century medicine between womanhood, hysteria, and the mysteries of reproduction, see Smith-Rosenberg (205–6) and Barker-Benfield (280–94).

4. In the few texts that portray female protagonists that fit my definition of the corporate androgyne—Dreiser's *Sister Carrie* and David Graham Phillips's *Susan Lennox, Her Fall and Rise* (1917), for instance—there is a strong sense that the male novelist projects himself into a female character that is endowed with many of the author's biographical traits. Thus, Carrie shares many features of Dreiser's other autobiographical personae—Eugene Witla in *The "Genius"* and the narrator of *Newspaper Days*.

Chapter 14: On the Threshold of the Metropolis

1. Peter Conn describes the ambivalent outlook of artists in the pre–World War I period as the effect of a "divided mind" (iii), torn between values of the past and the future—typically, between "the myth of individualism" (13) versus "'Collective Man'" (13). Conn's emphasis on ambivalence is well taken, but I also believe that such a clear-cut binarism is too simple to account for the identities constructed in

naturalist novels of education: in these works, boundaries are both marked out and transgressed.

2. Rachel Bowlby provides a survey of the generally negative criticism of which Dreiser's novel has been the object (118–20). She mentions that The *"Genius"* has been condemned for failing to transcend its autobiographical content or for offering an undignified and loosely organized documentary account of the literary market. The novel's critique of the institution of marriage elicited calls for censorship; this put H. L. Mencken, Dreiser's friend, in the delicate position of having to campaign in favor of a text that he found indefensible on aesthetic grounds (see Elias 187, 196–97).

3. The conflation of the artisan category with the pastoral ideology of the yeoman farmer is legitimate in this context, since Dreiser himself makes no distinction between the values of the small town and the work ethic of the urban lower-middle classes. In *Sister Carrie*, for instance, Carrie Meeber's rural hometown as well as her thrifty urban in-laws are viewed with the same condescension—a negative judgment that befalls all those who do not have an intuitive perception of market forces.

4. *An Amateur Laborer* is the title of an autobiographical manuscript in which Dreiser describes the period of his life that corresponds to Eugene Witla's stay in the carpenter shop. Amy Kaplan uses this text as evidence of the author's anti-proletarian bias (104–39).

5. Robert Elias mentions that, during the censorship controversies surrounding The *"Genius,"* Dreiser was the target of xenophobic attacks focusing on his German origins. Elias indicates that H. L. Mencken, a German-American himself, "insisted that . . . any controversy [Dreiser] would involve himself in would arouse considerable anti-German sentiment" (197; see also 188).

6. The figure of Dillon—the Wall-Street-sponsored advocate of social engineering—is a striking fictional embodiment of the coalition of liberals and corporate leaders that, according to Weinstein, acted as a leading force behind the reforms of the Progressive Era (see Weinstein).

7. See Coleridge: "And I blessed them unaware" ("Mariner" 4.279; Coleridge 192). In a later passage of *The Harbor,* Bill's lament recalls the death-in-life theme of the mariner's spell: "Like the Ancient Mariner I sat there dully on the pier watching the life of the ocean go past" (175).

8. Michel de Certeau—like Poole's Dillon—argues that it is only from such a panoptic vantage point that the urban tangle can be reordered into legible patterns (*Invention* 171). In another type of reading, Peter Conn compares Dillon's skyscraper to an ivory tower—a semi-religious retreat from which artists look down on the industrial scene with contempt (112). Yet this interpretation places, I think, too much emphasis on the narrator's presumed detachment toward the harbor. I believe instead that Poole's naturalist gaze partakes in the tropes of fascination and complicity typical of the naturalist perception of social space.

9. In his discussion of "Panopticism" (*Discipline* 196–228), Michel Foucault shows how the design of Jeremy Bentham's model prison—the Panopticon—ensures maximum surveillance and discipline through a careful architectural management of the controlling gaze. Foucault's argument suggests that a network of surveying vision is inherently an instrument of coercion.

Conclusion

1. A techno-psychedelic approach to cyberpunk is elaborated in Scott Bukatman's *Terminal Identity*, where the author contends that postmodern science fiction constructs "a new subject position," allowing subjects to "intersect the cyberscapes of contemporary existence" (9). In this perspective, computer technology is an agent of psychological expansion comparable to drugs. For a discussion of the link between magic and information technology, see also Erik Davis's "Techgnosis, Magic, Memory, and the Angels of Information."

Works Cited

Adams, Henry. *The Education of Henry Adams*. 1918. *Novels, Mont Saint Michel, The Education*. Ed. Ernest Samuels and Jayne N. Samuels. New York: Library of America, 1983. 715–1192.

Addams, Jane. *Twenty Years at Hull-House*. 1910. Rpt., New York: New American Library, 1981.

Austin, J. L. *How to Do Things with Words*. Oxford: Oxford University Press, 1962.

Bachelard, Gaston. *La Psychanalyse du Feu*. Paris: Gallimard, 1949.

Bakhtin, Mikhaïl Mikhailovich. *The Dialogic Imagination: Four Essays by M. M. Bakhtin*. Ed. Michael Holquist. Trans. Caryl Emerson and Michael Holquist. Austin: University of Texas Press, 1981.

———. *Esthétique et Théorie du Roman*. Trans. Daria Olivier. Paris: Gallimard, 1978.

Bannister, Robert. *Social Darwinism: Science and Myth in Anglo-American Thought*. Philadelphia: Temple University Press, 1979.

Barker-Benfield, G. J. *The Horrors of the Half-Known Life: Male Attitudes toward Women and Sexuality in Nineteenth-Century America*. New York: Harper and Row, 1976.

Bederman, Gail. *Manliness and Civilization: A Cultural History of Gender and Race in the United States, 1880–1917*. Chicago: University of Chicago Press, 1995.

Bell, Bernard W. *The Afro-American Novel and Its Tradition*. Amherst: University of Massachussets Press, 1989.

Bell, Michael Davitt. *The Problem of American Realism: Studies in the Cultural History of a Literary Idea*. Chicago: University of Chicago Press, 1993.

Benjamin, Walter. *Charles Baudelaire: A Lyric Poet in the Era of High Capitalism*. Trans. Harry Zohn. London: NLB, 1973.

———. *Illuminations: Essays and Reflections*. Ed. Hannah Arendt. New York: Schocken Books, 1969.

———. *Reflections: Essays, Aphorisms, Autobiographical Writings*. Ed. Peter Demetz. New York: Schocken Books, 1978.

Berthoff, Warner. *The Ferment of Realism: American Literature, 1884–1919.* New York: Free Press, 1965.

Boies, Henry M. *Prisoners and Paupers: A Study of the Abnormal Increase of Criminals and the Public Burden of Pauperism in the United States—the Causes and Remedies.* New York: G. P. Putnam's Sons, 1893.

Bonaparte, Marie. *The Life and Works of Edgar Allan Poe: A Psychoanalytic Interpretation.* London: Imago, 1949.

Bowlby, Rachel. *Consumer Culture in Dreiser, Gissing, and Zola.* New York: Methuen, 1985.

Bukatman, Scott. *Terminal Identity: The Virtual Subject in Post-Modern Science Fiction.* Durham: Duke University Press, 1993.

Bullard, Arthur. *Comrade Yetta.* New York: Macmillan, 1913.

Burke, Edmund. *A Philosophical Enquiry into the Origin of Our Ideas of the Sublime and Beautiful.* 1757. Ed. James T. Boulton. Oxford: Basil Blackwell, 1987.

Burke, Kenneth. *The Philosophy of Literary Form.* 1941. Rpt., Berkeley: University of California Press, 1973.

Butler, Judith. *Bodies That Matter: On the Discursive Limits of "Sex."* New York: Routledge, 1993.

Cahan, Abraham. *The Rise of David Levinsky.* 1917. Rpt., New York: Harper and Row, 1960.

———. *Yekl: A Tale of the New York Ghetto.* New York: D. Appleton and Co., 1896.

Camus, Albert. *The Rebel.* Trans. Anthony Bower. London: Hamish Hamilton, 1953.

Carrouges, Michel. *Les Machines Célibataires.* Paris: Chêne, 1976.

Cather, Willa. *O Pioneers!* 1913. Rpt., Boston: Houghton Mifflin, 1941.

———. *The Song of the Lark. Early Novels and Stories.* 1915. Ed. Sharon O'Brien. New York: Library of America, 1987. 291–706.

Chase, Richard. *The American Novel and Its Tradition.* London: G. Bell and Sons, 1958.

Chesnutt, Charles Waddell. *"The Wife of His Youth" and Other Stories of the Color Line.* 1899. Rpt., Ann Arbor: University of Michigan Press, 1978.

Chodorow, Nancy. *The Reproduction of Mothering: Psychoanalysis and the Sociology of Gender.* Berkeley: University of California Press, 1978.

Chopin, Kate. *The Awakening.* (1899). In *"The Awakening" and Selected Short Stories.* New York: Penguin Group, 1984. 43–176.

Coleridge, S. T. "The Rime of the Ancient Mariner" (1798). In W. Wordsworth and S. T. Coleridge, *The Lyrical Ballads.* Ed. Michael Mason. London: Longman, 1992. 177–205.

Conn, Peter. *The Divided Mind: Ideology and Imagination in America, 1898–1917.* Cambridge: Cambridge University Press, 1983.

Cott, Nancy. *The Bonds of Womanhood: "Woman's Sphere" in New England, 1780–1830.* New Haven: Yale University Press, 1977.

Crane, Stephen. *Maggie: A Girl of the Streets.* 1893. Rpt., New York: W. W. Norton, 1979.

———. "New York City, 1892–94." *Prose and Poetry.* Ed. J. C. Levenson. New York: Library of America, 1984.

Cronon, William. *Nature's Metropolis: Chicago and the Great West.* New York: W. W. Norton, 1991.

Davis, Erik. "Techgnosis, Magic, Memory, and the Angels of Information." *Flame Wars: The Discourse of Cyberculture*. Ed. Mark Dery. Durham: Duke University Press, 1994. 29–60.

De Bolla, Peter. *The Discourse of the Sublime: Readings in History, Aesthetics, and the Subject*. London: Basil Blackwell, 1989.

de Certeau, Michel. *L'Invention du Quotidien*. Paris: Union Générale d'Éditions, 1980.

Deleuze, Gilles, and Felix Guattari. *L'anti-Oedipe: Capitalisme et Schizophrénie*. Paris: Les Editions de Minuit, 1972.

Denning, Michael. *Mechanic Accents: Dime Novels and Working-Class Culture in America*. London: Verso, 1987.

Den Tandt, Christophe. "Amazons and Androgynes: Overcivilization and the Redefinition of Gender Roles at the Turn of the Century." *American Literary History* 8 (1996): 639–64.

———. "Invoking the Abyss: The Ideologies of the Postmodern Sublime." *Revue Belge de Philologie et d'Histoire* 73 (1995): 803–22.

Derrida, Jacques. "Signature, Event, Context." In *A Derrida Reader: Between the Blinds*. Ed. Peggy Kamuf. New York: Columbia University Press, 1991. 80–111.

———. *"Speech and Phenomena" and Other Essays on Husserl's Theory of Signs*. Trans. B. Allison. Evanston: Northwestern University Press, 1973.

Dinnerstein, Dorothy. *The Mermaid and the Minotaur*. New York: Harper and Row, 1976.

Doane, Janice, and Devon Hodges. "Undoing Feminism: From the Preoedipal to Postfeminism in Anne Rice's *Vampire Chronicles*." *American Literary History* 2 (1990): 423–42.

Douglas, Ann. *The Feminization of American Culture*. New York, Avon Books, 1978.

Douglas, Mary. *Purity and Danger: An Analysis of Concepts of Pollution and Taboo*. New York: Routledge and Kegan Paul, 1966.

Dreiser, Theodore. *An Amateur Laborer*. Ed. Richard W. Dowell. Philadelphia: University of Pennsylvania Press, 1983.

———. *The Financier*. 1912. Rpt., Harmondsworth, U.K.: Penguin Books, 1986.

———. *The "Genius."* 1915. Rpt., New York: New American Library, 1984.

———. *Newspaper Days*. 1922. Rpt., New York: Beekman Publishers, 1974.

———. *Sister Carrie*. 1900. Rpt., New York: W. W. Norton and Co., 1970.

———. *Sister Carrie*. 1900. Rpt., Harmondsworth, U.K.: Penguin Books, 1986. Pennsylvania edition.

———. *The Stoic*. Garden City, N.Y.: Doubleday and Co., 1947.

———. *The Titan*. 1914. Rpt., New York: New American Library, 1965.

Dugdale, Richard L. *The Jukes: A Study in Crime, Pauperism, and Heredity*. 1875. Rpt., New York: G. P. Putnam's Sons, 1910.

Eagleton, Terry. "Capitalism, Modernism, and Postmodernism." *New Left Review* 152 (1985): 32–47.

———. *Ideology: An Introduction*. London: Verso, 1991.

Elias, Robert. *Theodore Dreiser, Apostle of Nature*. Ithaca: Cornell University Press, 1970.

Ferguson, Frances. "The Nuclear Sublime." *diacritics* 14:2 (Summer 1984): 4–10.

Fine, David M. *The City, the Immigrant, and American Fiction, 1880–1920*. Metuchen, N.J.: Scarecrow Press, 1977.

Fisher, Philip. "Acting, Reading, Fortune's Wheel: *Sister Carrie* and the Life History of Objects." *American Realism: New Essays.* Ed. Eric J. Sundquist. Baltimore: Johns Hopkins University Press, 1982. 259–77.

Foucault, Michel. *Discipline and Punish: The Birth of the Prison.* Trans. Alan Sheridan. New York: Vintage Books, 1979.

French, Warren. "Introduction." In Frank Norris, *Vandover and the Brute* (1914). Lincoln: University of Nebraska Press, 1978. vii–xvi.

Freud, Sigmund. *Group Psychology and the Analysis of the Ego.* 1921. Trans. James Strachey. Rpt., New York: Liveright Publishing, 1967.

———. *Three Essays on the Theory of Sexuality.* 1905. In *The Essentials of Psychoanalysis.* Ed. Anna Freud. Trans. James Strachey. London: Penguin, 1986. 277–375.

Frow, John. *Marxism and Literary History.* Oxford: Basil Blackwell, 1986.

Frye, Northrop. *Anatomy of Criticism.* Princeton: Princeton University Press, 1957.

Fuller, Henry Blake. *The Cliff-Dwellers.* 1893. Rpt., New York: Irvington Publishers, 1981.

———. *With the Procession.* 1895. Rpt., Chicago: University of Chicago Press, 1965.

Fuller, Robert C. "Mesmerism and the Birth of Psychology." In *Pseudo-Science and Society in Nineteenth-Century America.* Ed. Arthur Wrobel. Lexington: University Press of Kentucky, 1987. 205–22.

Gallagher, Catherine. "More about 'Medusa's Head.'" *Representations* 4 (Fall 1983): 55–57.

Garland, Hamlin. *A Spoil of Office.* New York: D. Appleton and Co., 1897.

Gibson, William. *Count Zero.* London: HarperCollins, 1993.

———. *Mona Lisa Overdrive.* New York: Bantam Books, 1989.

———. *Neuromancer.* New York: Ace Books, 1984.

Gilman, Charlotte Perkins. *The Home: Its Work and Influence.* 1903. Rpt., Urbana: University of Illinois Press, 1972.

———. *The Living of Charlotte Perkins Gilman: An Autobiography.* 1935. Rpt., Madison: University of Wisconsin Press, 1991.

———. *Women and Economics.* 1898. Rpt., New York: Harper and Row, 1966.

———. "The Yellow Wallpaper" (1892). In *"The Yellow Wallpaper" and Other Writings.* New York: Bantam Books, 1989. 1–20.

Goodwyn, Lawrence. *The Populist Moment: A Short History of the Agrarian Revolt in America.* Oxford: Oxford University Press, 1978.

Gottesman, Ronald. "Introduction." In Upton Sinclair, *The Jungle.* New York: Viking Penguin, 1985. vii–xxxv.

Habegger, Alfred. *Gender, Fantasy, and Realism in American Literature.* New York: Columbia University Press, 1982.

Hales, Peter Bacon. *Silver Cities: The Photography of American Urbanization, 1839–1915.* Philadelphia: Temple University Press, 1984.

Hall, Bolton. *A Little Land and a Living.* New York: Arcadia Press, 1908.

Haller, Mark H. *Eugenics: Hereditarian Attitudes in American Thought.* New Brunswick: Rutgers University Press, 1984.

Haskell, Thomas L. *The Emergence of Professional Social Science: The American Social Science Association and the Nineteenth-Century Crisis of Authority.* Urbana: University of Illinois Press, 1971.

Herrick, Robert. *The Common Lot.* 1904. Rpt., New York: Macmillan, 1913.

————. *Together.* 1908. Rpt., Greenwich, Conn.: Fawcett Publications, 1962.

————. *The Web of Life.* New York: Macmillan, 1900.

Hertz, Neil. "Medusa's Head: Male Hysteria under Political Pressure." *Representations* 4 (Fall 1983): 27–54.

————. "The Notion of Blockage in the Literature of the Sublime." In *Psychoanalysis and the Question of the Text: Selected Papers from the English Institute, 1976–77.* Ed. Geoffrey Hartman. Baltimore: Johns Hopkins University Press, 1978. 62–85.

Higham, John. *Strangers in the Land: Patterns of American Nativism, 1860–1925.* New Brunswick: Rutgers University Press, 1955.

Hofstadter, Richard. *The Age of Reform: From Bryan to F.D.R.* New York: Random House, 1955.

————. *Social Darwinism in American Thought.* 1944. Rpt., Boston: Beacon Press, 1955.

Horney, Karen. "The Dread of Woman: Observations on a Specific Difference in the Dread Felt by Men and Women Respectively for the Opposite Sex." *International Journal of Psychoanalysis* 13 (1932): 348–60.

Horowitz, Daniel. *The Morality of Spending: Attitudes toward the Consumer Society in America, 1875–1940.* Baltimore: Johns Hopkins University Press, 1985.

Howard, June. *Form and History in American Literary Naturalism.* Chapel Hill: University of North Carolina Press, 1985.

Howe, Fredric C. *The City, Hope of Democracy.* New York: Scribner's Sons, 1905.

Howells, William Dean. *A Hazard of New Fortunes.* 1890. Rpt., Oxford: Oxford University Press, 1990.

————. *The Rise of Silas Lapham.* 1885. Rpt., Boston: Houghton Mifflin, 1957.

James, Henry. *The Bostonians.* 1886. Rpt., London: Penguin, 1986.

Jameson, Fredric. *The Political Unconscious: Narrative as a Socially Symbolic Act.* Ithaca: Cornell University Press, 1981.

————. *Postmodernism; or, The Cultural Logic of Late Capitalism.* Durham: Duke University Press, 1991.

Jeffrey, Kirk. "The Family as Utopian Retreat from the City: The Nineteenth-Century Contribution." *The Family, Communes, and Utopian Societies.* Ed. Sallie TeSelle. New York: Harper Torchbooks, 1981. 21–41.

Johnson, James Weldon. *The Autobiography of an Ex-Coloured Man.* 1912. Rpt., New York: Hill and Wang, 1960.

Kant, Immanuel. *The Critique of Judgment.* Oxford: Clarendon Press, 1952.

Kaplan, Amy Beth. "Romancing the Empire: The Embodiment of American Masculinity in the Popular Historical Novel of the 1890s." *American Literary History* 2 (1990): 659–90.

————. *The Social Construction of Realism.* Chicago: University of Chicago Press, 1988.

Kaplan, Harold. *Power and Order: Henry Adams and the Naturalist Tradition in American Fiction.* Chicago: University of Chicago Press, 1981.

Kazin, Alfred. *On Native Grounds: An Interpretation of American Prose Literature.* New York: Reynal and Hitchcock, 1942.

Kristeva, Julia. *Pouvoirs de l'Horreur.* Paris: Éditions du Seuil, 1980.

Kropotkin, Pyetr Alekseyevitch, Prince. *Fields, Factories, and Workshops.* 1913. Rpt. New York: B. Blom, 1968.

Lears, T. J. Jackson. *No Place of Grace: Antimodernism and the Transformation of American Culture, 1880–1920.* New York: Pantheon Books, 1981.

Le Bon, Gustave. *The Crowd: A Study of the Popular Mind.* 1895. Rpt., Harmondsworth, U.K.: Penguin Books, 1964.

Leverenz, David. *Manhood and the American Renaissance.* Ithaca: Cornell University Press, 1989.

London, Jack. *The Abysmal Brute.* New York: Century Co. 1913.

———. *Before Adam.* 1907. Rpt., Mattituck, N.Y.: Amereon House, n.d.

———. *"The Call of the Wild," "White Fang," and Other Stories.* New York: Viking Penguin, 1986.

———. *The Iron Heel* (1908). *Novels and Social Writings.* Ed. Donald Pizer. New York: Library of America, 1982. 319–553.

———. *Martin Eden.* 1912. Rpt., Harmondsworth, U.K.: Penguin Books, 1985.

———. *The People of the Abyss* (1903). *Novels and Social Writings.* Ed. Donald Pizer. New York: Library of America, 1982. 1–184.

———. *The Sea-Wolf* (1904). In *"The Sea-Wolf" and Other Stories.* London: Penguin Books, 1989. 17–274.

———. *"South of the Slot"* (1914). *Novels and Stories.* Ed. Donald Pizer. New York: Library of America, 1982. 817–33.

———. *The Valley of the Moon.* 1912. Rpt., New York: Macmillan Co., 1928.

Lukács, Georg. *The Lukács Reader.* Ed. Arpad Kadarkay. Oxford: Blackwell, 1995.

———. *"Narrate or Describe."* In *"Writer and Critic" and Other Essays.* Ed. and trans. Arthur D. Kahn. New York: Grosset and Dunlap, 1970. 10–148.

———. *Studies in European Realism.* London: Hillway, 1950.

———. *The Theory of the Novel.* London: Merlin, 1971.

Lynch, Kevin. *The Image of the City.* Cambridge: MIT Press, 1960.

Lyotard, Jean-François. *La Condition Postmoderne.* Paris: Éditions de Minuit, 1979.

———. *The Differend: Phrases in Dispute.* Trans. Georges Van Den Abbeele. Manchester: Manchester University Press, 1988.

———. *The Inhuman: Reflections on Time.* Cambridge: Polity Press, 1991.

———. *Leçons sur l'Analytique du Sublime.* Paris: Galilée, 1991.

———. *The Lyotard Reader.* Ed. Andrew Benjamin. Oxford: Basil Blackwell, 1989.

———. *The Postmodern Explained.* Minneapolis: University of Minnesota Press, 1992.

Marcus, Steven. *"Reading the Illegible."* In *The Victorian City: Images and Realities.* Ed. H. J. Dyos and Michael Wolff. London: Routledge and Kegan Paul, 1973. 257–76.

Markels, Julian. *"Dreiser and the Plotting of the Inarticulate Experience."* *Massachussets Review* 2 (Spring 1961): 431–48.

Martin, Ronald E. *American Literature and the Universe of Force.* Durham: Duke University Press, 1981.

Marx, Karl. *Economic and Philosophic Manuscripts of 1844.* Trans. Martin Milligan. New York: International Publishers, 1964.

Marx, Leo. *The Machine in the Garden; Technology and the Pastoral Ideal in America.* Oxford: Oxford University Press, 1964.

Matthiessen, F. O. *Theodore Dreiser.* New York: Sloane, 1951.

McDermott, John. *"Nature, Nostalgia, and the City: An American Dilemma."* In *The Family, Communes, and Utopian Societies.* Ed. Sallie TeSelle. New York: Harper Torchbooks, 1981. 1–20.

McKinsey, Elisabeth. *Niagara Falls: Icon of the American Sublime.* Cambridge: Cambridge University Press, 1985.

Michaels, Walter Benn. *The Gold Standard and the Logic of Naturalism.* Berkeley: University of California Press, 1987.

Mishra, Vijay. *The Gothic Sublime.* Albany: SUNY Press, 1994.

Nietzsche, Friedrich. *Beyond Good and Evil* (1886). Trans. R. J. Hollingdale. London: Penguin Books, 1990.

———. *The Genealogy of Morals: An Attack* (1887). *"The Birth of Tragedy" and "The Genealogy of Morals."* Trans. Francis Golffing. New York: Doubleday, 1956. 147–299.

———. *Twilight of the Idols; or, How to Philosophize with a Hammer* (1889). In *Twilight of the Idols/The Anti-Christ.* Trans. R. J. Hollingsdale. London: Penguin Books, 1990. 29–122.

Norris, Frank. *The Literary Criticism of Frank Norris.* Ed. Donald Pizer. Austin: University of Texas Press, 1964.

———. *McTeague: A Story of San Francisco.* 1899. Rpt., Harmondsworth, U.K.: Penguin, 1985.

———. *The Octopus.* 1901. Rpt., Harmondsworth, U.K.: Viking Penguin, 1986.

———. *The Pit.* New York: Doubleday, Page & Co., 1903.

———. *Vandover and the Brute.* 1914. Lincoln: University of Nebraska Press, 1978.

Palmer, Bruce. *Man over Money; The Southern Populist Critique of American Capitalism.* Chapel Hill: University of North Carolina Press, 1980.

Parrington, Vernon Louis. *The Beginnings of Critical Realism in America, 1860–1920.* New York: Harcourt, Brace & Co., 1930.

Parry, David. M. *The Scarlet Empire.* Indianapolis: Bobbs Merrill, n.d.

Patten, Simon Nelson. *The New Basis of Civilization.* New York: Macmillan, 1907.

Patterson, James T. *America in the Twentieth Century: A History.* San Diego: Harcourt, Brace, Jovanovich, 1989.

Penley, Constance. "Feminism, Film Theory, and the Bachelor Machines." *m/f* 10 (1983): 39–56.

Phillips, David Graham. *The Second Generation.* New York: Grosset and Dunlap, 1906.

———. *Susan Lennox, Her Fall and Rise.* 1917. Rpt., London: D. Appleton & Co., 1928.

Pickens, Donald K. *Eugenics and the Progressives.* Nashville: Vanderbilt University Press, 1968.

Pizer, Donald. *The Novels of Theodore Dreiser: A Critical Study.* Minneapolis: University of Minnesota Press, 1976.

———. *Realism and Naturalism in Nineteenth-Century American Literature.* Carbondale: Southern Illinois University Press, 1966.

Poe, Edgar Allan. "A Descent into the Maelstrom" (1841). In *The Complete Tales and Poems.* New York: Vintage Books-Random House, 1975. 127–40.

Poole, Ernest. *The Harbor.* New York: Macmillan, 1915.

Rideout, Walter. *The Radical Novel in the United States: Some Interrelations of Literature and Society.* 1956. Rpt., New York: Columbia University Press, 1992.

Riis, Jacob A. *How the Other Half Lives: Studies among the Tenements of New York.* 1890. Rpt., New York: Dover Publications, 1971.

Rosenblatt, Roger. *Black Fiction.* Cambridge: Harvard University Press, 1874.

Rotundo, Anthony. *American Manhood: Transformations in Masculinity from the Revolution to the Modern Era.* New York: Basic Books, 1993.

Rubin, Gayle. "The Traffic in Women: Notes on the 'Political Economy of Sex.'" In *Toward an Anthropology of Women.* Ed. Rayna R. Reiter. New York: Monthly Review Press, 1975. 157–210.

Ryan, Mary. *Cradle of the Middle-Class: The Family in Oneida County, New York, 1790–1865.* Cambridge: Cambridge University Press, 1981.

Searle, John R. *Speech Acts: An Essay in the Philosophy of Language.* London: Cambridge University Press, 1969.

Sedgwick, Eve Kosofsky. *Between Men: English Literature and Male Homosocial Desire.* New York: Columbia University Press, 1985.

———. *The Epistemology of the Closet.* New York: Harvester Wheatsheaf, 1991.

Seltzer, Mark. *Bodies and Machines.* New York: Routledge, 1992.

Sinclair, Upton. *The Jungle.* 1906. Rpt., Harmondsworth, U.K.: Penguin Books, 1984.

———. *The Metropolis.* 1907. Rpt., Long Beach, Calif.: By the Author, 1923.

Sklar, Martin. *The Corporate Reconstruction of American Capitalism, 1890–1916.* Cambridge: Cambridge University Press, 1988.

Smith, Henry Nash. *Virgin Land: The American West as Symbol and Myth.* 1950. Rpt., Cambridge: Harvard University Press, 1970.

Smith-Rosenberg, Carroll. *Disorderly Conduct: Visions of Gender in Victorian America.* Oxford: Oxford University Press, 1985.

Starr, Kevin. "Introduction." In Frank Norris, *The Octopus.* Harmondsworth, U.K.: Penguin Books, 1986. vii–xxxiv.

Sterling, Bruce. *Heavy Weather.* New York: Bantam Books, 1996.

Strong, Josiah. *Our Country: Its Possible Future and Its Present Crisis.* New York: American Home Missionary Society, 1885.

Suvin, Darko. *Pour une poétique de la science fiction: Etudes en théorie et en histoire d'un genre littéraire.* Montreal: Presses de l'Université de Québec, 1977.

Tabbi, Joseph. *The Postmodern Sublime: Technology and American Writing from Mailer to Cyberpunk.* Ithaca: Cornell University Press, 1995.

Taylor, Nicholas. "The Awful Sublimity of the Victorian City: Its Aesthetic and Architectural Origins." In *The Victorian City: Images and Realities.* Ed. H. J. Dyos and Michael Wolff. London: Routledge and Kegan Paul, 1973. 431–47.

Teller, Charlotte. *The Cage.* New York: D. Appleton & Co., 1907.

Todorov, Tzvetan. *Introduction à la Littérature Fantastique.* Paris: Éditions du Seuil, 1970.

Tompkins, Jane. *Sensational Designs: The Cultural Work of American Fiction, 1790–1860.* New York: Oxford University Press, 1985.

Trachtenberg, Alan. "Experiments in Another Country: Stephen Crane's City Sketches." In *American Realism: New Essays.* Ed. Eric J. Sundquist. Baltimore: Johns Hopkins University Press, 1982. 138–53.

———. *The Incorporation of America.* New York: Hill and Wang, 1982.

———. "Who Narrates? Dreiser's Presence in *Sister Carrie.*" In *New Essays on "Sister Carrie."* Ed. Donald Pizer. New York: Cambridge University Press, 1991. 87–127.

Trotsky, Leon. "Letter to Joan London." In Jack London, *Le Talon de Fer (The Iron Heel).* Paris: Union Générale d'Éditions, n.d. 25.

Veblen, Thorstein. *The Instinct of Workmanship; and the State of the Industrial Arts.* New York: Augustus Kelley, 1964.

———. *The Theory of the Leisure Class.* 1899. Rpt., New York: Modern Library, 1934.

Voloshinov, V. N. *Marxism and the Philosophy of Language.* New York: Seminar Press, 1973.

Walcutt, Charles. *American Literary Naturalism: A Divided Stream.* Minneapolis: University of Minnesota Press, 1956.

Wardley, Lynn. "Woman's Voice, Democracy's Body, and *The Bostonians.*" *English Literary History* 56 (1989): 639–65.

Weinstein, James. *The Corporate Ideal in the Liberal State, 1900–1918.* Boston: Beacon Press, 1968.

———. *The Decline of Socialism in America.* New York: Monthly Review Press, 1967.

Weiskel, Thomas. *The Romantic Sublime: Studies in the Structure and Psychology of Transcendence.* Baltimore: Johns Hopkins University Press, 1976.

Wharton, Edith. *The House of Mirth.* 1905. Rpt., New York, Penguin, 1986.

White, Morton, and Lucia White. *The Intellectual vs. the City: From Thomas Jefferson to Frank Lloyd Wright.* Cambridge: Harvard University Press, 1962.

Whitman, Walt. *Leaves of Grass.* 1876. Rpt., New York: Random House, 1981.

Wiebe, Robert. *The Search for Order, 1877–1920.* New York: Hill and Wang, 1968.

Williams, Raymond. *The Country and the City.* New York: Oxford University Press, 1973.

Wilson, Christopher. *The Labor of Words.* Athens: University of Georgia Press, 1985.

Wilson, Rob. *American Sublime: The Genealogy of a Poetic Genre.* Madison: University of Wisconsin Press, 1991.

Wolf, Bryan Jay. *Romantic Re-Vision: Culture and Consciousness in Nineteenth-Century American Painting and Literature.* Chicago: University of Chicago Press, 1982.

Wolff, Cynthia Griffin. "Introduction." In Edith Wharton, *The House of Mirth.* New York: Penguin, 1986. vii–xxvi.

Yaeger, Patricia. "Toward a Female Sublime." In *Gender and Theory: Dialogues on Feminist Criticism.* Ed. Linda Kauffman. Oxford: Basil Blackwell, 1989. 191–211.

Zaretsky, Eli. *Capitalism, the Family, and Personal Life.* 1976. Rpt., New York: Harper & Row, 1986.

Žižek, Slavoj. *The Sublime Object of Ideology.* London: Verso, 1989.

Zola, Émile. *L'Argent.* 1891. Rpt., Paris: Gallimard, 1980.

———. *Le Docteur Pascal.* Paris: Fasquelle, n.d.

———. "The Experimental Novel" (1880). In *Documents of Modern Literary Realism.* Ed. George J. Becker. Princeton: Princeton University Press, 1963. 161–96.

Index

Department stores, 13, 57

De Quincey, Thomas, 211

Derrida, Jacques, 7, 168

Determinism. *See* Forces and deterministic currents

Dialogization, 132, 174, 232, 247, 248, 249; of urban space, 11, 31, 168; in turn-of-the-century fiction, 17, 18; and ethnicity in Howells's *Hazard*, 21, 28, 30; as theoretical paradigm, 48. *See also* Bakhtin, Mikhail

Différance, 168

Differend (of postmodernity), 48, 49. *See also* Lyotard, Jean-François

Dime novels, 181, 183

Dinnerstein, Dorothy, 95

Doane, Janice, 259n3

Documentary discourse, 17, 19, 33, 35, 36, 125, 174–75, 247; as dialogized component of naturalism, 17, 19–20. *See also* Naturalism; Realism

Domestic fiction, 113

Domestic sphere, 27, 49, 129, 135, 145, 184, 185, 201, 202; and Howellsian realism, 20, 23; in Norris's *Pit*, 83–84; in London's *Valley*, 101, 103; in Addams, 111; and individualistic rebellion in Herrick, 115–17; and hypnosis in James's *Bostonians*, 161–62, 167; and artistic education, 192; and bohemia, 222, 225, 239. *See also* Gender; Public sphere

Domus: defined by Lyotard, 50

Dorfman, Ariel, 260n3

Dos Passos, John, 254n9

Double consciousness, 143, 233

Douglas, Ann, 162

Douglas, Mary, 88, 206

Douglass, Frederick, 232

Dreiser, Theodore, 8, 21, 22, 32, 47, 70, 71, 109, 121, 126, 138, 152, 159, 196, 206, 215, 219, 229, 235, 246, 249, 251n1, 253n9; *The "Genius,"* 3–4, 15, 19, 66–67, 70, 190, 194, 215, 219–24, 225, 233, 234, 243; *Sister Carrie*, 8–9, 18–20, 33–41, 55–69, 70, 75, 147, 151–52, 205, 232, 245, 252n9, 256–57n1, 263n4; *The Titan*, and vitalism, 62; *Newspaper Days*, and vitalism, 62; *The*

Financier, 131–132; and bohemia, 218; *An Amateur Laborer*, 264n4

Dubofsky, Melvyn, 124

Du Bois, W. E. B., 233

Dugdale, Richard, 139, 146

Eagleton, Terry, 256n6

Eisenstein, Sergei, 45

Elias, Robert, 61

Emerson, Caryl, 253n6

Engels, Friedrich, 38

Entrepreneurial ideology, 213–14, 216, 224, 239. *See also* Producers' ideology; Work ethic

Ethnicity, 9, 12, 210, 225, 245; in Howells, 27–28, 30; in London's *Valley*, 98–99; in Fuller, 110; and naturalist gothic, 132; and atavistic disourse, 141, 143, 146–47, 149, 151. *See also* Immigrants; Nativism; Primitivism; Race

Eugenics, 124, 128–30, 139, 145. *See also* Atavism; Darwinism; Ethnicity; Primitivism

Evolution, 183, 197; in Dreiser's *Sister Carrie*, 61; and naturalist gothic, 130, 131, 135–37; and trickster figures, 206, 208, 209, 215. *See also* Darwinism

Failed sublime, 66, 90, 95, 151, 211; defined by Yaeger, 43–44

Farmers Alliance, 72, 79, 80

Farming. *See* Agriculture

Farrell, James T., 253n9

Fascism, 152, 155

Feminine sublime, 225, 228, 229; defined by Yaeger, 225

Femininity: linked to economic degeneration, 87–90, 128, 130, 175; and work, 103, 105, 202; and crowds, 154, 160, 168; and middle-class culture, 190–93; and trickster figures in Gilman, 204–6; and access to professional status, 209; and overcivilization, 210–11, 213–16; and matriarchal empowerment, 228–30

Feminism, 117, 161–63, 166, 168, 171, 192, 185, 201

Ferenczi, Sandor, 242n6

Ferguson, Frances, 252n7

Christophe Den Tandt is an assistant professor at the Université Libre de Bruxelles (Free University of Brussels), where he teaches English and American literature as well as theory. His research interests include American fiction and cultural studies.

NEW FROM

Illinois

We are pleased to send you a review copy of

THE URBAN SUBLIME IN AMERICAN LITERARY NATURALISM

CHRISTOPHE DEN TANDT

Publication date: October 12, 1998

Price: Cloth, $49.95   **Paper, $18.95**

Please send two copies of published reviews to the Publicity Department.

UNIVERSITY OF ILLINOIS PRESS
1325 South Oak Street • Champaign, IL 61820
phone: (217) 244-4689 • fax: (217) 244-8082
www.press.uillinois.edu